VISUALIZING
PROJECT MANAGEMENT

SECOND EDITION

VISUALIZING PROJECT MANAGEMENT

A MODEL FOR BUSINESS AND TECHNICAL SUCCESS

SECOND EDITION

KEVIN FORSBERG

HAL MOOZ, PMP

AND

HOWARD COTTERMAN

FOREWORD BY NORMAN R. AUGUSTINE
RETIRED CHAIRMAN AND CEO
LOCKHEED MARTIN CORPORATION

JOHN WILEY & SONS, INC.
NEW YORK · CHICHESTER · WEINHEIM · BRISBANE · SINGAPORE · TORONTO

This text is printed on acid-free paper. ∞

Copyright © 2000 by John Wiley & Sons, Inc.
Published by John Wiley & Sons, Inc.

All rights reserved. Published simultaneously in Canada.

Reproduction or translation of any part of this work beyond that
permitted by Section 107 or 108 of the 1976 United States Copyright
Act without the permission of the copyright owner is unlawful.
Requests for permission or further information should be addressed
to the Permissions Department, John Wiley & Sons, Inc.

This publication is designed to provide accurate and authoritative
information in regard to the subject matter. It is sold with the
understanding that the publisher is not engaged in rendering legal,
accounting, or other professional services. If legal advice or other expert
assistance is required, the services of a competent professional person
should be sought.

Library of Congress Cataloging-in-Publication Data:

Forsberg, Kevin.
    Visualizing project management 2d Edition / Kevin Forsberg,
Hal Mooz & Howard Cotterman.
        p.   cm.
    Includes bibliographical references.
    ISBN 0-471-35760-X (alk. paper)
    1. Project management.   I. Mooz, Hal.   II. Cotterman, Howard.
III. Title.
HD69.P75F67   1996
658.4′04—dc20   95-52250

Printed in the United States of America

10 9 8 7 6 5 4 3 2

To Cindy, Connie, and Maureen
who provided more support
than they should have had to.

FOREWORD

There are a thousand reasons for failure but not a single excuse.
Mike Reid

It is every manager's unending nightmare: In today's world of increasing complexity, there is less and less tolerance for error. We see this daily in the realms of health care, product safety and reliability, transportation, energy, communications, space exploration, military operations, and—as the above quote from the great Penn State football player Mike Reid demonstrates—sports. Whether the venue is the stock market, a company's customer base, consumers, government regulators, auditors, the battlefield, the ball field, or the media, "No one cares"—as the venerated quotation puts it—"about the storms you survived along the way, but whether you brought the ship safely into the harbor."

Over the course of my own career in aerospace, I have seen an unfortunate number of failures of very advanced, complex—and expensive—pieces of equipment, often due to the most mundane of causes. One satellite went off course into space on a useless trajectory because there was a hyphen missing in one of the millions of lines of software code. A seemingly minor flaw in the electrical design of the Apollo spacecraft was not detected until Apollo 13 was 200,000 miles from Earth, when a spark in a cryogenic oxygen tank led to an explosion and the near-loss of the crew. A major satellite proved to be badly nearsighted because of a tiny error in grinding the primary mirror in its optical train. And, as became apparent in the inquiry into the Challenger disaster, the performance of an exceedingly capable space vehicle—a miracle of modern technology—was undermined by the effects of cold temperature on a seal during a sudden winter storm. Murphy's Law, it would seem, has moved in lock-step with the advances of the modern age.

THEORETICALLY, SUCCESS IS MANAGEABLE

In the grand old days of American management, when it was presumed that all problems and mistakes could be controlled by more rigorous managerial oversight, the canonical solution to organizational error was to add more oversight and bureaucracy. Surely, it was thought, with more managers having narrower spans of control, the organization could prevent any problem from ever happening again. Of course, this theory was never confirmed in the real world—or, as Kansas City Royals hitting instructor Charlie Lau once noted regarding a similar challenge, "There are two theories on hitting the knuckleball. Unfortunately, neither one works."

The problem with the strategy of giving more managers fewer responsibilities is that no one is really in charge of the biggest responsibility: Will the overall enterprise succeed? I recall the comment a few years ago of the chief executive of one of the world's largest companies, who was stepping down after nearly a decade of increasingly poor performance in the marketplace by his company. He was asked by a journalist why the company had fared so poorly under his tutelage, to which he replied, "I don't know. It's a mysterious thing."

My observation is that there is no mystery here at all. After decades of trying to centrally "manage" every last variable and contingency encountered in the course of business, *Fortune 500* companies found themselves with 12 to 15 layers of management—but essentially ill-prepared to compete in an increasingly competitive global marketplace. Or, as I once pointed out in one of my Laws, "If a sufficient number of management layers are superimposed on top of each other, it can be assured that disaster is not left to chance."

A NEW LOOK AT PROJECT MANAGEMENT

Today's leaders in both the private and public sectors are rediscovering the simple truth that every good manager has known in his or her heart since the first day on the job: *Accountability* is the one managerial task that cannot be delegated. There must be *one* person whose responsibility it is to make a project work—even as we acknowledge the importance of teamwork and "worker empowerment" in the modern workplace. In other words, we are rediscovering the critical role of the *project manager*.

The importance of the project manager has long been noted in our nation's military procurement establishment, which has traditionally considered the job to be among the most important and most difficult assignments in peacetime. Performed properly, the project management role, whether in the military, in civilian government, or in business, can make enormous contributions and can even affect the course of history.

Challenges of this technology-focused project management role are particularly noteworthy for the insights they provide into the broader definition of project management. Perhaps the greatest of these is inherent in technology itself. In the effort to obtain the maximum possible advantage over a military adversary or a commercial competitor, products are often designed at the very edge of the state of the art. But as one high-level defense official noted in a moment of frustration over the repeated inability of advanced electronic systems to meet specified goals, "Airborne radars are not responsive to enthusiasm." In short, managerial adrenaline is not a substitute for managerial judgment when it comes to transporting technology from the laboratory to the field.

Despite considerable tribulations—or, perhaps *because* of them—the job of the technology-focused project manager is among the most rewarding career choices. It presents challenging work with important consequences. It involves the latest in technology. It offers the opportunity to work with a quality group of associates. And over the years, its practitioners have generated a large number of truly enormous successes.

THE LURE OF PROJECT MANAGEMENT

This brings me to the broader observation that the project manager's job, in my opinion, is one of the very best jobs anywhere. Whether one is working at the Department of Defense, NASA, or a private company, the project manager's job offers opportunities and rewards unavailable anywhere else. Being a project manager means integrating a variety of disciplines—science, engineering, development, finance, and human resources—accomplishing an important goal, making a difference, and seeing the results of one's work. In short, project management is "being where the action is" in the development and application of exciting new technologies and processes.

The principles of successful project management—picking the best people, instilling attention to detail, involving the customer, and, most importantly, building adequate reserves—are no secret, but what is often missing in the literature on the subject is a comprehensive, easy-to-understand model. This is one of the many compelling aspects of *Visualizing Project Management*. The authors have taken a new, simplified approach to visualizing project management as a combination of sequential, situational management actions incorporating a four-part model—common vocabulary, teamwork, project cycle, and project management elements. The beauty of their approach is that they portray management complexity as process and discipline simplicity.

Kevin Forsberg, Harold Mooz, and Howard Cotterman are eminently qualified to compose such a comprehensive model for successful project management. They bring a collective experience unmatched in the commercial sphere. One author has spent his entire career in the high-tech commercial world; the two others have more than 20 years each at a company (Lockheed Corporation, which is part of the new Lockheed Martin Corporation) that established a reputation strongly supporting the role of the project manager. Collectively, the authors have had many years successfully applying their "visualizing project management" approach to companies in both the commercial and the government markets. Their technical skill and work-environment experience are abundantly apparent in the real-world methodology they bring to the study and understanding of the importance of project management to the success of any organization.

SUMMARY

As corporate executives and their counterparts in the public sector expect project managers to assume many of the responsibilities of functional management—indeed, as we look to project managers to become "miracle workers" pulling together great teams of specialists to create products of enormous complexity— we need to make sure that the principles and applications of the project management process are thoroughly understood at all levels of the organizational hierarchy. This book will help executives, government officials, project managers, and project team members *visualize,* then successfully *apply* the process. I recommend this book to all those who aspire to project management, those who must supervise it in their organizations, or even those who are simply fascinated with how leading-edge technologies make it out of the laboratory and into the market.

—Norman R. Augustine
Retired Chairman and CEO
Lockheed Martin Corporation

ABOUT THE AUTHORS

Kevin Forsberg, Ph.D., is co-principal and co-founder of the Center for Systems Management which serves international clients in project management. Dr. Forsberg draws on 27 years of experience in applied research, system engineering, and project management, followed by 17 years of successful consulting to both government and industry. While at the Lockheed Palo Alto, California, Research Facility, Dr. Forsberg served as deputy director of the Materials and Structures Research Laboratory. He earned the NASA Public Service Medal for his contributions to the Space Shuttle program. He was also awarded the CIA Seal Medallion in recognition of his pioneering efforts in the field of project management training. Dr. Forsberg received his B.S. in Civil Engineering at Massachusetts Institute of Technology and his Ph.D. in Engineering Mechanics at Stanford University.

Hal Mooz, PMP, is co-principal and co-founder of the Center for Systems Management, one of two successful training and consulting companies he founded that specialize in the disciplines associated with project management. Mr. Mooz has won and successfully managed highly reliable, sophisticated satellite programs from inception to operations. His 22 years of experience in program management was followed by 18 years of experience installing project management into federal agencies, government contractors, and commercial companies. He is co-founder of the Certificate in Project Management at the University of California at Santa Cruz. He was awarded the CIA Seal Medallion in recognition of his pioneering efforts in the field of project management. Mr. Mooz received his ME degree from Stevens Institute of Technology.

Howard Cotterman is president of Cognitive Corporation, which specializes in computer-based training. He is also the managing director of the Center for Systems Management. Mr. Cotterman has held key posts and managed a broad range of projects from real estate development, to publishing, to the computer and semiconductor industries. His 34 years of project management experience began with the development of IBM's first microprocessor in the mid-1960s and includes development and manufacturing projects at NCR, Intel, and Rockwell International. Mr. Cotterman received his B.S. and M.S. degrees in Electrical Engineering from Purdue University.

PREFACE TO THE SECOND EDITION

The positive response to the first edition of *Visualizing Project Management* has been gratifying and has justified the publisher's support of this second edition. We have continued to simplify and clarify the complexity of project management and system engineering and present these ideas to help you manage your projects successfully. We and our expert cadre of consultants at the Center for Systems Management have now trained over 30,000 project management practitioners, and we have consulted with over 100 corporations. We have confirmed by our training, consulting, and mentoring that the processes and techniques of *Visualizing Project Management* are current and are equally applicable to any environment where doing it right the first time and every time is important.

The mantra for project management 2000 has become "better, faster, cheaper." Enlightened project managers will ask "than what?" Better, faster, cheaper than ad hoc is not difficult; but better, faster, cheaper than an efficient, honed process is very challenging. Our process model will help you achieve these broad objectives but, more importantly, will help you avoid bypassing important controls and ending up with a faster, cheaper failure. While many projects must be right the first time and our process is directed at this outcome, today's market pressures force a fast and good enough result to capture market share. We address the issue of achieving fast with reduced formality and of achieving good enough with requirements management in Chapter 9 "Applying the Process."

We have added exercises throughout for those who use the book as a text to support training. We have also added a CD-ROM with a software version of our process model, including all four essentials of project management. This tool, called *Visual Project Management (Visual PM),* is being used by our clients to assist the project teams in tailoring the process to meet their needs. At our clients' sites, Visual PM incorporates their corporate templates and guidelines which usually already exist (unused) in manuals on the corporate shelves. Visual PM facilitates point-and-click access to their project-unique project cycle and documentation. The CD-ROM contains a guided tour of a generic version of a commercial project cycle, vocabulary definitions, and sample document templates. In practice, Visual PM would be on an intranet web site for accessibility by all members of the corporate team. Those interested in more information are invited to visit our web site at CSM.com.

KEVIN FORSBERG, Truckee, CA
HAL MOOZ, Tiburon, CA
HOWARD COTTERMAN, Truckee, CA

October 1999

ACKNOWLEDGMENTS

By 1989, we were successful with careers of project management behind us and seven years of successful consulting to reinforce our credibility. In 1989, we were selected by Lucent Technologies (at the time part of AT&T) and, independently, by several government agencies including the National Aeronautics and Space Administration (NASA), to team with their experts and develop a process to enhance their already enviable record of successfully developing and fielding some of the most extraordinary and technically advanced projects ever conceived. This joint effort and our clients' on-going drive to be the absolute best in the world produced the processes that we have documented in *Visualizing Project Management*. For a decade, they have supported the development of new ideas. Our process has been routinely enhanced to reflect these improvements. We extend our appreciation to our initial supporters and thank our many clients and students who have significantly influenced and enhanced our concepts over the years.

We particularly wish to acknowledge the following significant contributors: Len Malinowski for his contributions to the process development, quality of content, ability to remain centered and objective, and above all for demonstrating the power of teamwork to the overall result. We also wish to thank Rich Roy for his significant enrichment of the process, Joe Keogh, Lee McMillion, Bob Teague, and Reg Heitchue for sharpening the message and clearing out the extraneous. Darrell Hull, Frank Hoban, and Ed Hoffman provided sustained support necessary for success. We especially thank John Chiorini for sharing his experiences and helping us clarify the focus of our messages. We thank Shirley Devan and Jeff Owen for their creativity in developing the many illustrations. Finally, we thank Frank Passavant for his careful review and thoughtful edit of the final draft.

K.F.
H.M.
H.C.

CONTENTS

PART II
THE ESSENTIALS OF
PROJECT MANAGEMENT

4   Project Vocabulary   **49**

5   Teamwork   **59**

6   The Project Cycle   **75**

INTRODUCTION

A SUCCESSFUL FUTURE DEPENDS ON SUCCESSFUL PROJECTS

Whether you're a middle manager on the endangered list or already up to your armpits in alligators as a project manager, your future may well depend on achieving success in the challenging project environment. In his *Fortune* article,[1] Thomas Stewart likened the deepening cuts in middle management to the extinction of the dinosaur, with project managers evolving to rule the corporate jungle. "Like his biological counterpart, the project manager is more agile and adaptable than the beast he's displacing, more likely to live by his wits than by throwing his weight around. Says William Dauphinais, a partner at Price Waterhouse: 'Project management is going to be huge in the next decade. The project manager is the linchpin in the horizontal/vertical organizations we're creating.' Project management is 'the wave of the future,' says an in-house newsletter from General Motors' technology and training group, which exhorts, 'We need to raise the visibility and clout of this job responsibility!'"

The project manager may well be the hero of the American workplace as Tom Peters, author of *In Search of Excellence*, asserts in his more recent book, *Liberation Management*. He observes that, even though he is a self-avowed "middle manager basher," most of the people attending his training seminars are themselves middle managers. Says Peters, "Middle management, as we have known it since the railroads invented it right after the Civil War,

> "The project manager is the linchpin in the horizontal/vertical organizations we're creating."

Project management techniques have evolved from various niches to be the mainstream and mainstay of management, in general.

Success in the dynamic project world depends on integrating the best techniques available with what's valid among conventional wisdom.

is dead. Therefore middle managers as we have known them are cooked geese." His answer to his clients facing a dead end, ". . . create projects."

What's all this fuss about projects? After all, a project can be any temporary undertaking carried out to achieve specified results within well-defined cost, schedule, and technical boundaries. Well, it's those precise boundaries, coupled with that temporary organization, that give project management its unique challenges and rewards. To see the picture, visualize the intensity and hubbub of a theater production, a building construction site, or a new product development.

Near-maximum productivity improvements have already been wrought from executive and external pressures to work harder and longer, and with capital improvements such as computers. In fact, automation of day-to-day tasks is one trend that's driving the middle manager to extinction. Now project management is being widely recognized as the next productivity frontier. Recent trends have moved this most complicated of management processes to center stage. The concepts described here are the precursors of future management practices.

IT'S ALARMINGLY COMMON FOR PROJECT TEAMS TO FAIL

Although the vital role of projects has been widely acknowledged, project teams continue to fail. Some do well, but most do not. Yet, the most basic techniques have been available, as Stewart quips, literally from day one, ". . . the first practitioner having been God, who gave himself six days in which to turn the void into the world, then turned operations management over to Adam, who promptly made a hash of it. (Unlike corporate project managers, however, God got to define what he meant by 'six days' and had unlimited resources.)"

In our experience, failure often results from fundamental confusion over precisely what is involved in successfully managing a project from inception through completion. While excellent managers are usually cognizant of the full scope of management thinking, others limited by one-dimensional thinking often make uninformed decisions from the wrong theory. At best, this locks them into mediocre performance. At worst, it leads to project failure.

Being temporary, projects often bring together people unknown to each other. The newly formed group usually includes specialists motivated by the work itself and their individual contributions. Teams of highly skilled technicians make costly errors —even fatal ones—simply because the members fail to understand or follow a disciplined, systematic approach to project management. This factor remains most critical to project success: the availability of an effective and intuitive project management process—one that the project group will quickly buy into and build their team upon.

> The most critical success factor is the availability of an effective and intuitive project management process.

YOU CAN'T RELY ON PERSONAL EXPERIENCE AND INTUITION ALONE

No matter how much intuition and experience you have, you can't rely on personal experience alone as you navigate through the increasingly complex and dynamic project environment. On the other hand, management excellence cannot be taught any more simply than professional quarterbacking, Olympic gymnastics, or being a great artist. No matter how much innate management talent you start with, you need input from others as well as your own experiences to attain excellence.

> Our field-tested model helps you to understand every piece of the project puzzle and to visualize how each fits into the overall picture.

Our own management roles range from high-tech CEOs to general contractors, from industry leaders to new ventures. As professional trainers, our clients hail from the ranks of Lucent Technololgies, AT&T, Emerson Electric, GTE, government agencies such as NASA, and dozens of other organizations which through over 30,000 trainees are now realizing the benefits of our project management model. Having successfully completed many complex government and commercial projects, we developed this text by combining our own experiences as managers and trainers with those of our clients. Providing hundreds of real case studies, our clients challenged us to perfect techniques and tools that they could propagate upward, downward, and laterally throughout their own organizations. They spurred us to confront tradition constructively—to challenge conventional wisdom here as we have in our training programs.

It is difficult, even for the most experienced project team, to effectively manage a complex process without a complete understanding of every piece, and an ability to visualize how each part fits into the overall picture. We introduce intuitive models in Part I to enable you to visualize the relationships before getting involved in the supporting application details of Part II.

As in solving any puzzle, it helps to know how many pieces there are. Rather than present the full inventory of management techniques, we decompose them into 10 essential and unambiguous management elements. We separate the planned, sequential project cycle events from those situational management and leadership elements that we portray in an orthogonal, three-dimensional model.

Those of you considering a commitment to project management can use this foundation to support and enhance your own experiences. If you're already an experienced manager, we're confident our model and visual aids will clarify your management thinking, extend your comfort zone, and make dramatic performance improvements—yours as well as your organization's.

These are just some of the ways this book will make a difference.

Improvements should be measured both on a personal and an organizational basis.

ENDING UP WITH THE GOLDEN GOOSE

Not every manager and every organization can benefit from creating projects during this time of transition. If you are unable to cope with things such as matrix ambiguities and responsibility without authority, you may be better off focusing on a support management role or supervising repetitive operations. By becoming a project manager, you'll trade job insecurity for a host of other uncertainties, including the very nature of your next project. On the other hand, if you thrive on adventure or aspire to the ranks of executive or general management, projects are your best training ground. Achieving the payoff depends more on your personal attitude than position—be it an executive, as one interfacing with project teams, or as a project manager or team member.

Regardless of your position or your speciality, you can ensure a successful future through project management.

Fortunately, the efforts you make now to revitalize the project environment, or to create one, can pay high dividends to your entire organization. The project team can be a catalyst for culture changes that may be needed elsewhere. This team catalyst can also become the most significant competitive edge a firm can wield in this technology-driven, time-compressed era. Whereas technology is surprisingly easy to clone, a well-integrated, highly productive project culture, tailored to your needs, is an invaluable proprietary asset.

Whereas technology is surprisingly easy to clone, an integrated, highly productive project culture, tailored to your needs, can be your proprietary golden goose.

PART ONE

VISUALIZING PROJECT MANAGEMENT: REALIZING SUCCESS

This book has been organized to achieve two goals: (1) your visualization of what project management is all about at the concept level; then (2) defining how to apply those concepts, together with the tools to do the tailoring.

Part One enables you to visualize the major relationships. We progressively assemble a composite view of the project management process much as the video camera does for dynamic sports such as gymnastics and football. The sports fan initially sees the total activity—the gymnastics routine or the collective movements of the football team. Then, zooming in for a close-up or replaying in slow motion, the viewer sees the precise maneuvers and subtle techniques that result in an Olympic or Superbowl performance. In this way, Part Two gets you involved in the supporting application details.

Finally, by zooming out in Chapter 8, you regain the broad perspective, but now with the awareness of details needed to appreciate the complexities of the total performance. Chapter 9, added in this edition, discusses selected issues in applying the process in today's environment.

1

WHY IS PROJECT MANAGEMENT A CRITICAL ISSUE?

It is best to do things systematically, since we are only human and disorder is our worst enemy.

Hesoid,
8th century B.C.

THE FUTURE OF MOST ORGANIZATIONS DEPENDS ON SUCCESSFUL PROJECTS

Whether for survival or to sustain market leadership, projects are the key in the new era of world competition. Projects are essential to the vital aspects of any business:

- Developing new products and services that meet customer needs.
- Shortening time-to-market for new developments (as evidenced by the recent international drive for "better, faster, cheaper").
- Improving efficiency and productivity.
- Strengthening competitive positions in national or world markets.

For some businesses, such as construction and aerospace, projects are the only product.

3

The Hubble Telescope is one of the most highly publicized project failures *and* successes (repair mission).

IT'S ALARMINGLY COMMONPLACE FOR PROJECT TEAMS TO FAIL—SOME DO WELL, BUT MOST DO NOT

Almost daily we are made aware of projects that have failed or not met customer expectations. Past examples include the Denver International Airport which suffered from both software and construction deficiencies, the Challenger disaster, the AT&T telephone system shutdown, the Hubble Space Telescope, and many others. Concurrent with these troubled projects are those that meet or exceed expectations. The Olympics are perhaps the best examples. They routinely accomplish difficult objectives on time and usually with substantially—sometimes surprisingly—higher profits. (Los Angeles' Olympics profit was $100,000,000—ten times that expected.)

Project performance is very team-dependent.

Widely varying project results would lead one to conclude—quite correctly—that project success is too often dependent on the specific team. Since projects and project teams are temporary, their performance may be incorrectly attributed to the luck of the draw. But any team can succeed when it is committed to the fundamentals of project management and insists on applying them consistently and systematically.

WHY DO PROJECTS HAVE A DISMAL PERFORMANCE RECORD?

Project Management is not well-understood.

Failure often results from fundamental confusion over precisely what is involved in managing a project successfully from inception through completion. Even experienced managers often disagree on important aspects, like the blind men that encounter the elephant and reach different conclusions concerning the nature of the beast. In the parable, the man feeling the tail concludes the elephant is like a rope, while the man holding the trunk decides the elephant is like a snake, and so forth. Project reality is such a complex organism that personal experience alone provides a biased view.

In an atmosphere of confusion, indiscriminately adding people usually compounds poor performance.

In an atmosphere of confusion—internally and externally—it's no wonder that projects are often poorly implemented. Typically, waste, inefficiency, and costly errors are compounded as hoards of new personnel are added in a futile attempt to recover from the incorrect practices that caused the failures.

Many projects fail by repeating either the technical or business mistakes of others, which we refer to as *Lessons Learned.* For example, the SeaSat Satellite failed in orbit when an arc across the solar array slip rings caused a catastrophic power supply failure. A prior project at the same company had solved this problem, discovered in a thermal vacuum chamber test before the launch. A *Lessons Learned* analysis developed by the project team after a project is completed would be invaluable to other project managers, present and future. But there is usually no mechanism for the lessons to get into the hands (and minds) of those who would benefit most. Furthermore, project teams are dispersed to other projects just at the time they should be documenting those learning experiences. Perhaps Thoreau had this predicament in mind when he queried, "How can we remember our ignorance, which our growth requires, when we are using our knowledge all of the time?" Of all the project management concepts, *Lessons Learned* from prior failures and successes is the most neglected. Project requirements should include such lessons, but even when documented, they're usually not readily accessible.

Lessons Learned from prior failures and successes are too often neglected.

To succeed, the project team needs training and support from above. Unfortunately, relatively few companies comprehend the full power of project management. The more difficult the times, the greater the need to effectively manage projects. Successful companies of all types have discovered that a transition to project management is essential to improve or sustain high business performance. So why do troubled companies appear reluctant to make necessary cultural changes? As managers rise in the organization, they often suffer a gradual loss of perspective regarding the change process itself. Too many executives are reluctant to leave their comfort zones and depart from tradition. They typically don't embrace or emphasize disciplined project management on any level. Their behavior can range from being reactive to showing no interest as contrasted with the ideal proactive management attitude (Table 1.1).

WHY IS PROJECT MANAGEMENT SO DIFFICULT?

Several major challenges, unique to projects, add to the demanding business environment discussed above. In this section we

TABLE 1.1　Upper Management Frequently Gives Lip Service to Project Management

	Proactive ☺	Reactive 😐	Slow React 🙁	Lip Service 🙁 🙁	No Interest 🙁 🙁 🙁
Project Training	All levels	Project team	Managers only	None	None
Management Support	Continuously involved	Reference manual	Reluctant	Impossible edicts	Sink or swim
Management Process	Up-to-date	Standard	As customer demands	Counter-productive involvement	None
Funding & Budgets	Planned	Controlled	By variances	No budget authority	Excess spending with cash cow
Project Mgr Authority	Fully empowered	Selective delegation	Reluctant to delegate	Responsibility w/o authority	Unspecified
Project Controls	Comprehensive and effective	Basic	Force fit	Arbitrary	Uncontrolled
Communications	Open to broad scrutiny	Formal	Defensive	Avoided	Closed to any scrutiny

highlight the difficulties inherent in a project's temporary nature, those inherited from misguided management, and others contributed by the need for nontraditional organizations.

For simple projects or complex, the only certainty is uncertainty in the increasingly demanding project environment. Our training programs continually provide us with candid, in-depth visibility into dozens of projects each month which reveal trends that threaten government and commercial enterprises alike. Some austerity measures are a one-way road. Here are a few of the more familiar signs of the times:

Uncertainty . . . is the only certainty.

- Layoffs and early retirement.
- Attrition without replacement.
- Dependence on overtime and outsourcing.
- Merging of organizations and cultures.

Plans don't scale by demanding more and more from less and less.

Marketplace shifts often force abrupt changes of direction. Longer projects face particularly elusive targets. Budget and contingency planning rarely account adequately for market shifts and schedule slips—a double-edged sword. A prolonged project can face inflated labor and material costs, and then eroded market prices when it eventually shoulders its way into the marketplace. Competitive danger signs include:

Tougher competition demands shorter time-to-market and squeezes the break-even point.

- Greater market-window risks.
- More contenders carving available markets.
- Reduced profit margins.
- Plethora of emerging technologies.

Conditions such as inflation/recession cycles, lack of borrowing power, and stockholder pressures have always existed, but not to the degree they do now, especially when coupled with technology shocks and dealing in unstable international markets, together with worldwide competition. Diversionary pressures include:

Outside influence, often distracting, is becoming relentless.

- High rate of technology change.
- More attention to legal, ethical, and fair conduct.
- Greater international involvement.
- Internet-based worker mobility.

Reaching new heights of efficiency and productivity, while laudable, may overtax the means. When carried to extreme, this can be divisive and divert teams from their primary goals leading to:

Inside pressure is being compounded by the other trends.

- Stressful, conflict-ridden atmosphere.
- Higher demands from a shrinking staff.
- More generalization and reorganizations.
- Worker unrest.

Productivity improvements wrought from automation and from pressure to work harder and longer need to be replaced by the elimination of costly errors through disciplined project management.

Inadequate skills. It's rare to find personnel with the requisite set of broad skills.

Staffing challenges contribute significantly to the difficulty of project management. Selecting the right project manager is critical to project success. The project manager must fulfill the requirements of the customer or user, must answer to senior management by generating a fair return on investment, and must provide a stimulating, positive work environment for the project team. Project managers must be skilled in technical, business, legal, financial, and personnel matters. Above all, project managers must be selected for their leadership qualities. They must be able to deal with all levels, from stakeholders who are often international and multicultural, to an internet-based workforce.

Project management is made difficult by the urgent need for a new group to achieve proficiency as a team. The temporary nature of project teams often brings together people who have little or no experience working with one another. Furthermore, people who are attracted by project assignments are generally motivated by intangible factors such as the work itself or the technical challenge, rather than being part of the team. The newly formed group usually includes specialists who have excelled as individual contributors. Some key team members may even be working part-time. This independence—both managerial and technical—conflicts with the interdependence required for teamwork.

Project managers must often overcome stigma resulting from a lack of training or inherited from previous misapplication of the most vital project management methods. To the uninitiated, a structured process can appear to be overbearing and bureaucratic—even to slow progress and stifle creativity. As in most complex processes, a partial implementation or one crippled by ignorance is worse than none at all. People who use the techniques or tools must be skilled enough to apply them for maximum effectiveness and to achieve support from the team. Misapplied techniques and tools will often lose their effectiveness and poison others against them—possibly forever. This pollution has been happening for years. Unfortunately, the personnel base has been poisoned against good techniques as well as bad. The negative biases are most likely to come from those with:

- Misperceptions based on flawed project management implementations.
- Bad experiences resulting from flawed processes.
- Misinterpretations of the causes of prior failures.

The nature of teams.
Teams are formed of a diverse group of talented individuals with little or no experience working together.

Negative bias.
Team members may be biased against good tools by bad prior experience.

The personnel base has been poisoned against good techniques as well as bad.

- Inadequate training.
- Fears that controls will constrain creativity.

Project controls are often perceived as constraining creativity.

Fears about tight controls are a major source of negative bias, particularly from the technical community, which often confuses project controls with lack of creative freedom. This bias may have resulted from arbitrary controls that didn't make sense or were never explained. Experienced managers know, however, that appropriate controls enhance rather than inhibit creativity. Such controls free the project team to be creative in finding solutions, rather than being distracted by the day-to-day confusion of misdirected project activity. Our surveys, summarized next and addressed in Chapter 8, were taken over many years and across diverse industries. They reveal that, in the absence of a strong project management culture, the most effective techniques are often not considered important for project success. Even worse, the project team is likely to be biased against the very techniques critical to project success, believing they aren't beneficial and should be avoided.

Opinions about project management, like those about Management by Objectives and Total Quality Management, are seldom neutral. People tend to be either fully committed or extremely negative, depending on their own experiences or perceptions. We designed a survey to be administered to participants entering our training classes. The survey measures the participants' candid attitudes about "how they value" a selected group of important project management techniques prior to receiving training. The results are summarized in Chapter 8. The wide range of responses, with most techniques falling below the 50 percent acceptance level, suggests that the majority of project personnel will not cause these tools to be incorporated into their organization or even support them if they are installed by others. With so many flawed and incomplete implementations of project management, it's no wonder negative attitudes continue to propagate. The project manager faces the challenges of assessing both individual and team attitudes on each issue and converting the negative and neutral attitudes into passionately positive ones. We address this challenge in Chapter 8.

The project manager faces the challenge of converting the negative and neutral attitudes into passionately positive ones.

Projects are quite different from traditional operations. A common form of project is historically exemplified by a construction

Projects defy tradition. Traditional management methods simply don't apply.

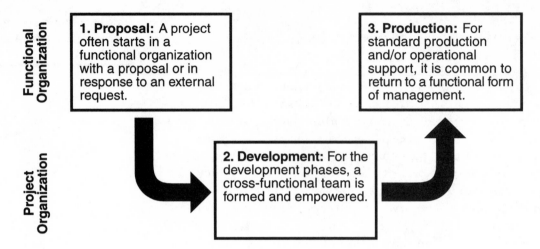

FIGURE 1.1   The evolution of a typical project.

industry project or by DOD- and NASA-contracted developments that typically create projects among many geographically and nationally dispersed companies. When the project team has completed its objectives, it is disbanded and its members seek new assignments through their skill center home organization. Still other project organizations are formed by one company at the core which then uses other companies and subcontractors as skilled resources. In all cases, project team members typically serve two managers, the project manager performing as their task manager and a permanent functional manager who guarantees the technical performance of the temporary resource.

The evolution of a typical project, such as a new product or new business development, usually follows three steps as shown in Figure 1.1.

Traditional management approaches deal well with the first and third of these three steps. They do not do well during step two—the heart of project management. Traditional working conditions have meant stability, continuity, and security. Conventional wisdom and traditional management textbooks have emphasized the need for the manager to create a productive work environment and a consistent climate including:

Conventional wisdom seldom holds true for projects. In many cases, it's dead wrong.

- Stable work environment.
- Minimum of conflict among employees.
- Ambitious employees driven to be their personal best by perks and personal competition.
- Simple, clear reporting structure and organization.
- Responsibility matched with authority.
- Maximum creative freedom.

There's very little that's conventional in the project environment. So conventional wisdom seldom holds true. In many cases, it's dead wrong.

As depicted by Figure 1.2, projects are as important to institutions as leaves are to a tree. Traditional management models focus on the enduring organizations—the roots—such as functional departments. By contrast, project management is more narrowly focused on the specific objectives of the project at hand. Like task forces and other temporary groups, project teams are drawn from various long-term permanent organizations. But unlike other temporary groups, projects are managed to a defined plan including a budget, schedule, and specific output—usually a product or service. Projects are requirements-driven. The customer or user defines the requirements to be met by the project

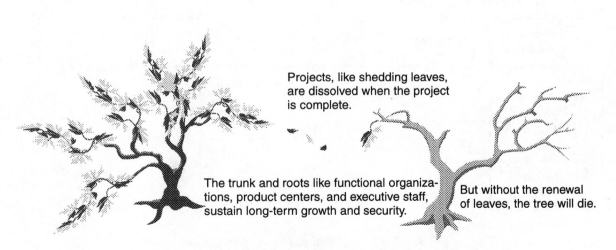

Projects, like shedding leaves, are dissolved when the project is complete.

The trunk and roots like functional organizations, product centers, and executive staff, sustain long-term growth and security.

But without the renewal of leaves, the tree will die.

FIGURE 1.2 Projects are like the leaves on a tree.

> Projects should not be forced into traditional structures used for repetitive or long-term work.

> Project Management is difficult to describe succinctly.

team. This may be done through an intermediary, such as the marketing organization.

Unlike the activities that occur wholly within traditional, functional organizations, project work depends on lateral flow. Therefore, projects lend themselves to some form of matrix organization, such as shown in Figure 1.3. Horizontal dotted line interfaces need to be encouraged and strengthened rather than used reluctantly as exceptions to the linear chain of command.

The nontraditional aspects and complexity of project management make it difficult to instill in others and install as a culture. This is exacerbated by the mixed heritage discussed earlier and the lack of training. Even when training is available, it is often based on models that are oversimplified and inadequate. For example, many models confuse and intermix sequential activities and ongoing processes. In the next chapter, we address the role of models in concisely describing project management and the specific limitations of current models.

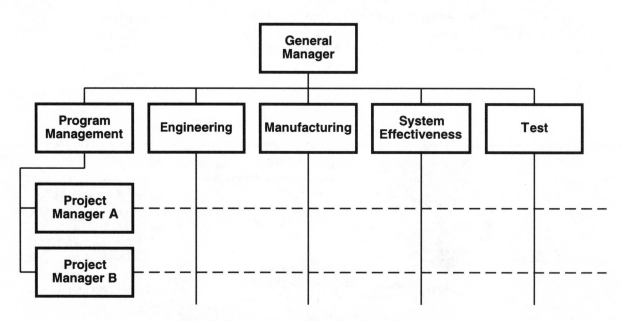

FIGURE 1.3   Typical matrix organization.

EXERCISE: PROJECT SUCCESSES
AND FAILURES

Based on your personal experiences and readings on projects, make a list of successful projects and those considered unsuccessful:

1. Describe at least three causes of their success or failure.
2. What was done to make the successful projects succeed? What should have been done to prevent failure in the unsuccessful projects?
3. What conditions create an environment for project success? For project failure?

Note from the text that the Hubble Space Telescope was initially a failure, but the Hubble repair mission was very successful. Note also that the Concorde Supersonic Transport, while technically a success, is a business failure requiring ongoing subsidies to remain in operation. The Chunnel (the tunnel connecting England and France) is another technical success that falls short of its business goals. Remember that over-budget, late, technical successes are *not* considered successful projects.

2

WHY MODEL PROJECT MANAGEMENT?

The power of a science seems quite generally to increase with the number of symbolic generalizations its practitioners have at their disposal.

Thomas Kuhn,
The Structure of Scientific Revolutions

WHY MODEL ANYTHING?

From road maps to wind tunnels, models help us to avoid costly errors and dead ends.

- *Models help to explain how things work.* Abstractions can be personalized and explained by math models or expressions. What young student of science hasn't been enlightened by a physical model of the reciprocating engine or of a molecule?
- *Models can broaden our perspective* as does a desktop globe or a model of the solar system.
- *Models provide a common conceptual frame of reference* just as the common vocabulary does for communications.
- *Models can express rules more simply,* often replacing explicit rules or providing a strong complement.
- *Models clarify relationships, identify key elements, and consciously eliminate confusion factors.* In Thomas Kuhn's words, ". . . all models have similar functions. Among other things they supply the group with preferred and permissible analogies or metaphors."

Models enable us to visualize the big picture. Visualization can be as powerful a technique for achieving high performance and success in business as it is in fields such as sports. Top athletes first perform successfully in their minds before competing. They experience their winning achievement visually—see it—even feel it. NASA researcher, Dr. Charles Garfield, reports that most peak performers are visualizers. Businesspeople who need to persuade others, such as sales personnel or entrepreneurs, benefit from visualizing their situation and the response they expect. Visualization—a right brain activity—is a vital characteristic of leadership, another right brain activity. We employ this technique to gain insight into the logical and systematic project management process—a left brain activity. Visualization can broaden your perspective on all aspects of your job. Lead from your right, manage with your left.

Improved visualization and intuition can be developed with time and training.

Psychologists agree that most people have insight and creative abilities far beyond those used routinely. Albert Einstein is just one of many people believed to have overcome traditional Western society left-brain learning patterns. He was able to "see" three-dimensional pictures in his mind before he wrote equations. He emphasized the importance of visualization to his own working methods when he said, "The words of the language as they are written or spoken do not seem to play any role in the mechanism of thought. The psychical entities which serve as elements in thought are certain signs which can be voluntarily reproduced and combined." Experts now believe that visualization, and the subsequent intuition improvements from right-brain thinking, can be developed with time and training.

It's empowering, even for the most experienced project manager, to comprehend the complex project management process with a complete understanding of every piece, and an ability to visualize how each fits into the overall project picture. But many practitioners and even trainers don't see the big picture. Furthermore, current approaches to project management lack sufficient clarity and detail to be applied routinely and effectively by the project team. This void leads to problems, including the single most common and high impact one, that of insufficient understanding of user requirements. This often results in deficient initial design, painful redesigns, and expensive time delays (Figure 2.1).

THE FAR SIDE   By GARY LARSON

FIGURE 2.1 Visualization without confirmation through a common language can produce a flawed vision of reality. The results can be equally misleading whether we see the world through the optimist's rose-colored glasses or through a "bugy" lens as this Far Side cartoon depicts. (THE FAR SIDE ©️ 1994 FARWORKS, INC./Dist. by UNIVERSAL PRESS SYNDI-CATE. Reprinted with permission. All rights reserved.)

With a well-defined project management process depicted by a model, it becomes relatively easy to:

- Convey to the team how the project will be managed.
- Communicate with others about the health and progress of the project.
- Assess the risk of alternate paths and take advantage of emerging opportunities.

THE ESSENTIALS OF A PROJECT MANAGEMENT MODEL

Several experts have identified the general criteria for an effective model, to which we have added specific criteria for project management:

- *Explicitly—and operationally—defined* as to structures, variables, and relationships.
- *Obviously valid and intuitive* to all project stakeholders. If a model has to be studied each time it's applied, it has minimal—perhaps even negative—value.
- *General applicability* throughout the project environment in a way that accounts for the complexity and dynamics of the project process and the special role that project requirements play.
- *Validated empirically* in the real project world.

To implement an effective process, the model must be intuitive because it is impossible to install if it can't be quickly understood and affirmed (it is difficult to install even if it is affirmed). Installing a well-defined "best in class" project management culture, based on the model defined in this book, coupled with training and certifying key team members, can dramatically improve the success rate of projects. To deliver as predicted, project-intensive organizations must ultimately come to this realization.

The first step toward defining an explicit model is to establish a vocabulary. In this chapter, we have already used several terms that likely conjure up differing images, depending on each reader's background. Examples are analogies, metaphors, systems, paradigms, and the term "model" itself used many times in this section.

The definitions that follow, from *The American Heritage Dictionary of the English Language, Third Edition,* explain the terms within the context used in this book:

Analogy: Similarity in some respects between things that are otherwise dissimilar. A comparison based on such similarity.

Construct: A concept, model, or schematic idea. A concrete image or idea.

> It is difficult to install a process if the model can't be quickly understood and confirmed.

> The model defined in this book, fully-installed as a culture, can dramatically improve your project success rate.

Depict: To represent in a picture or sculpture. To represent in words; describe.

Intuition: The act or faculty of knowing or sensing without the use of rational processes; immediate cognition. Knowledge gained by the use of this faculty; a perceptive insight.

Map: Something that represents with clarity.

Metaphor: A figure of speech in which a word or phrase that ordinarily designates one thing is used to designate another, thus making an implicit comparison. One thing conceived as representing another; a symbol.

Model: A schematic description of a system, theory, or phenomenon that accounts for its known or inferred properties and may be used for further study of its characteristics.

Paradigm: An example that serves as pattern or model.

Process: A series of actions, changes, or functions bringing about a result: the process of digestion; the process of obtaining a driver's license.

Relationship: A logical or natural association between two or more things; relevance of one to another, connection. The way in which one person or thing is connected with another.

Structure: Something made up of a number of parts that are held or put together in a particular way. The way in which parts are arranged or put together to form a whole. The interrelation or arrangement of parts in a complex entity.

System: A group of interacting, interrelated, or interdependent elements forming a complex whole. An organized set of interrelated ideas or principles. A set of objects or phenomena grouped together for classification or analysis. An organized and coordinated method; a procedure.

THE LIMITATIONS OF CURRENT MODELS

This section focuses on the need to avoid adoption of any model based on a superficial relationship. We often hear strong preferences voiced for one model to the exclusion of all others. This is dangerous. It is important to take advantage of the wide array of management models by understanding their limitations and then applying them appropriately. For example, some models are useful primarily for visualization and comprehension, while others are better suited for day-to-day management.

In this section, we critique several popular models. This has two purposes:

- To use the strengths and contributions of each model to enhance the visualization process.
- To be aware of the important omissions in popular portrayals of the project flow.

We will begin by revisiting a classic: Henri Fayol's[1] widely accepted management principles, originally published in 1916, outline what is necessary for effective general management. His 5 elements:

Planning,
Organizing,
Coordinating,
Commanding,
Controlling

continue to be popularized by today's project management practitioners as they struggle to accurately describe and model the nature of project management. Combined with Fayol's 5 elements, his 14 principles provide a structure for management direction:

1. Division of work.
2. Responsibility matched to authority.
3. Discipline.
4. Unity of command.
5. Unity of direction.
6. Subordination of the individual's interests to the general interest.
7. Remuneration of personnel.
8. Centralization.
9. Scalar chain (line of authority).
10. Order.

> Most management models are based on Henri Fayol's 5 elements and 14 principles.

11. Equity.
12. Stability of tenure of personnel.
13. Initiative.
14. Esprit de corps.

Four principles among Fayol's 14 are often missing in the project environment.

Project managers perform the traditional management functions of planning, organizing, coordinating, directing, and controlling. The fact that most of the management texts written since 1916 are based on the Fayol structure, with only minor variations and embellishments, is a tribute to the timelessness of this conventional wisdom. We will often refer to this classical model, confirming the general principles that apply to project management and identifying those that do not. Four principles among Fayol's 14 principles, namely responsibility matched to authority, unity of command, scalar chain of command, and stability are often omitted because some believe they are not desirable or cannot be achieved in the project environment. This is but one reason a new structure is needed for project management. We will return to this subject in Chapter 3 when we define the project management elements.

There is no universally accepted approach to managing the technical aspect of projects.

Next, we will summarize four current models or structures representing the technical aspect of managing projects. While these models are popular portrayals of the technical project cycle and enhance the visualization process, they all have important omissions. Part of the problem is that there is no widely understood or universally accepted approach to managing the technical aspect of projects. Furthermore, some popular approaches err in the sequencing of project events. More importantly, they fail to differentiate between sequence-driven and situation-driven management aspects. Viewing the project solely as a sequence of events paints a distorted and biased image of the overall project management process.

Most approaches fail to differentiate between sequential and situational events.

These last two problems became apparent when we set out to model the technical processes that drive the project cycle. We started with a commonly accepted circular diagram (Figure 2.2), previously used by a leading government agency to manage complex technical projects. This model, with its visible flaws, proved highly instructive. In this and other two-dimensional models, continuously present situational activities, such as risk analysis/ management, are incorrectly shown as sequential events.

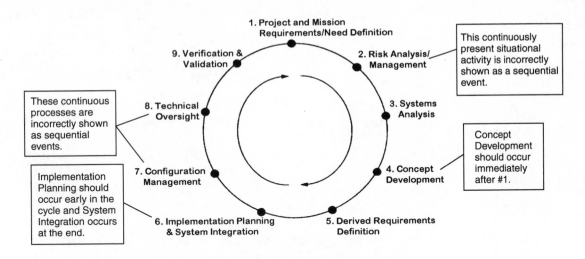

FIGURE 2.2   This circular model has several flaws.

Some models, such as one Department of Defense representation of the technical aspect of their project cycle (DOD STD 2167A), depict hardware-related events as independent from software-related events (Figure 2.3). The false conclusion that these two vital project paths can and should be managed separately

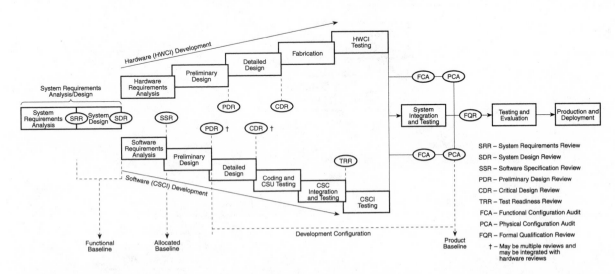

FIGURE 2.3   Hardware-related events, in the upward path, are erroneously separated from the software events in the downward path.

until final system integration has resulted in the failure of many projects. This model was in use for several decades, but was abandoned in the mid-1990s, when the Department of Defense directed its staff and contractors to use commercial standards for software development.

Figure 2.3 and the waterfall model (Figure 2.4) assume that work downstream should not begin until upstream uncertainties are resolved and major reviews (control gates) have been satisfied. This well-known graphic representation, developed by Dr. Winston W. Royce,[2] presents the software project cycle as a series of diagonal steps vertically paced from upper left to lower right. This process has been designated the waterfall model, since project activity flows from the top to the bottom in discrete, sequential, linear phases. In complex, high-risk projects this is inappropriate. Rona Stillman, a computer scientist at the U.S. General Accounting Office, maintains that "The waterfall model

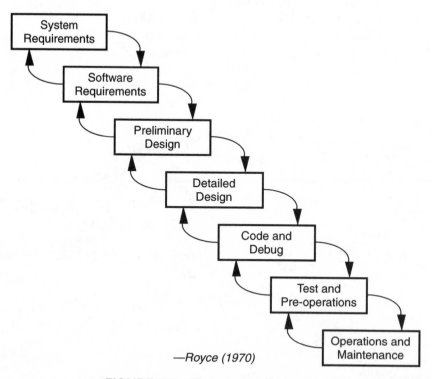

—*Royce (1970)*

FIGURE 2.4   The waterfall model.

is risk-averse. It encourages unrealistic cost and schedule estimates and the appearance of problem-free development." There is often a need to initiate software design and coding, as well as hardware modeling, earlier in the project cycle to ensure that the requirements are properly understood and to prove technical feasibility. For these reasons, many organizations have not embraced

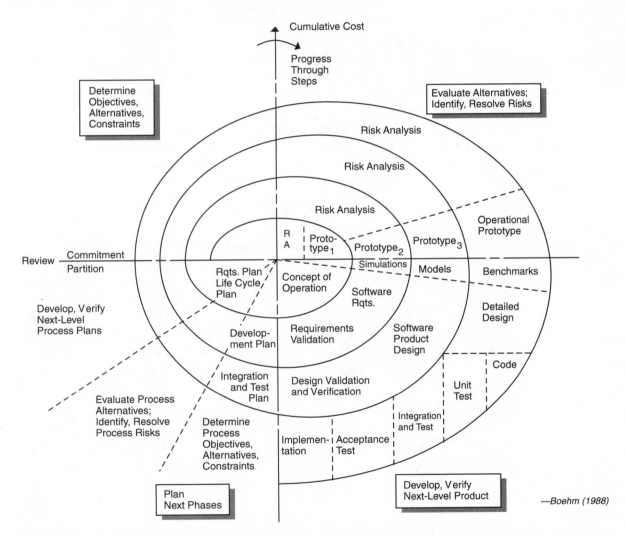

FIGURE 2.5   The spiral model. (Barry Boehm, "A Spiral Model of Software Development and Enhancement," reprinted in *System and Software Requirements Engineering,* an IEEE tutorial by R. H. Thayer and M. Dorfman. © 1990 IEEE. Used by permission.)

these and similar models. They are not adaptable to most real life situations.

The spiral model (Figure 2.5) attempts to address the previous problems. Developed by Dr. Barry W. Boehm,[3] this model is widely used in software development projects. To resolve the deficiencies mentioned above, Dr. Boehm addresses the need for early requirements understanding and feasibility modeling. While the model does achieve his objective of risk mitigation, the spiral representation can be confusing. The radial time base is inconsistent with traditional left-to-right time representation and the model obscures the reviews necessary to control the evolving baseline. A second shortcoming is that risk management is portrayed as a series of analyses (in the upper left quadrant) preceding and delaying low-risk product development rather than offering the option of performing risk management as an ongoing, parallel part of the development process.

EXERCISE: PROJECT MANAGEMENT MODELS

Using project management and system engineering texts, professional organization standards, handbooks, training company literature, and conference proceedings, perform research of available project management and system engineering models. Make observations of functional bias and of how sequential activities are depicted differently from situationally applied processes. As an example, concept development is a sequential event in the process while change control is situationally applied at any point in the cycle.

3

VISUALIZING PROJECT MANAGEMENT

Hundreds of people can talk for one who can think, but thousands can think for one who can see. To see clearly is poetry, prophecy, and religion—all in one.

John Ruskin,
Modern Painters

THE FOUR ESSENTIALS FOR EVERY PROJECT

The dictionary defines a team as a group of people working or playing together. But anyone watching a swarm of 6-year-olds playing at soccer, with each child focused on his or her own performance, knows that this definition is incomplete.

Imagine the challenges faced by a newly formed orchestra, composed of highly trained specialists, each capable of a solo performance (Figure 3.1). When they come together for a short-term engagement, they depend on four essentials:

- Common *vocabulary* of musical symbols.
- Commitment to *teamwork*.
- Musical score (*project cycle* plan).
- Conductor and baton movements (leadership and *management elements*).

FIGURE 3.1 Our image of a great project team is an orchestra, each member capable of solo performances, but committed to teamwork.

The several hundred successful techniques and tools fit naturally into ten homogeneous groups.

We developed the overall model described in this chapter to provide an easily-referenced visual depiction of the project management process. To aid in understanding and communication, the model had to differentiate between practices that are ever present, those that are sequential, and those that are situational. As we visualize the structure of each essential and the relationships among them, vocabulary and teamwork are seen as perpetual properties of a project, while the project cycle and management elements embody the sequential and situational properties, respectively (Figure 3.2).

We decomposed the project management process portion of our model into fundamental and unambiguous components. We continued the decomposition process until we identified the most

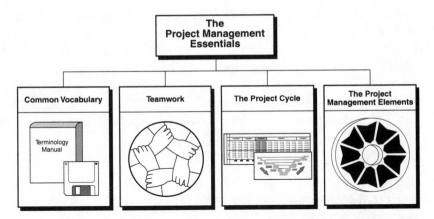

FIGURE 3.2 The project management essentials. *Vocabulary* **and** *Teamwork* **are perpetual properties of projects. The** *Project Cycle* **and** *Management Elements* **embody the sequential and situational properties, respectively.**

fundamental components: three Project Cycle Aspects and ten Project Management Elements. In the case of the Management Elements, we listed every technique and tool that we and other project management practitioners have used successfully. Several hundred were identified. The next step was to categorize the techniques according to how they are used. For instance, the work breakdown structure, WBS dictionary, project network diagrams, critical path analysis, scheduling, estimating, and others naturally fit into a planning group. Similarly, the techniques of measuring overrun, under-run, earned value, and others naturally fit within a group we called Project Status. We iterated the total group until all techniques and tools fit naturally into homogeneous specialities, forming a ten-element structure.

Techniques and tools that provided multiple benefits were located where most significant. For instance, phase transition reviews (known as *control gates*) provide the team with visibility as to what is happening, but the most significant benefit of control gates is to provide project baseline control. Therefore, control gates are categorized as a Project Control technique.

We've validated our model by extensive user experience, having used it to train thousands of project management practitioners. Our graduates confirm this model's unique ability to succinctly

Our model has been installed, validated, and refined by highly experienced project managers who report significant performance improvements through application of the model.

The trends toward specialists, each with their own language, coupled with the global and temporary aspects of projects, necessitate the definition of a common vocabulary for each project—even small ones.

convey the necessities for project management success. Clients report that they have significantly improved project performance by basing their culture on this model. We are further gratified with feedback that this concept has helped even the most experienced project managers better understand their role and become even more effective in their career.

After their introduction below, each of the following four chapters focuses on one essential.

A COMMON VOCABULARY—CONSPICUOUS BY ITS ABSENCE

In the previous section, we identified the four essentials through the imagery of an orchestra. When we remove any one of those essentials, a very different picture appears. If you've ever had to recover lost luggage in a foreign country without a common language, you can imagine the disaster that can be bred by misunderstanding.

We are constantly reminded of the consequences of vocabulary breakdown in our training sessions, which vary across a wide range of industries. Some terms we use to teach the practice of project management are confused with similar or identical terms used in the context of a particular business or technical field. For example, the term "proactive" has a prominent role in our project management vocabulary. Our usage reflects the term as defined by *The American Heritage Dictionary of the English Language; Third Edition:*

> Acting in advance to deal with an expected difficulty; anticipatory: not reactive, but proactive steps to combat terrorism.

This usage confuses some people. "Proactive," as used in psychology, refers to a type of memory interference where newly learned facts contribute to forgetting older information, a significant project management problem that we'll return to later.

Another prominent project management word, "status," has nothing to do with stature. The project management context is usually unambiguous, but what troubles some people is our use of "statusing" as a verb. Project Statusing, one of our ten project management elements, is defined in the last section of this chapter.

We will define terms and jargon as we introduce them, a practice that we encourage for every project team. Vocabulary problems lead to conflict and can destroy teamwork. Therefore, a common vocabulary is necessary before you can effectively communicate about the project and develop teamwork.

PROJECT TEAMWORK

Teamwork is often defined as working together to achieve a common goal. However, this definition falls short of the scope of project teamwork. The work portion of teamwork—that is, the creative effort needed—is usually not well understood. Because of this, real teamwork is only partially achieved.

Each of the following fundamentals must be developed and nurtured:

- Common goals.
- Acknowledged interdependency and mutual respect.
- A common code of conduct.
- Shared rewards.
- Team spirit and energy.

Most project teams, including the stakeholders, fail to adequately address these teamwork factors. Of these five factors, the most often overlooked is the common code of conduct. All too often, managers assume that a code of conduct is implied and understood even though it hasn't been explicitly defined and agreed to. This can lead to tension and separation among the team members, destroying teamwork. Many authors, including Jackman[1] and Kinlaw,[2] have addressed the issues involved in achieving successful teamwork.

Without a commitment to and implementation of teamwork, daily project activity would resemble rush hour in the subway. And it's difficult to imagine a talented group of musicians making good music without a common score and a conductor. Even in "self-directed" teams, the leadership role is filled circumstantially by strict adherence to proven teamwork processes. And while it is possible for a leaderless group to become a team, it is a time-consuming process at best and likely to fail in today's rapid-paced

Conflict and confusion may drive team members into incorrect practices—even to performing incorrect work.

The visual evidence of teamwork . . .

The coffeepot is never left empty for teammates!

project environments. With company survival riding on project successes, we doubt any CEOs would gamble on the odds of creating effective leaderless project teams—any more than preseason ticket buyers would gamble on the emergence of a conductor-less orchestra.

With a common vocabulary established within the team, the team can then engage in informed discussions about the project cycle.

THE SEQUENTIAL PROJECT CYCLE

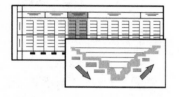

Successful project cycles, usually embodying a proven strategy and lessons learned, serve as a template to achieving consistency from project to project.

All projects have a cycle. It may not always be documented and it may not be understood, but there is a sequence of phases through which the project passes in pursuit of the project opportunity (Figure 3.3).

Professional project management organizations usually have a standard or template project cycle that includes their preferred approach. The cycle is tailored to the special characteristics of the project at hand. The resultant project cycle becomes the parent or driver and shapes the spine of the logical project network that will be developed during planning.

The cycle usually has Periods (such as Study, Implementation, and Operations), and Phases within the periods (such as Concept Definition and Verification). Phases include activities such as Trade-Off Candidate Concepts, products such as System Concept Document, and control gates or phase transition reviews such as System Concept Review (Figure 3.4).

Known by a variety of names that help to characterize it, the project cycle has been called: budget cycle, acquisition cycle, implementation cycle, and others. A complete project cycle usually contains all of these—the framework of the project strategy and the overall tactical approach.

There are three aspects of the project cycle that can be envisioned as layers. Each layer—Business, Budget, and Technical—uses the common phases but contains its own set of events. The interwoven events for the three aspects constitute the total project cycle also known as the opportunity cycle. The project cycle should span from user wants to project deactivation or reduced scope in accordance with the project objectives (Figure 3.5).

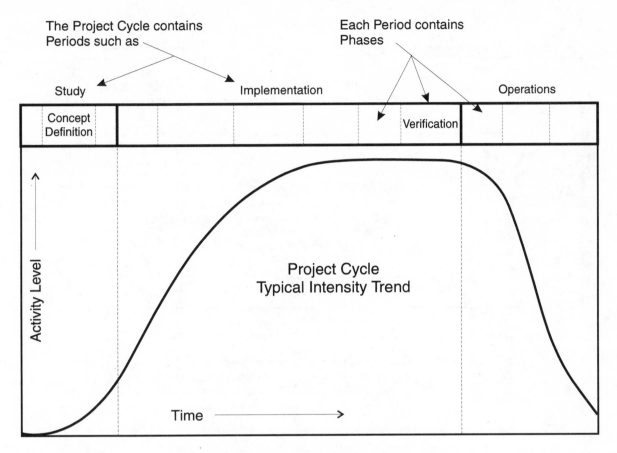

FIGURE 3.3   The sequential project cycle.

The business aspect contains the strategy for accomplishing the opportunity including the business case to justify the very pursuit of the opportunity. The business aspect includes the development of the top level "should cost" estimate for the concept under consideration, and it must be matched to the executive or customer "target cost." Events include approval of the overall program plan and contracting and subcontracting processes.

The budget aspect contains the management approach for securing and managing the funding of the project. It includes development of the detailed project component "should cost" estimates and events associated with applying for and getting approval for the project funds.

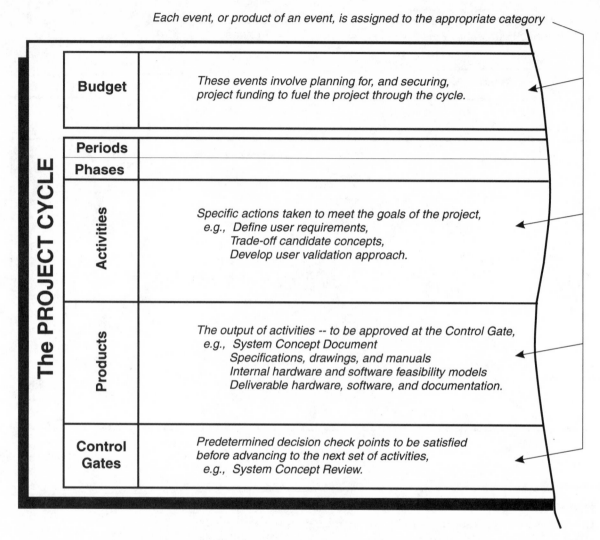

FIGURE 3.4 Our recommended format for the project cycle.

The technical aspect identifies the activities and events required to provide the optimum technical solution in the most efficient manner, a system engineering responsibility. Development strategy such as incremental or evolutionary and delivery strategy such as single or incremental should be reflected by the technical aspect of the cycle.

The technical aspect of the project cycle is best visualized as a Vee.

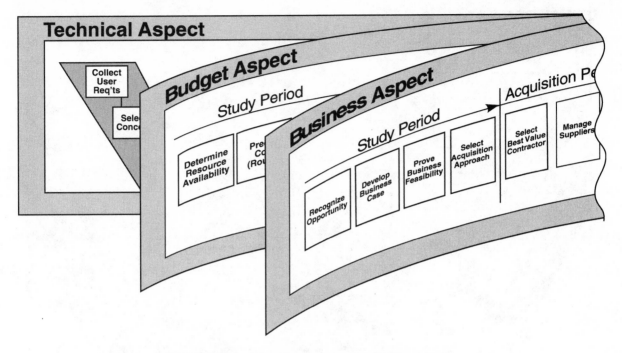

FIGURE 3.5   The three aspects of all projects.

The technical aspect includes the sequences for decomposition, definition, integration, and verification as shown in a simplified version (Figure 3.6). The process is best visualized when portrayed in a Vee format, rather than purely horizontal, to illustrate decomposing from system requirements and concepts down to detailed part and assembly processes and then upward consistent with fabrication and integration of the system elements into the completed system. Also included are the activities associated with opportunity and risk management. The basic Vee shape is similar to NASA's Software Management and Assurance Program approach that was used for a while in the late 1980s. The significant advance in visualization of the technical aspect of the project cycle[3] is the accurate portrayal of opportunity and risk management within the basic Vee model.

Work should not progress beyond a decision point until the project manager and the buyer agree to baseline the progress and implement formal change control to the new baseline. Unlike the

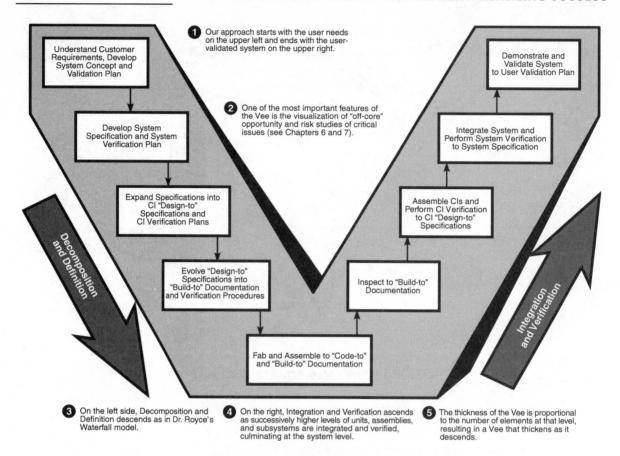

FIGURE 3.6   The basic Vee model.

commonly held view of the Waterfall model, there is no prohibition against doing exploratory design and analysis at any point in the cycle to investigate or prove concepts being considered. Unlike the spiral model, the Vee opportunity and risk investigations are done in parallel rather than sequential to the overall development process.

Hardware and software requirements-understanding models and/or technical feasibility models are encouraged at the outset to reduce project cycle risk. The use of the Vee to illustrate these fundamental and vital concepts is found in Chapters 6 and 7.

At each decomposition level, there is a direct correlation between activities on the left and right sides of the Vee. This is

The right side of the Vee directly corresponds to the left—the rationale for the shape.

deliberate. For example, the method of verification to be used on the right must be determined on the left for each entity and should be baselined to ensure verification methods are known and provided for. This reduces the chances that requirements are specified in a way that cannot be measured or verified.

The relationship between the sequence of project events (in the plane of the Vee) and the situationally-applied processes, is illustrated by orthogonal planes (Figure 3.7a and b).

We define the System Engineering Process to be the application of the Decomposition Analysis and Resolution (DA&R) Subprocess and the Verification Analysis and Resolution (VA&R) Subprocess to the technical aspect of the project cycle. Chapter 6 will address the system engineering process in more detail.

THE SITUATIONAL PROJECT MANAGEMENT ELEMENTS

Technical, schedule, and cost performance do not naturally work together. They are opposing forces that require compromise based on knowledge of the project's priorities and health. The management elements, summarized here, provide the necessary techniques and tools that can be situationally applied to manage the project throughout the project cycle.

Many texts and organizations attempt to apply the Fayol model to projects (reviewed in the last chapter and depicted in the first column of Table 3.1). While the Fayol model and its recent derivatives (second column) have a timeless validity to ongoing general management, they have critical deficiencies related to project management and the relatively short duration of projects. They fail to address the unique role of Requirements as the project initiator and driver. Even more significantly, they do not provide enough detail to manage highly complex project processes, particularly those of high-risk, high-technology projects. In order to provide greater comprehension of what is required, we have expanded these models. The resulting 10 elements, applied to every phase of the cycle, identify those indispensable responsibilities of project management that are too often misunderstood, minimized, or ignored in practice. This is not simply

> Technical, schedule, and cost performance are opposing forces that require compromise.

> Our model adds details that too often are misunderstood, minimized, or ignored in practice.

> Lack of attention to these details is precisely the kind of omission that dooms projects.

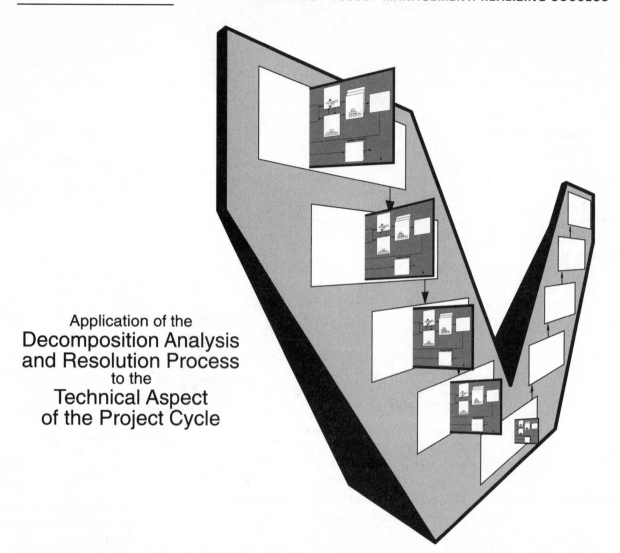

Application of the
**Decomposition Analysis
and Resolution Process**
to the
**Technical Aspect
of the Project Cycle**

FIGURE 3.7a The Decomposition Analysis & Resolution (DA&R) subprocess plane represents those activities that must be performed situationally as the project proceeds down the left side of the Vee. This DA&R subprocess is repeated at all levels of system decomposition and definition for each design decision that requires trade-off analysis. It will be repeated many times within a phase to satisfy the requirements for the corresponding core control gate.

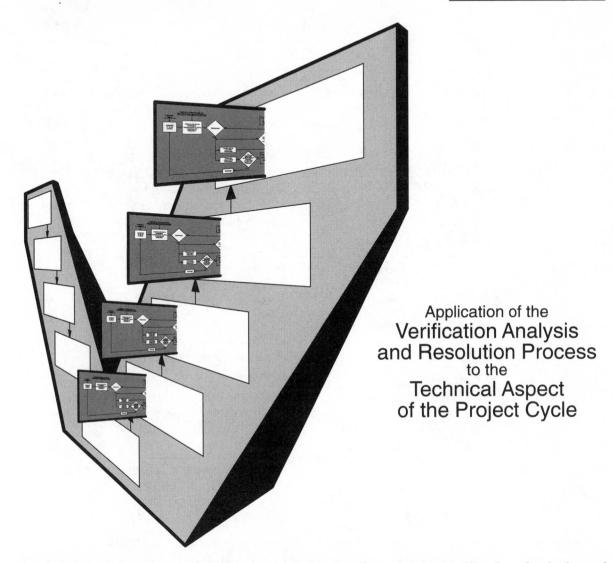

Application of the
**Verification Analysis
and Resolution Process**
to the
**Technical Aspect
of the Project Cycle**

FIGURE 3.7b The counterpart of the DA&R subprocess is the Verification Analysis and Resolution (VA&R) subprocess, an iterative process repeated throughout the integration and verification sequence as illustrated in the diagram.

TABLE 3.1 Relating the Ten Elements to Traditional Models

Fayol (1916)	Recent Derivatives	Our Ten Element Model	Rationale for Expansion	Major Focus
		Requirements	Failure to manage requirements, which initiate and drive projects, is the major cause for failure.	
Organizing	Organizing	Organizing		
	Staffing	**Project Team**	Teams are newly formed for each project and include subcontractors and outsourcing.	Formulate *Proactive*
Planning	Planning	Planning		
		Opportunity and Risk Management	Usually ignored in the project environment and a significant cause of project failures.	
		Project Control	Often improperly implemented as monitoring. Many failures are due to a lack of proper controls.	
Controlling	Controlling	**Visibility**	Visibility systems must be designed and implemented to keep all stakeholders informed.	Variance control
Coordinating		**Status**	Hard measurement of progress and variance, as opposed to the more typical activity reporting.	*Reactive*
Commanding	Directing	**Corrective Action**	Innovative actions required to get back on plan.	
		Leadership	Creation of team energy to succeed to the plan.	Motivate

another academic reorganization. Lack of attention to these details leads to omissions that doom projects.

The added and changed elements are shown in bold. For project control, the distinction between being proactive and reactive, noted in the last column, is particularly significant. Project Control embodies those techniques that help ensure that events happen as planned, and that unplanned events do not happen (proactive), whereas the three variance control elements define the means for detecting and correcting unplanned results (reactive).

Because they are situational, the techniques must be applied responsively, relative to the active project phase and the specific team or individual circumstances at the time. An example is the Organization Options element that is applied frequently as the project moves from phase to phase and changes its organization form to best satisfy the objectives of the active phase. Similarly, the element of Project Visibility will apply those techniques best suited to the active project cycle phase.

The ten project management elements are the team's toolbox (Figure 3.8) and, therefore, should contain the best and most effective methods in each category. This implicitly depends on the team being skilled in the application of all of the techniques and tools—which is often not the case. Projects do fail by misapplication of excellent techniques.

The ten elements are summarized next and are discussed in detail in Chapter 7.

Project Requirements covers both the creation and management of requirements. It includes requirement identification, substantiation, concept selection, decomposition, definition, integration, verification, and validation. Techniques and tools include decomposition analysis and resolution, requirements traceability, accountability, modeling, and others. While we do not discuss in this book the details of system engineering methods necessary to determine system requirements through data modeling, process modeling, and behavior modeling, there are many excellent references such as the text by Buede, *The Engineering Design of Systems,* which will guide those in search of more detail.[4] This element is situational rather than sequential since new requirements are apt to be introduced at almost any point in the project to be managed concurrently with the requirements driving development.

Situational management depends on the appropriate application of each technique . . . skillfully.

Projects sometimes fail by misapplication of excellent techniques.

Project Requirements

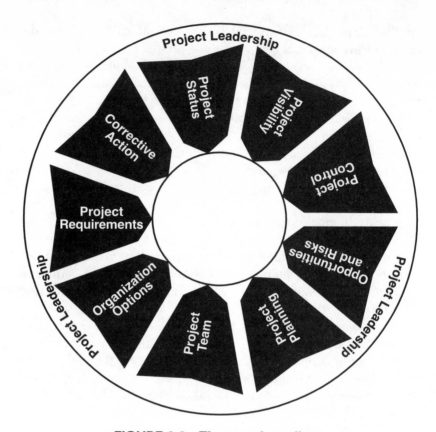

FIGURE 3.8   The team's toolbox.

Organization Options considers the strengths and deficiencies of various project structures (wiring diagram), for example, how each resolves accountabilities, responsibilities, and promotes teamwork and communications. Complex projects do not have to result in complex structures, and there is no single "best" organization. There are many options including matrix, integrated product teams, and integrated project teams—even "skunk works." (The "skunk works" is a name adopted by a highly creative and innovative aircraft development organization; the skills they developed are transportable and we will be referring to them in future chapters.[5, 6]) This element is personnel-independent and provides the basis for selecting and changing the structure appropriately as the project progresses through project cycle phases from concept to deactivation.

The *Project Team* element addresses staffing the organization. Selection criteria consider character traits, qualifications, and the specific skills demanded by the challenges of each project phase. Competency models that include necessary attributes and qualifications should form the basis of selection for key positions such as the project manager, the business manager, the system engineer, the planner, and the subcontractor manager. The best management approach may require that some key players be changed as the project progresses through the cycle.

Project Planning starts with the team's conversion of project requirements into team task authorizations including delivery schedules and resource requirements. But it doesn't end there. Too often planning is done once and is then forgotten as the project strays from its intended path. Plans must be kept current, reflecting new information and actual progress. The planning process should include both manual and computer tools which support the development of the best tactical approach for accomplishing project objectives consistent with the project cycle constraints. We encourage the use of the powerful technique *cards-on-the-wall* described in Chapter 7.

Opportunity and Risk management is an important part of the overall planning process, yet it is often ignored. This jeopardy, together with the need for focused attention and the uniqueness of the associated techniques and tools, justifies treatment as a separate element. This element encompasses the identification, evaluation, and management of both opportunities and their associated risks. It includes techniques for determining and managing the planned actions to enhance the opportunities and to mitigate the risks. Opportunities and risks may be identified at any point in the project cycle, so the techniques and tools of this element must be applied perceptively as the project progresses through the cycle. It is not uncommon for both of these factors to be ignored by the project team and many projects have failed as a result.

Project Control is often misunderstood because many projects have a project controls organization that reports activity and status rather than actually controlling anything. Controlling the

project is necessary to ensure that planned events happen as planned and that unplanned events don't happen at all. In our method, proactive control is recognized as process control where every aspect that needs to be controlled must have a control standard, a control authority, a control mechanism, and a variance detection system. Using schedule control as an example, the standard is the master schedule, the authority is the business manager, the mechanism is the change board, and the variance detection is schedule status. Categories of controlled processes may include security, safety, requirements, manufacturing processes, software development environment, schedule, cost, and so on. Reactive control consists of corrective action initiated in response to unacceptable variances. Many projects fail when control systems are not established or are circumvented.

Project Visibility encompasses all of the techniques used by the project team and stakeholders to gather data and disseminate information so as to ensure that the project team communicates effectively and is informed as necessary about relevant project activity. It includes manual techniques like MBWA (management by walking around) and project information centers as well as electronic techniques such as voice mail, e-mail, and video conferencing. The visibility system and associated techniques must be designed to serve the active project phase, the organizational structure, and geographic complexity.

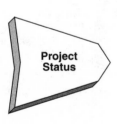

Project Status is frequently confused with project activity rather than performance metrics. Project status is not simply activity, but comprehensive measurements of performance against the plan to detect unacceptable variances and determine the need for corrective action. Status should encompass schedule, cost, technical, and business progress. The evaluation and measurement should also include the rate of change of the variance if not corrected. Earned value and other systems are included in this technique and tool set.

Corrective Action is the culmination of variance management and emphasizes that reactive management is necessary and proper for effective project management. Corrective Actions are the actions taken to return the project to plan and usually take place during Project Statusing, or shortly thereafter. The techniques may include overtime, added work shifts, an alternate technical approach, new leadership, and so on. Projects that

ignore variances and fail to implement corrective action are usually out of control.

Project Leadership is the most important of the 10 project management elements. Leadership is the mortar that holds together all other elements of project management and ensures that all the others are properly implemented and effectively used. It represents the ability to inspire—to ensure that project members are motivated on both the individual and team level to deliver as promised within the desired project management culture. Leadership emphasizes doing the right things, while doing things right is a primary management responsibility. Leadership depends on the skillful application of techniques such as handling different personalities and maturity levels, and team composition and rewards. History has confirmed that, without strong leadership, the team is likely to stray from sound fundamentals and implement high-risk, failure-prone short cuts. If the team members are fully trained in the worth of the elements and are believers in the process, then the need for strong leadership is reduced.

VISUALIZING THE PROJECT MANAGEMENT PROCESS

Presenting the project management elements in two-dimensional table form is useful for discussing the relationships among them. However, to illustrate the more complex relationship between the situationally-applied management elements and the sequential project cycle, we need to employ a third dimension (Figure 3.9).

Once a project cycle is defined, each of the three aspects must be managed situationally by the application of the project management elements. As an example, Project Requirements, one of the 10 management elements, occurs throughout the cycle as the original requirements evolve in detail and as new requirements are introduced into the project irrespective of the phase of the cycle currently being managed. Similarly, Project Planning occurs in each and every phase in order to prepare for the subsequent phases. We will return to this model as we implement the process in Part Two.

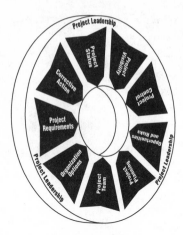

We begin by depicting the first nine project management elements as the spokes of a wheel, held intact by its rim, Project Leadership (the tenth element).

The sequential gated project cycle can be visualized as an axle. If the project is to succeed in business as well as technical terms, the three aspects of the project cycle must be simultaneously managed, as depicted by the three core sections of the axle.

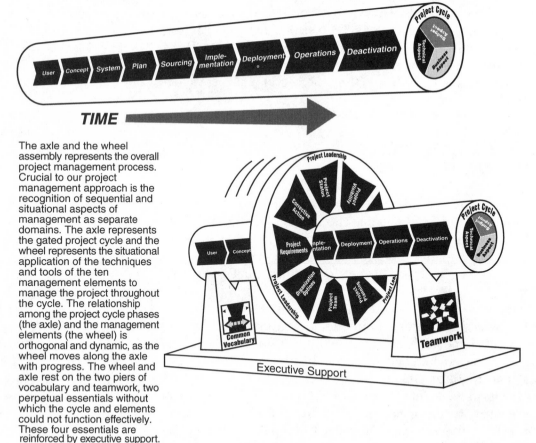

The axle and the wheel assembly represents the overall project management process. Crucial to our project management approach is the recognition of sequential and situational aspects of management as separate domains. The axle represents the gated project cycle and the wheel represents the situational application of the techniques and tools of the ten management elements to manage the project throughout the cycle. The relationship among the project cycle phases (the axle) and the management elements (the wheel) is orthogonal and dynamic, as the wheel moves along the axle with progress. The wheel and axle rest on the two piers of vocabulary and teamwork, two perpetual essentials without which the cycle and elements could not function effectively. These four essentials are reinforced by executive support.

FIGURE 3.9   The orthogonal model.

EXERCISE: PROJECT MANAGEMENT TECHNIQUES

Make a list of every project management technique that you can think of. Then group them according to the ten project management elements. When a technique serves more than one element, locate it in the element with the highest order benefit. For instance, a Project Review often provides visibility, status, and corrective action for problems; however, the primary purpose is to determine project status. A Corrective Action Review focuses on specific problem areas and addresses progress against the corrective action plan; thus corrective action is the highest order purpose, even though visibility and status are essential parts of an effective Corrective Action Review.

Example:

Requirements	*Organization Options*
Specification	Functional Organization
Traceability	Integrated Product Team
Standards	Matrix Organization

PART TWO

THE ESSENTIALS OF PROJECT MANAGEMENT

In Part One we presented a bird's-eye view of the management playing field—environment, concepts, roles, and goals. Part Two zooms in on application details in depth. In Chapter 8 we assess the future implications.

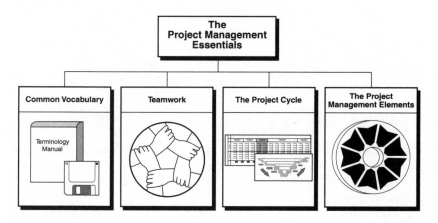

4
PROJECT VOCABULARY

Precision of communication is important, more important than ever, in our era of hair-trigger balances, when a false, or misunderstood word may create as much disaster as a sudden thoughtless act.

James Thurber,
Lanterns and Lances

A disaster such as that described by Thurber occurred when the term *qualified* was not understood and not responded to during the prelaunch readiness review of the space shuttle Challenger, leading to the O-ring failure and causing the tragic deaths of seven astronauts.[1]

TO SUCCEED AT PROJECT MANAGEMENT, YOU FIRST HAVE TO COMMUNICATE CLEARLY

We can't discuss the other three project management essentials—Teamwork, the Project Cycle, and the 10 Elements—without a common vocabulary. The successful practice of project management involves areas of conflict that can only be resolved with clearly defined terms. For example, communications problems lead to conflict and destroy teamwork; therefore, a common vocabulary is necessary before you can develop teamwork.

To press a suit means one thing to a tailor, and something very different to a lawyer.

TO COMMUNICATE CLEARLY, YOU FIRST HAVE TO THINK CLEARLY

To communicate precisely, you have to think clearly and use a common vocabulary.

John Beckley[2] articulates the essence of clarity, "It isn't hard to write something which, if a person takes the time to study it, is absolutely clear. But writing that has to be studied is not good communication. The meaning of good writing is so immediately clear and obvious, it doesn't have to be studied."

Beckley tells the following story about a man who wrote to a government bureau asking if hydrochloric acid could be used to clean the tubes in his steam boiler. This was the bureau's reply:

> "Uncertainties of reactive processes make the use of hydrochloric acid undesirable where alkalinity is involved."
>
> In appreciation, the man wired back: "Thanks for the advice. I'll start using it next week."
>
> Washington wired back urgently, but still in the bureaucratic jargon: "Regrettable decision involves uncertainties. Hydrochloric acid will produce sublimate invalidating reactions."
>
> This extra courtesy prompted this acknowledgment: "Thanks again. Glad to know it's O.K."
>
> Finally, another urgent, but unmistakable, message: "DON'T USE HYDROCHLORIC ACID! IT WILL EAT HELL OUT OF YOUR TUBES!"

"Snow jobs"—intended or not—can backfire. Your words may mean something quite different to your listener.

We've historically criticized lawyers and politicians for their confusing, often incomprehensible, prose. It seems intended to obscure rather than to clarify events. But in a similar fashion, managers and technical people often try to sound managerial or technical.

Jargon needs to be used as a means, rather than becoming an end, for communicating.

Unfortunately, Orwellian "doublespeak" has proliferated to all segments of politics and business, often in the form of jargon that finds us blaming everything on "paradigms" or a lack of "infrastructure." On the other hand, capitalizing on new technologies and practices can be facilitated by carefully defined jargon.

All too frequently, when an engineer sounds as if he's speaking a foreign language—one composed mostly of acronyms—it's because he wants to.

Acronyms can simplify communication if they are uniformly understood by the team. Remember to leave the jargon behind and to spell out the acronyms when making presentations or writing for audiences outside the project environment. If acronyms are used, define them as they are introduced and provide a glossary. We've included a Glossary for the acronyms used in this book.

The truly impressive communicator doesn't set out to impress anybody—just tries to get ideas across in the simplest, clearest fashion. Such a person is likely viewed as an outstanding communicator and project contributor.

WE ALL SPEAK ENGLISH, DON'T WE?

Many words, which are viewed as synonyms in common usage, have unique and distinct meanings in a technical sense. Stress and strain, commonly used interchangeably to refer to personal anxiety, refer to quite different technical phenomena, as do the project management terms, verification and validation. Few people confuse "bread" with its chief ingredient, "flour," but the ingredient, "cement," is often used incorrectly to refer to "concrete." Not many people care, but the distinction is critical if you are a civil engineer or a building contractor.

The assumption that we have a common language, when we don't, can have far worse consequences than trying to communicate nonverbally. After all, as jargon and jabberwocky proliferate, the language of choice will often revert to that more trustworthy standby: body language.

A leading corporation recently asked us to participate in a team session convened to identify for a major new project the opportunities, associated risks, and appropriate actions. It was the first time the complete team had been brought together so the project manager opened the meeting with a 40-minute overview of the project. We jotted down some 20 terms we didn't understand and later asked the team members which of the terms they understood. Over half the group didn't understand any of the 20 terms. Without a clarifying reference, the team didn't get the important message the project manager was trying to convey. But each remained silent assuming the others knew. The most dangerous assumption was on the part of the project manager who assumed everyone understood.

A major U.S. corporation recently signed a contract with a foreign government to rebuild that country's entire communication structure without understanding the meaning or implications of many of the contract provisions.

To prevent misunderstandings, one U.S. government agency includes electronic and printed versions of their terminology

The listener's ego may discourage seeking clarification.

It can be very costly to assume people understand when they don't.

manual with their Request For Proposal so that all proposals are based on the same definitions. Such techniques are now proliferating to other project environments.

EACH PROJECT NEEDS ITS OWN TERMINOLOGY BASELINE

In order to make this point in our training sessions, we ask the class to define several commonly used terms. We frequently select the following five from a substantial list of misunderstood terms:

Prototype, Baseline, Qualification, Verification, Validation

The class usually erupts into a great debate as they argue among themselves as to the correct meanings. The debate continues inconclusively until our project management terminology manual is used to clarify the meanings. There is a need for a common vocabulary, which should exist at the project level, since:

- Schools don't have, and consequently don't teach one.
- Most companies don't have a common vocabulary.
- Words are used differently across projects, companies, and industries.
- Terminology manuals, when they exist, are often imprecise.
- There is little effort to fix the problem.

The process of creating a terminology manual of any kind is not trivial. Consider the plight of James Murray when he agreed in 1878 to take the assignment as editor to create the Oxford English dictionary.[3] The job had been scoped several years earlier as a two-year project involving 60 thousand definitions. It was completed 50 years later with over six *million* definitions (estimating project size and duration has never been easy). However the process we use today to build a terminology manual is not unlike that used by Murray, where multiple sources must be consulted to create a meaningful document.

When building a project management terminology manual, one would think that, in the present era, existing sources in the disciplines supporting projects would provide a strong starting point. However, in reviewing one 387-page dictionary of mechanical design, we could not find common project terms such as prototype, engineering model, mock-up, specification, or qualification.[4] Yet, it is the mechanical designer who must implement those concepts on any project involving hardware. The software profession has been more aware of the need for accurate definitions; four of these five terms were found in the appendix to a software tutorial.[5]

When we turned to a well-respected reference from the project management field, we were flabbergasted to find that the word "requirements" did not even appear.[6] We think "requirements" are so important that we have devoted an entire section of Chapter 7 to the topic. On the other hand, PMI uses "scope" to refer to requirements. Thought these words are not identical in meaning, this clearly illustrates the need for terms to be carefully defined on your project. It also emphasizes the need for completeness. "Requirements" is a term widely used in high-technology industries, and "scope" is widely used in the construction field.

A terminology database, tailored to the project at hand, can go a long way toward fixing the problem. It needs to consider the terminology appropriate to the industry, company, and the specific project. The cardinal rule in constructing a project vocabulary is to make sure every item added is justified. It must contribute more to understanding than it detracts as potential excess verbiage. Try first to use ordinary language to represent a needed concept, using short words where possible. Only if the resulting expression is unduly burdensome, should a new term or acronym be coined or borrowed from a related field or industry. In the latter case, the use of the existing nomenclature should clarify, rather than mislead, through its similarities.

We surveyed several widely used terminology manuals (including NASA, DoD, and IEEE) and found them to be unclear and imprecise, often "relating" terms to other terms rather than explicitly defining them. This led us to develop a terminology database for our training courses. The result is over 1,000 definitions for acronyms, terms, control gates, and documents.

Prototype and *Model* are commonly used terms in product development projects. The traditional definition of "prototype" infers a model built by manufacturing under engineering surveillance. It

> A secondary benefit of a project terminology database is the rise in everyone's sensitivity to the need for precise communications.

> Why use "utilize" when you could utilize "use"?

> Desktop computers now make it easy to provide access to the project's terminology manual as a shared database.

is built to released drawings with production-worthy parts and processes and serves as model for manufacturing to replicate. This is the definition that was intended by the customer for a government development project. But the contractor interpreted "prototype" to mean an engineering model that could be based on commercial or even consumer parts bought at the local Radio Shack—a costly mistake. To avoid this surprise, their project terminology database should have included the necessary definitions. The following definitions are excerpts from our own terminology database:

Model—Engineering. A technical demonstration model constructed to be tested in a simulated or actual field environment. The model meets electrical and mechanical performance specifications, and either meets or closely approaches the size, shape, and weight specifications. It may lack the high-reliability parts required to meet the reliability and environmental specifications, but is designed to readily incorporate such changes into the prototype and final production units. Its function is to test and evaluate operational performance and utility before making a final commitment to produce the operational units. Also called an Engineering Development Model.

Model—Mock-up. A physical demonstration model, built to scale, used early in the development of a project to verify proposed design fit, critical clearances, and operator interfaces.

Model—Production. A production demonstration model, including all hardware, software, and firmware, manufactured using production drawings, production tools, fixtures and methods. Generally, the first article of the production unit run initiated after the Production Readiness Review (PRR). A Prototype model, also built from production drawings may precede the PRR, to provide confidence to authorize fabrication of the production model.

Prototype—Hardware. A specification-compliant production readiness demonstration model developed under engineering supervision that represents what manufacturing should replicate. All design engineering and production engineering must be complete and the assembly must be under configuration control. Prototype acceptance test data are presented at the Production Readiness Review (PRR).

In software, models such as screen designs or algorithm demonstration are often referred to as prototypes, hence the ambiguity of the term needs to be explicitly noted in the definition:

The term "rapid prototyping" has lost all meaning—it is seldom rapid or prototyping.

> *Prototype—Software.* An imprecise term, currently with multiple meanings. A "rapid prototype" is usually a software requirements demonstration model, which provides a simulated representation of the software system functionality and operator interface. The model facilitates early Customer-Supplier agreement of the system design approach. A software prototype may also be a technical demonstration model. Except with "Evolving Prototypes," the code is usually discarded once the model has served its purpose.

Baselines are the progressively documented set of functional, performance, and physical characteristics, mutually agreed upon by Customer and Provider, that define the evolving definition of the "to be delivered" item, as well as the project management plan for the project. (Note: Items that have not been mutually agreed upon between Customer and Provider are not part of the Baseline.) Four baselines are typically established during system development. The first three are the System Specification Baseline, "Design-to" Baseline, and "Build-to" Baseline. The last is the "As-built" baseline.

Qualification is the process of testing and analyzing hardware and software from components on up to the fully integrated system to prove that the design will survive the anticipated accumulation of acceptance test environments plus its expected handling, storage, and operational environments *plus a specified qualification margin.* Qualification usually includes temperature, vibration, shock, salt spray, software stress testing, and other testing.

Verification is proof of compliance with specification performance requirements. Verification may be determined by test, analysis, inspection, or demonstration.

Validation is the process of proving that the system meets the needs of the User. (Is the User smiling?)

SOME *CRITICAL* CONTROL GATES HAVE CRITICALLY CONFUSED TITLES

While the definition of control gates involves more than terminology, some titles themselves have been a source of confusion. We will use this section to clarify particularly egregious nomenclature. Control gates will be discussed in more depth in the next chapter.

Professional societies have defined control gates that are common to both government and commercial projects. Since these definitions are being broadly adopted by commercial industry in international environments, it is important to alert new users to misleading nomenclature. Some control gate titles are incorrectly based on their position relative to design approval (e.g., being "preliminary" to or "critical" to design approval). There is no universal set of terms all agree to. The Preliminary Design Review is also called an Initial Design Review by some, and a High Level Design Review by others. Moreover, the intent of these three reviews is similar, but not identical. The terminology we have selected is in wide use and clearly represents the concepts we wish to convey.

The *Preliminary* Design Review (PDR) is actually the *final* "design-to" specification and verification plan review. PDRs are really Performance Guarantee Gates because test and analytical evidence should prove that all performance numbers are achievable and no significant performance risk remains, and the end product will satisfy the customer. But in many PDRs you can count on only three things: coffee, donuts, and pictorials of the project approach. Specifications (major evidence to be evaluated) are often conspicuous by their absence, as are verification plans, having not yet been developed. Because it's "prelim," the audience is easily contented, but should not be. This confusing terminology may well cause the team to not provide their milestone requirements. Countless hours are wasted in PDRs that don't satisfy the criteria for the review.

All control gates are the *final* points for important project decisions. Even though one of the better-known control gates is called CDR—Critical Design Review (which is the "build-to" design review), all control gates are critical events in the project cycle. CDRs are really Production Guarantee Gates because test and demonstrations should prove that building and coding to the

> There is nothing preliminary about the Preliminary Design Review. It would be better called the Performance Guarantee Gate.

> There is nothing uniquely critical about the Critical Design Review. It would be better called the Production Guarantee Gate.

proposed documentation is achievable with acceptable risk, and the end product will satisfy the customer. That is, the design approach and processes are well understood and are repeatable.

The most critical of all design reviews is the System Concept Review where the system concept is approved, thereby committing to the associated lifecycle costs and risks of the concept selected.

The most critical control gate is the System Concept Review.

A FEW WORDS FOR THE BOOK (THIS BOOK, THAT IS)

In general, we will define the jargon and terms used in the book, as they are introduced. Here are a few exceptions. The meaning of terms such as customer and provider, as used in the Software Prototype definition above, seem obvious. But when users, buyers, and sellers enter the picture, roles can be confused. For example, a major airline may be the customer for an airplane that has many users, such as crew and passengers. The major airline, as the customer, may define the user requirements. Small charter services are both final buyers and users, but they would probably buy a "standard" airplane defined by the manufacturer. In this case, we designate the customer (as seen by the development project team) to be the aircraft manufacturer's marketing department. Since we use these terms liberally in the remaining chapters, we include their definitions here.

User The final party for whom the service or product is being provided. There are many types of users; here are some examples: product user, operational user, service user, future user. All four types drive the user requirements and provide constraints on the product.

Customer The buyer of the project team's product or service. The customer is responsible for defining the user requirements through interaction with the intended user (for contracts) or knowledge of the user community (for proprietary products or services).

Provider The final seller in the project chain, usually the project team itself.

Buyers All the intermediate parties in the project chain which must be satisfied by the corresponding sellers. For example, the project manager can be viewed as the buyer of services provided by a support organization or other contractor/seller.

Sellers All the intermediate parties in the project chain which respond to the buyers.

Stakeholder Any individual, group, or organization that can affect, or be affected by, the project.

YOU CAN LEAD A HORSE TO WATER . . .

"Accountability" is an important part of every project's vocabulary.

Project managers should hold their teams accountable to the project vocabulary. It is reasonable to have team members certify that they have read the project terminology baseline and that they are committed to using it.

EXERCISE: VOCABULARY

Develop a list of project-related terms and phrases used in your project environment that may be causing confusion and/or misunderstanding. With other team members redefine these terms with the objective of providing precise clarity in meaning.

Example:

Verified: Performs as specified.
Validates: Buyer loves it.

5

TEAMWORK

**One man may hit the mark, another blunder; but heed
not these distinctions. Only from the alliance of the one
working with and through the other, are great things
born.**

Saint-Exupéry,
The Wisdom of the Sands

Team effectiveness relies on many things: chemistry, attitudes,
and motivational sources. Achieving real teamwork depends on:

1. Forming a group capable of becoming a team,
2. Creating and sustaining a teamwork environment, and
3. Inspiring teamwork growth through leadership.

In this chapter, we focus on the second of these, creating and sustaining a teamwork environment, which is also the second essential
to successful project management. In Chapter 7, we address the
project management elements for team formation and leadership.
Team formation emphasizes the techniques for selecting the right
people and defining their roles—an ongoing process throughout
the project cycle. The motivational techniques needed to sustain
the project team are an integral part of Leadership.

Of all the challenges facing
project teams, the greatest
involves the people
themselves.

WHY DO SO MANY TEAMS FAIL?

Teamwork, so essential to effective project performance, receives
considerable attention today. We want our project staffs to become

Few terms are as evocative of today's desired work setting as "team" and "teamwork."

empowered teams—perhaps even self-directed teams. We organize our work groups into Integrated Project or Product Teams. We use Red Teams for peer review and Tiger Teams to solve problems. To manage quality achievement, we team with our customers. We have Continuous Improvement Teams. We agonize over the impact of telecommuting on teamwork. And then with all this emphasis on team and teamwork, we still collect groups of workers, tell them they're empowered, leave them alone, and hope that a functioning team somehow emerges from that forced proximity of a small conference room or an Internet-facilitated discussion.

When teamwork fails, it's seldom due to lack of good intentions.

If that wished-for team fails to emerge from that self-discovery process, maybe we'll organize an event called a "team build," at an off-site location. The staff discusses goals and generates mission statements. The event is full of good social activities—perhaps the traditional "build a tower out of drinking straws"—even some outward-bound type of outdoor experience like a "trust fall." Then, full of sociable camaraderie, we go back to work and watch the team that started to jell so nicely in the woods or at the conference site fall quickly and quietly apart, back into the group of individuals with whom we started. (See Figure 5.1.)

Once a group is formed, the people tend to believe they are a team, even when they're not.

Failure usually results from a lack of knowledge about how to get work done as a team. Inadequate leadership fails to create the environment in which teams can flourish. Furthermore, potential team members are seldom trained to share their efforts to accomplish team goals. The team may assume they know more about teamwork than they do. So we need to be able to differentiate between superficial teamwork and the real thing.

THE FUNDAMENTALS OF AN EFFECTIVE TEAMWORK ENVIRONMENT

Effective teams share several common characteristics. They can articulate their common goal which they are committed to achieve. They acknowledge their interdependency coupled with mutual respect. They have accepted a common set of boundaries on their actions—a common code of conduct for the performance of the task. They have accepted the fact that there is one reward

The special recognition usually given to the "team" portion of teamwork makes members aware of the need for cooperation.

Yet many teams fail.

Most team efforts fail because of insufficient attention to the ⟨WORK⟩ involved.

FIGURE 5.1   The "work" in teamwork.

they will all share. Add team spirit and a sense of enjoyment when working together, and the result can be a smoothly functioning team.

Our metaphor for a team, depicted in Chapter 3, is an orchestra, with a common score and a conductor. Both need direction from a commonly defined script (project plan or score) and need direction from a single point of accountability for setting the tempo of the project. However, having a conductor just wave the baton (or a project manager authorize tasks, its functional equivalent in today's project environment) is insufficient to build and sustain a team.

> The image of an orchestra reflects today's real project environment and the real nature of operating project teams.

Our dilemma today is that we can't take the time or risk for self-directed group discovery. And merely having a project manager and a kick-off event is insufficient to sustain real teamwork. So, where do the shared goals, the sense of interdependency, the common code of conduct, and the shared rewards come from? That's the work of creating teamwork.

COMMON GOALS

From a classical management definition, project team members usually represent a heterogeneous group of people from various

> Significant involvement leads to a sense of responsibility for—and, therefore, commitment to—project goals.

functional responsibilities. For this reason as well as the nature of project people and the teamwork culture, each team member wants involvement and proactive participation in management activities. These include planning, measuring, evaluating, anticipating, and alerting others to potential problems.

Building teamwork begins with clearly defining the group objectives and outlining the various roles and responsibilities required to accomplish the objectives. Gaining consensus on the top level goal is often easy. You must probe to the second or third tier to reveal and resolve conflicts. With the visibility of that team activity, ask each member of the group, "Do you really want to be a member of this team?" "Yes" identifies a potential team member.

ACKNOWLEDGED INTERDEPENDENCY AND MUTUAL RESPECT

We concur with Stephen Covey's assertion: "The cause of almost all relationship difficulties is rooted in conflicting or ambiguous expectations around roles and goals."[1] In the team environment, mutual respect, relationships, roles, and interdependencies are inextricable and develop in concert.

At the beginning, one very revealing team effort is defining roles. After team orientation and goal setting, the task of preparing personal job descriptions provides a maturity calibration point and offers an important way of getting feedback and confirmation regarding team role perceptions. These steps are the vehicle for the team to acknowledge interdependency and to establish expectations:

- Define the specific functions, tasks, and individual responsibilities.
- Develop an organizational structure and define team interdependencies.
- Define the scope of authority of each member.

All roles and mutual dependencies need to be acknowledged by all project members.

Some roles are informal, including personal activities such as tutor, interpreter, cheerleader, or troubleshooter. While there are usually formal, written responsibilities for project managers and leaders, team members' roles are too frequently informal. In her book, *Star Teams, Key Players,* Jackman[2] emphasizes the responsibility of each team member for ensuring the outstanding performance of the team—by becoming a key contributor. As each member is added to the team, it is a wise, proactive practice for that new member to define his/her roles and to have those roles acknowledged by the rest of the team and the project manager. Then the roles are adjusted as appropriate, to create team synergy and minimize discord.

Later, in the planning process, the Cards-on-the Wall technique (discussed in Chapter 7) provides a unique team building opportunity. As the schedule network evolves, interdependencies are easily recognized.

You can have very well-defined responsibilities, but if the interdependencies are not acknowledged, there is no basis for teamwork—only well-structured individual effort. For interdependencies to be recognized, there must be an acceptance of, and respect for, the roles that must be filled by each team member.

Like teamwork itself, mutual respect is easier said than done. You need to be aware of, acknowledge, and accommodate both strengths and weaknesses—yours and others'.

Role biases can be a major roadblock to respect. And that can even lead to potholes, as one of the authors learned long ago when mixing asphalt for a road resurfacing project. The contractor personnel took great pleasure in fooling the state inspector. A faulty scale allowed too much sand in the mix, causing the inspector to approve every bad batch. The workers thought it was a great joke until they depended on those roads. Many years later, the potholes are still a grim reminder of our deficient mix, and especially, of our deficiency in appreciating the inspector's vital role.

In a production environment, manufacturing often sees quality assurance (QA) as an enemy to be circumvented, rather than a vital member of the team necessary to project success. Conversely, QA has been known to stop production lines just to exercise their authority.

The space shuttle tile program (which developed and produced the external heat shield for the orbiter vehicle) demonstrates how teamwork, based on mutual respect, can mean the difference between success and failure. In the transition from research to production, problems occurred that no one knew how to solve. Manufacturing and QA personnel worked together very

> **Mutual Respect means accepting the need for the role performed by each team member and respecting their competency, especially if it is outside your field of expertise.**

effectively, helping each other resolve the many technical challenges. Responsibilities for traditional QA tasks were even shifted between organizations when people on the production line found a better way. A true cooperative and lasting team spirit, based on mutual respect, was developed between manufacturing and QA.

Though respect is earned, it begins by putting one's critical attitude aside and giving others the benefit of the doubt, without being condescending or patronizing. By keeping an open mind, you can acquire respect for your lack of specific skills, for another's competency, and for traditionally adversarial roles.

A COMMON CODE OF CONDUCT

> The right time to address legal and ethical issues is while they are only potential problems—before they become a career-limiting lesson learned. When it comes to conduct, just as in planning, an ounce of prevention is worth a pound of cure.

While legal and ethical issues have been receiving widespread attention in the news media, most of that has focused on government contracts where many watchdog organizations are hard at work. These more formalized government guidelines demonstrate the scope of the issue. We are now seeing this investigative process moving swiftly into the commercial arena, software piracy being just one example. The most obvious conduct issues are usually well-documented by company or government policies. But they may not be well known to all team members. And the gray (or ambiguous) areas, especially those involving contractor and customer interfaces, may not be understood or interpreted consistently. The project manager is responsible for reviewing these issues, together with the relevant company policies, to ensure that all team members are sensitized to potential problems. Figure 5.2 provides an overview of key legal conduct issues to review with the team.

Ethical conduct issues are more difficult to enumerate. Ultimately, one has to depend on personal values to navigate through the possible conflicts that can occur between company practices, laws/regulations, and management direction. When dichotomies persist, these guidelines may help:

> Ask yourself: "Would I be embarrassed if my behavior appeared on the front page of the newspaper?"

- Seek higher management guidance to confirm difficult choices for conflicts among the various codes of conduct.

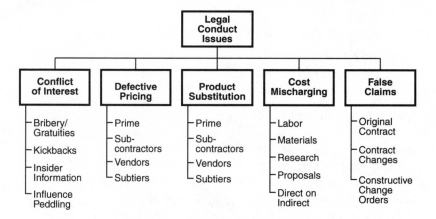

FIGURE 5.2 Legal conduct issues.

- If asked to operate in a potentially improper manner, make sure that the request is written and verify it with the cognizant authority. Do nothing that violates your personal ethics.
- Report any improper conduct, anonymously if necessary.

To be effective, a common code of conduct needs to:

- Resolve potential sources of conflict.
- Clear the air on gray areas.
- Cover areas not covered by other standards such as:
  —Working on new scope in response to an oral request.
  —Threshold value of a change proposal.

Categories to consider include:

> Customer relations.
> Personal use and care of company property.
> Attendance and work hours.
> Safety.
> Sexual harassment.
> Smoking, alcohol, and drug abuse.

Ask each potential member of the team: "Will you commit to abide by these rules of conduct?"
A "No" will surface issues to be resolved.

Gambling.

Falsification of records.

Acceptance of gifts.

Standards of quality.

SHARED REWARDS

Money spent on pizza for all may be more effective than a bonus given to the most outstanding contributor.

Shared recognition for all contributing team members on a successful project is often far more important than a cash bonus. People are motivated to do a good job and to cooperate with one another when they are confident that their individual, as well as team, performance will be publicly recognized and appreciated by their peers and their management.

Effective team cash rewards begin with fair and equitable compensation for each position on the team. You can devise awards which can be earned by the entire team or individual members. The concept of shared rewards suggests dividing a bonus pool by the number of participants. Shared cash awards should be given in small amounts so more can share or be spent on team recognition.

TEAM SPIRIT AND ENERGY

Instilling teamwork cooperation often begins with uninstalling the "me-first" competition culture deeply scripted in most people by their education and business experience.

This quality depends on personal attitudes as well as company culture and begins with:

- An agreement to pool resources.
- Interdependence rather than independence.
- Desire to do whatever is necessary to succeed.
- Placing team needs above one's own needs.
- Never asking the team to do what you are not willing to do.

Independent thinking alone is not suited to the interdependent project reality. Putting the team ahead of oneself, however, does not mean the elimination of strong "pacesetters." The driver-type personalities need to exercise their assertiveness and energy without dominating their teammates. This sometimes involves subtle leadership techniques.

TECHNIQUES FOR BUILDING AND SUSTAINING TEAMWORK: THE WORK OF TEAMWORK

Creating and sustaining effective teamwork requires on-going work on the part of all team members. Many team building efforts fail either because essential techniques are unknown or applied inappropriately by participants unaware of the situational nature of project management and leadership.

While team building is a total team responsibility, we will focus first on what the project manager can do to foster and nurture a fledgling team. First, we need to refine our image of the team as an orchestra led by the project manager. In the project reality, the project manager is both the composer and the conductor. To quote Peter Drucker,[3] "This task requires the manager to bring out and make effective whatever strength there is in his or her resources—and above all in the human resources—and neutralize whatever there is as weakness. This is the only way in which a genuine whole can ever be created."

Like any other development process, there is a gestation period involved. The project manager must avoid over-directing and smothering the team. On the other hand, too much freedom can cause a new team to founder. The project manager must:

- Clearly define unambiguous responsibilities.
- Define and communicate a project process and style.
- Delegate wherever possible.
- Empower the team to be accountable.
- Balance support with direction as required.
- Train the team, by example, to operate as a team.
- Deal with under-performers who drag the team down.
- Establish team-effort rewards.
- Design the tasks and work packages in a way to encourage teamwork.

The leadership techniques discussed next pertain especially to building teamwork.

Teams don't always need managers to do things right, but leaders always need teams doing the right things.

The project manager is the most responsible for sustaining a whole that is larger than the sum of its parts.

TEAM KICK-OFF MEETINGS

The kick-off meeting may
be the best opportunity the
project manager has to
communicate the project
vision to the team in
relationship to their work.

The kick-off meeting should be a working session. When properly led by the project manager, it can provide each team member with a sense of organization, stability, and personal as well as team accomplishment. Proper leadership includes a detailed agenda. In *Dynamic Project Management,*[4] the authors offer a detailed agenda for the team kick-off meeting. Emphasizing this opportunity to commit the team members to a common goal, they list eight meeting goals, which we have paraphrased below in items 1 and 4 through 10:

As in football, a successful
kick-off has the team lined
up and heading for the
common goal(post).

1. Introduce project team members.
2. Define the overall project (objectives, goals, strategies).
3. Describe key deliverables, key milestones, constraints, opportunities and risks.
4. Review the team mission and develop supporting goals interactively.
5. Determine reporting relationships and interactions with other teams.
6. Define lines of communication and interfaces.
7. Review preliminary project plans.
8. Pinpoint high-risk or problem areas.
9. Delineate responsibilities.
10. Generate and obtain commitment.

Video recording the kick-off meeting may provide an important resource for new members added later.

TEAM PLANNING AND PROBLEM SOLVING

Planning is a continuing
activity, not a one-time
event.

In a team context, these are excellent team building tools, offering opportunities for training, environment setting, and reinforcement. For planning and network development, we use a technique called "Cards on the Wall," described in Chapter 7, to involve the project team in the planning process. It facilitates team development of the tactical approach and buy-in on the planned actions. Once created, the plan will need to be revisited by the team at each phase transition point to ensure that it remains valid and that current plans incorporate previous lessons learned.

DEFINING AND COMMUNICATING A DECISION PROCESS AND STYLE

Even though leadership style and the decision process will vary with the project situation, most managers have a preferred or default style which needs to be communicated to the team. This is detailed in the section on leadership in Chapter 7. In many project environments, a consensus decision process fosters teamwork and is more effective than the extremes of unilateral or unanimous decision-making, depicted in Figure 5.3.

A consensus decision process consists of a thorough discussion until all team members have had a fair hearing and all members are

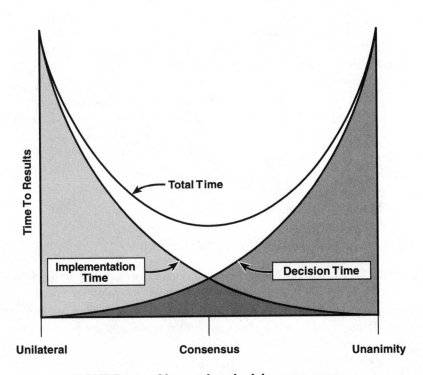

FIGURE 5.3 Alternative decision processes.

committed to accept and support the group decision. Reaching a consensus may require compromises, but it does *not* involve:

- Voting or averaging.
- Bargaining or trading-off.
- Steam-rolling or flipping a coin.

Consensus decision-making is most effective when:

- You don't know who has the expertise.
- Your facts are insufficient to decide and you need the judgment of a group of involved personnel.
- You need the commitment of the group for the implementation.

Setting the decision environment is not a one-time activity. Let's say you've decided to operate throughout the project on a consensus basis. You find that it works well for team planning of the project, but not as you get into the actual work. Individual contributors with differing work habits and desire for flexible work schedules make consensus building at each decision point cumbersome. Finally, as you hit a real crisis in the program, you can't wait for the team. You make a decision unilaterally and that irritates everyone on the project. The urgency of the situation called for a change in style—an important right for the leader. But teamwork suffered when you changed your style without letting the team know when or why the change was necessary. An effective leader would reveal the reasons when announcing the planned change.

> Management styles need to be appropriate to the situation. The key to success is in communicating your style appropriately as well.

PROJECT INFORMATION CENTERS

> The Project Information Center should portray timely, accurate, and relevant information.

Centers where staff can review current information on the project in near-real-time offer an efficient means to share information. Sharing information with the team is a way of reinforcing the vision and setting a good communications example. Current information also enhances the team's ability to reach a shared reward. But what information do you share and how often do you share it? Typical project dynamics suggest that selecting relevant information throughout the project is essential because as the project changes, so does the type of information needed, as well as its timeliness. Out-of-date status charts and schedules vividly reveal a lack of attention to the details of project management and the lack of importance you place on team communication.

DEALING WITH UNDER-PERFORMERS WHO DRAG THE TEAM DOWN

All too often project managers are reluctant to lose a warm body because of scarce human resources. This can be shortsighted. The under-performer may represent more of a drag than his or her contribution represents. It also sends the wrong message to the remainder of the team. They need to know exactly what kind of performance it takes to earn job security.

> When removing a team member, the manager needs to let the others know why—in direct, simple terms.

TEAM EVENTS AND CELEBRATIONS

These are opportunities for creative team building. Events that simulate the project environment through outdoor activities, for example, are extremely useful at start-up time. There is also a continuing need for team rebuilding throughout the project as new challenges are faced and especially as new project members join. The techniques, useful in the later stages of the project, should focus more closely on the actual project where lessons learned can be incorporated into the event.

> Be careful not to leave someone out!

Look for positive events and report them publicly at staff meetings and project reviews. Enlist the customer when appropriate. Go off-site . . . even pizza and milk (hey, it is good; try it) (no money is no excuse).

TRAINING

As formal courses or as an integral part of any team activity, training can contribute significantly to teamwork. Project management courses, such as those we conduct for our clients, are only the starting point for training—an on-going management responsibility. Senior team members should take any opportunities to reinforce the team principles presented in formal training sessions.

> Training is leadership.

REWARD ACHIEVEMENT

Good performance needs
to be rewarded—what gets
rewarded gets done.

Remember that rewards come in many forms and, wherever possible, recognize group contributions as did the shared rewards discussed earlier.

Rewarding achievement is the one technique that most consider easy to apply. There is a talent, however, in rewarding performance effectively. For example, if you like to start meetings by recognizing good performance, you're obliged to make sure you're aware of the supporting details. Many a compliment backfires by irritating someone else who contributed to the work while the recipient was just the most visible (or worse, the highest ranking). Paying for accomplishments is another traditional reward that has to be done judiciously.

REINFORCEMENT

Techniques used to remind team members of the continuing requirements of working as a team include: focusing on the common goal once established and accepted by the team; maintaining respect for the functions, roles, and positions within the team; acceptance of interdependencies; continued acceptance of the evolving common code of conduct; and adjusting the shared rewards as the project matures. The leader must emphasize the essentials of teamwork throughout the project. Posters and slogans around a team room (reminding people of important things) can be helpful.

WHEN IS YOUR GROUP REALLY A TEAM?

You need to confirm that
your leadership is working
on an on-going basis as
measured by observable
behavior.

Teamwork, like motherhood and apple pie, is something everyone claims to believe in. People tend to believe they're a team, even when they are not. It would be useful to have a means to assess if your team really is one. Kinlaw[5] has drawn on his decades of experience in working with both industry and government teams to create a "superior team development inventory (STDI)." His inventory questionnaire is presented in the appendix of his book for use by all.

The surest way to get off on a false start is to convene the troops for a kick-off session that is little more than a pep talk. It may feel good to you, but it won't last. Likewise, the surest way to a dead stop is to use teamwork techniques sparingly or only as reactions to problems.

Positive Indicators	*Negative Indicators*
A positive cooperative climate prevails.	A climate of suspicion and distrust exists.
Information flows freely between team members.	Information is hoarded or withheld.
No work is considered beyond an individual's job description. If it needs to be done and you can do it, then do it!	Finger-pointing and defensiveness prevails.
Interpersonal interactions are spontaneous and positive.	Counterproductive subgroups and cliques begin to form.
The collective energy of the team is high.	"Fear of failure" causes individuals to avoid or postpone making important decisions.
Real teamwork focuses the energy of a diverse group of individuals, having different personality traits and skills, to optimally accomplish a common goal.	The absence of teamwork doesn't lead just to low productivity, it creates a counterproductive environment which saps the energy of the group and demotivates the individuals.

EXERCISE: TEAMWORK

From your personal experience, identify those teams, of any type, that exhibited good and poor teamwork. For each team identified, evaluate to what extent they implemented the four fundamentals to effective teamwork, (1) Common goal, (2) Acknowledged interdependency, (3) Common code of conduct, and (4) Shared reward. Make recommendations for improving the teamwork of the poor performing teams.

TEAM STRUCTURE EXERCISE

Define the following terms:

- Functional team.
- Integrated product team.
- Integrated process team.
- Self-directed team.
- Leaderless team.
- Distributed team.

Discuss the strengths and weaknesses of each of the above, and evaluate personal experiences with these team structures in a project environment. Describe the suitability of these team structures for the following project types:

- Exploratory research.
- Quick reaction project.
- Large system development.
- New product development and production.

6

THE PROJECT CYCLE

Every step of progress the world has made has been from scaffold to scaffold, and from stake to stake.

Wendell Phillips,
Speech Oct. 15, 1851

This chapter is about project management scaffolding, the Project Cycle. It's about progressing from stake to stake—the Control Gates we introduced in Chapter 3. The foundation is the project cycle that reflects the sequential management approach for realizing the project opportunity (Figure 6.1).

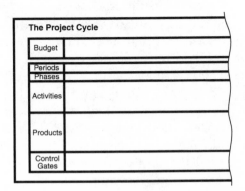
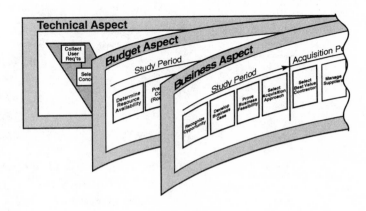

FIGURE 6.1   The project cycle format and the three aspects.

DEFINE A PROJECT CYCLE OR WANDER THROUGH THE INSTITUTIONAL FOREST

Even though all projects travel through a sequence of events, the road may not be mapped or the route may not be clearly understood.

In our training and project management experience, we often encounter the following types of project travelers,

1. Those who follow a project cycle and accept it because it's dictated by their customers or management.
2. Those who don't define a project cycle, having not previously heard of the concept.

The former tolerate the concept because compliance is directed, and the latter reject it because it appears too formal and bureaucratic. Both are victims of a failure to appreciate the power of the project cycle as a road map for an enterprise and as a flexible and effective risk management tool.

In the absence of a clear and desirable management approach to be taken on a project, and without the major milestones (control gates) for assuring progress and baseline approval, project teams are left to create their own sequence models or wander ad hoc hoping they are navigating correctly. In this competitive era requiring short time-to-market, the institutionalized project cycle becomes the time-proven lessons-learned road from which you can take shortcuts—but only if you know the regular route first.

An appropriate project cycle contributes significantly to doing the project right the first time.

The impact of not establishing a gated project cycle can be devastating, as the case of a national Health Maintenance Organization (HMO) constructing new medical facilities. Historically, in the absence of a defined project cycle, the HMO's management had not been intimately involved in important design decisions. When the facilities department undertook a project to build a new hospital, general opinions were gathered informally and no sign-off or baseline was required. There were no control gates to involve the appropriate stakeholders—such as doctors—and to get formal approvals at the right time and by the right stakeholders. For example, the doctors (the operational users) were not required to approve the dimensionally correct floorplan. As a result, after the hospital was built, the doctors didn't like it and directed considerable rearrangement of facility layout before anyone could move in, a costly rework.

In this chapter, we will present a template that can be applied to a wide range of projects, in both government and commercial environments. This framework can be used to proactively manage projects through a sequential management approach that is:

- Orderly,
- Methodical, and
- Disciplined.

Since not all events and features in our template pertain to a specific organization or project, you will need your own version. To define a project-specific cycle, each entry must be carefully considered, resulting in a conscious decision to include it or not. This avoids errors of omission while taking advantage of a comprehensive field-tested format.

A powerful way to build a tailored project cycle is to decide first on the appropriate periods (Study, Implementation, Operational) for your project. Second, identify the control gates needed to effectively manage the project. If phases are defined within a period, control gates are usually at the end of each phase, but they might also be beneficial within a phase. Third, you need to determine the products (documents, models, test articles, etc.) that must be in evidence at each control gate to give assurance that the project has met the goals of the phase or subphase, and is ready to move forward (exit and entry criteria). Fourth, having defined what must be produced within a phase, you can then identify the activities required to create those products. These data provide a framework for building the project network and schedule (discussed in Chapter 7). We will return to the tailoring process after reviewing the project cycle content.

Our project cycle template is divided into three periods: the Study Period, the Implementation Period, and the Operations Period. These periods correspond to the three major stages of the project as it progresses from an identified user need, through concept determination, implementation, and ultimately to production and/or user operation. Figure 6.2a depicts representative government and commercial periods and phases along with our project cycle template discussed next.

In their book, *Microsoft Secrets,* Cusumano and Selby describe the Microsoft project cycle for new product development.[1]

We define the project cycle as an orderly sequence of integrated activities, performed in phases, leading to success.

Any feature eliminated from a proven template should be justified.

Many disciplined companies follow some version of a project cycle that is divided into periods and further subdivided into phases.

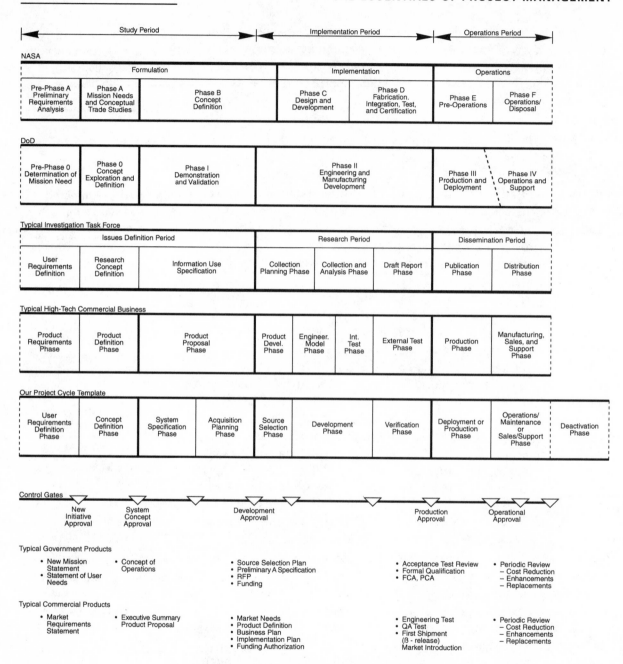

FIGURE 6.2a   Project cycle templates.

The Microsoft cycle, which typically lasts from 12 to 24 months, has three phases (Planning, Development, and Stabilization). Each of the phases has detailed activities, products, and control gates. The final control gate, at the end of the stabilization phase, has a title that should delight users of Microsoft products; it is called "Zero bug release." Although their terms differ somewhat from those used in Figure 6.2a, their description of the cycle fits exactly the model we have described here. The uniqueness lies in the determination of user needs, which initiates all cycles. This will be discussed in Chapter 7.

> Even though projects can be initiated very differently, they are subject to similar project management processes once the requirements are established.

The customer determines the need and user requirements and then contracts with the provider (ultimately, the project team) to develop the product or service. The customer could be a government agency, a commercial enterprise, or a company's internal marketing department.

Even in highly creative commercial organizations one must have a defined process, and must manage projects in a business-like fashion. The development of new attractions begins with "blue sky" explorations and concludes with a new exhibit or ride (Figure 6.2b). Many theme-park organizations, including Walt

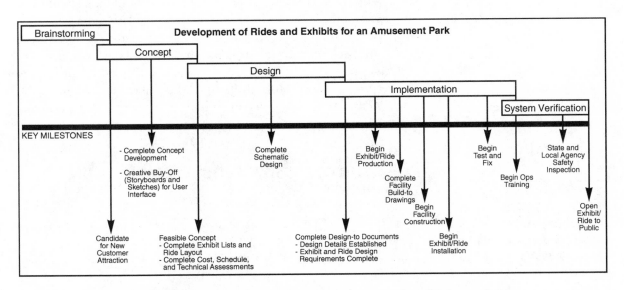

FIGURE 6.2b   Project cycle for amusement park exhibits and rides.

Disney Imagineering, follow a cycle like this.[2] Note that this cycle closely matches the processes envisioned in Figure 6.2a.

In government acquisition projects and larger corporation environments, there may be two or more project teams and project managers in succession. For example, in the case of a Department of Defense project, once a mission need is identified, a project champion is selected and a core team is formed to refine the user requirements and to produce the bidders documents. That core team often provides the project continuity throughout the three periods. The bidders will generally form their proposal preparation team, the core of which may continue through at least the implementation period.

Larger decentralized corporations often follow the government practice of having separate customer (e.g., product marketing) and provider (e.g., product development) teams. In this example, the marketing team prepares the user requirements for the product development team.

Another example comes from a major commercial supplier of large systems built up from their "standard" components. The sales team signs a contract (which should contain clear requirements). The implementation team manages the project after contract signing, and procures, installs, and verifies the system. The project cycle focuses on the activities and products related to the design modifications needed for the installation team to complete their effort and to verify the system before handing it to the operational team.

Smaller commercial projects are more likely to consist of just one project manager selected as soon as the scope and nature of the project is established. Even in this case, the size and composition of the team will usually change with the transitions from one period to the next.

> The project periods often represent natural boundaries to team responsibilities and composition.

THE STUDY PERIOD YIELDS A HIGH RETURN ON INVESTMENT

The study period determines the scope and funding of the project (Figure 6.3) and can therefore make or break most projects. Yet important study elements are typically circumvented in the rush to implementation. High-level government panels, such as the Hearth commission (1980) and Packard commission (early 1990s)

> A major cause of project failure is mono-focus on end product opportunities and inadequate attention during the study period to resolving development risks.

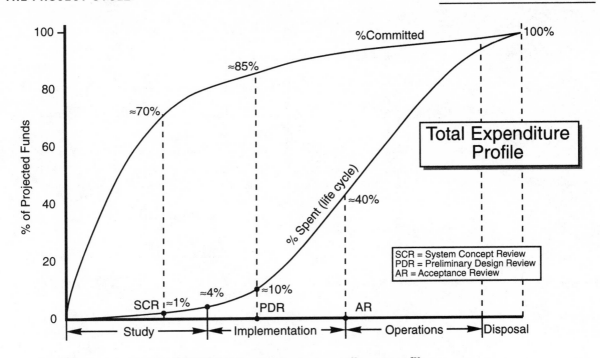

FIGURE 6.3   Typical expenditure profile.

concluded that hasty study periods, resulting in flawed or incomplete requirements, are the major cause of project failure. Their findings continue to be re-verified; the General Accounting Office (GAO) reported in 1999 that high-tech government projects continue to fail for low-tech reasons. Typically these low-tech reasons are flaws built in through incomplete study periods as well as improper implementation of an otherwise sound project management process.

The project team generally must engage in considerable analysis and negotiation in order to determine the appropriate requirements. A thorough study can often prevent the time lost and the funds wasted on requirements-driven rework as illustrated by Figure 6.4.

Our project cycle template consists of four study phases: User Requirements Definition; Concept Definition; System Specification; and the Acquisition Preparation Phase.

The major objective of the User Requirements Definition Phase is to determine exactly which of the user's many requirements

*User Requirements
Definition Phase*

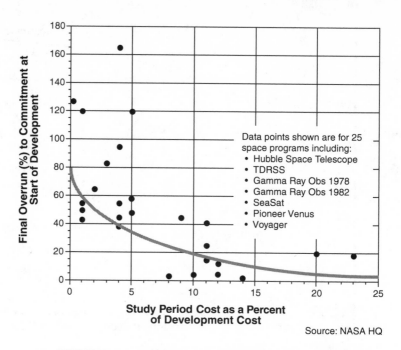

Data points shown are for 25
space programs including:
- Hubble Space Telescope
- TDRSS
- Gamma Ray Obs 1978
- Gamma Ray Obs 1982
- SeaSat
- Pioneer Venus
- Voyager

Source: NASA HQ

FIGURE 6.4   Twenty-five NASA program profiles.

will be included in and satisfied by the responsive project. In some cases, user requirements may be more comprehensive than can be reasonably incorporated into a single project. This phase is essential in both government and commercial projects since each is susceptible to over-specifying and grandiose expectations.

Concept Definition Phase

    The objectives of the Concept Definition Phase are to evaluate alternatives and to select the appropriate system concept, to develop the total lifecycle budgetary cost estimate, the target schedule, and finally, to identify and address areas of high risk. During this phase, funding actions are updated.

*System Specification
Definition Phase*

    The objective of the System Specification Definition Phase is to quantify the system and interface requirements for the selected concept, and to perform risk reduction actions in areas where technical feasibility is uncertain.

*Acquisition Preparation
Phase*

    The final phase of the Study Period is used to prepare for and initiate the Implementation Period. It includes the schedule for acquiring or developing the proposed system and ensures the availability of funding for the project. The Acquisition Preparation Phase is used to define the method of acquisition, identify participants in the acquisition process, and identify the candidate suppliers. The final step is to obtain executive approval to proceed with the project. For internal development projects, the final step in the Study Period is to present the business opportunity to executive management and secure their commitments.

THE IMPLEMENTATION PERIOD IS FOR ACQUISITION OR DEVELOPMENT

The Implementation Period consists of three phases: Source Selection, System Development, and Verification. In government projects, the Implementation Period may be referred to as the Acquisition Period. It sets the contractual foundation for the project, and initiates the process of building the buyer-seller team.

Source Selection Phase

The objective of the Source Selection Phase is to choose, through fair and open competition and through the comprehensive evaluation of contractor proposals, the highest value bidder. For acquisition projects, the buyer releases the Request for Proposal, receives and evaluates bidders' proposals, and negotiates a contract with the selected contractor. For internal developments, the Implementation Period may have one or more Source Selection phases for specific elements of the system; however, theses phases often occur after the "Design to" specifications are available.

System Development Phase

In both external and internal developments, the objective of the System Development Phase is to design and build the first article or develop the service concept.

Verification Phase

The Verification Phase is used to integrate, test, and verify the system or service in accordance with all specifications.

THE OPERATIONS PERIOD IS FOR FULFILLING THE USERS' NEEDS

During the Operations Period, the users' needs are fulfilled and the solution to the project challenge is realized. It consists of three phases—Deployment and Operations/Maintenance—for government acquisitions corresponding to Production and Sales/Support phases for commercial projects, and for both, the third phase is Deactivation.

Deployment and Operations/Maintenance Phases

In government or acquisition projects, the objectives of the Deployment Phase are to transfer the system from the contractor's facility to the operational location and to establish full operational capability. Operations and Maintenance, the second phase of the government cycle, consists of operating and maintaining the system in conformance with user requirements, and to identify system improvements for future implementation.

Production and Sales/Support Phases

In commercial projects, the objective of the Production Phase is to transfer the system to manufacturing operations, often accompanied by the formation of a new project team to emphasize the production engineering function. Finally, the system is delivered to users in the marketplace and the Sales and Support Phase begins. During this time, the project team handles any design changes justified by manufacturing or by market demands.

Deactivation Phase

Early planning for a deactivation phase is vital in certain projects. The NASA Skylab randomly fell to earth in an uninhabited part of Australia. Pieces of a Russian satellite fell uncontrolled onto Canada. Love Canal and other super-fund° sites are also examples of inadequate deactivation planning.

THE IMPORTANCE OF CONTROL GATES

A control gate requires formal review to evaluate status and obtain approval to proceed to the next control gate event according to the project plan.

We define a Control Gate as a management event in the project cycle, sufficiently important to be defined and included in the schedule by executive management, the project manager, or the customer. Control gates represent the major decision points in the project cycle. They ensure that new activities are not pursued until the previously scheduled activities, on which the new ones depend, are satisfactorily completed and baselined. The primary objectives of control gates are to:

° Super-fund refers to U.S. federal money set aside for high-priority environmental clean up.

- Ensure that all current phase activities and products are complete.
- Ensure that progressing to the next set of activities is based on hard evidence that the team is prepared and that the risk of proceeding is acceptable.
- Promote a buyer/seller synergistic team approach.

Control gates need to occur throughout the project phases to control all three aspects: business, budget, and technical. Too often reviews like Preliminary Design Review (PDR) and Critical Design Review (CDR) are conducted as technical reviews where in reality all control gates are also business reviews. Affordability and schedule realism are important decision criteria leading to appropriate concept selections and should be reviewed and updated at control gates. Failure to provide adequate checks along the way can set up subsequent phases for failure and is usually a major factor in cost overruns and delays. At each control gate, the decision options are:

> *Acceptable:* Proceed with project.
> *Acceptable with reservations:* Proceed and respond to identified action items.
> *Unacceptable:* Do not proceed; repeat the review when ready.
> *Unsalvageable:* Terminate the project.

Upon successful completion of a control gate, the appropriate agreements (usually in the form of a document—a product of a project cycle phase) are baselined and put under configuration management, requiring buyer/seller agreement to incorporate changes.

The definition of each control gate should identify the:

- Purpose of the control gate.
- Host and chairperson.
- Attendees.
- Place.
- Agenda and how the control gate is to be conducted.

Too few control gates allows the project to operate out of control. Too many overburden the project with unnecessary administration and can lead to the "design by viewgraph" syndrome.

Each control gate's definition should be included in the project's Terminology Database.

- Evidence that is evaluated.
- Actions.
- Closure method.

A broadly employed control gate, the System Requirements Review (SRR) is held whenever beneficial to confirm the provider's understanding of the buyer's requirements. It usually occurs near the beginning of the project cycle and again every time a new supplier is added to the project.

The consequences of conducting a superficial review, omitting a critical discipline, or skipping a control gate altogether, are usually long-term and costly. The executives at a leading conglomerate literally choked on their new product (a microwaveable meal) when they set out to investigate its market woes. They discovered 28 product deficiencies that should have been caught early in the project cycle, well before its introduction. A few of the more obvious flaws:

- When positioning the open carton to read the heating instructions, the contents spilled.
- The instructions, printed in black on a dark blue background, weren't legible.
- The specified microwave heating time was insufficient, but when the time was increased to adequately heat the food, some of the food migrated into the plastic container.

Control gate approval must include the appropriate disciplines and must be based on hard evidence of compliance.

In another example, a Lincoln car design separates the seat controls, placing some of them on the moving seat and the remainder on the dashboard. When the seat is reclined, the dashboard set could be out of reach. As in the previous case, control gates were skipped or critical skills omitted, such as Human Factors. This could be a result of inadequate concurrent engineering, addressed in the next chapter.

Even when appropriate control gates are held, there is little chance of success if the participants don't pay attention to the technical content. A neighbor of one of the authors had a custom-designed home built with an attached three-car garage. He requested that one bay be specifically designed to be extra wide (three meters) and extra high (three and a half meters) to accommodate his recreation vehicle. After the building was finished, and after he found his vehicle did not fit, he found the design error on the design drawings—which he had signed 10 months earlier. A costly mistake, but he is not alone. After completing a new post office building in a major U.S. city several years ago—at a cost of 140 million dollars—the city engineers found that post office trucks would not fit into the enclosed loading dock.

THE THREE ASPECTS OF THE PROJECT CYCLE: BUSINESS, BUDGET, AND TECHNICAL

The *Business* aspect (Figure 6.5) contains the necessary business events related to customer management, justifying the project, the overall business management events, and associated contractor and subcontractor management. These include the activities necessary to solicit, select, and manage vendors. The Business aspect starts with seeking project opportunities to help achieve the strategic objectives of the enterprise. Trade-offs are made to select those projects suitable for the organization's portfolio. To secure a position in the portfolio, projects must make sense as justified by the business case. The business case analyzes the project's fit within the organization's business objectives, the investment required, the expected market and market share, the profit expected, and the associated risks. It's essential that the business case is accurate in predicting both the need and the demand for the product and/or service and what customers will be willing to pay for it.

While many projects end up producing very successful results there are those that are based on faulty business cases that do not. Some examples are the supersonic transport, Concorde, that continues to be subsidized and operates at a loss. The English Channel tunnel that faced bankruptcy because of excessive construction costs and extensive competition by multiple less-expensive ways of crossing the channel. The Iridium communications system is a financial failure and filed for bankruptcy because subscribership is failing to meet expectations by a very large margin. Since Iridium phones are large and won't work indoors, it appears the users are staying with conventional, less expensive services.

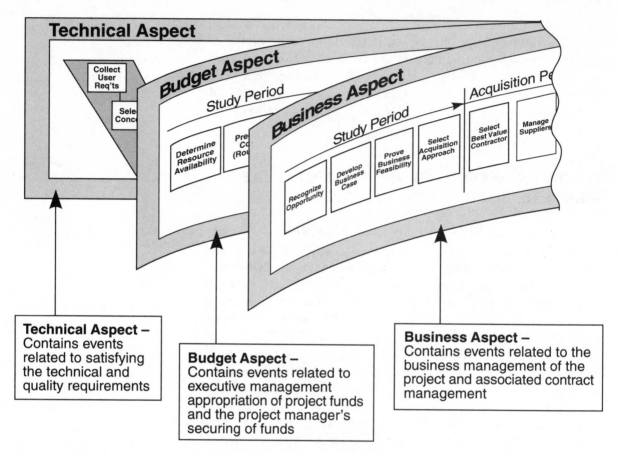

FIGURE 6.5 The three aspects of the project cycle: business, budget, and technical.

Each control gate throughout the project cycle should reaffirm the business case and be prepared to react to the everpresent dynamics of the marketplace.

The business aspect further reflects the approach to acquisition and fielding. If competitive source selections are required, they are provided for. During the acquisition period, the focus is on supplier management and trading off features and benefits in the marketplace as designers and producers seek to enhance the project concept. Then as production and fielding begin, the focus shifts to customer service and increasing value by continuous improvement in both service and product performance.

Incremental upgrades are the generally accepted way of implementing this approach.

The *Budget* aspect (Figure 6.5) depicts the activities and events necessary to fuel the project with funds throughout its project cycle. The executive's challenge is to allocate available funds among the active projects. The project manager's challenge is to secure the necessary funds for the project at hand.

Government and commercial organizations usually have to operate within a total budget, typically established on an annual basis. New project initiatives have to compete with ongoing projects for a share of the total budget. This reality may present difficult timing constraints, especially with increasingly narrow market windows.

The budget aspect for government projects is complex, involving both the executive and legislative branches. Whereas Congress used to focus primarily on new initiatives, deficit reduction pressures are placing increased emphasis on life-cycle costs. In the past, projects were often approved without knowledge of or realistic preparation for the operating costs.

The budget activities and business management activities are combined with the *technical* aspect (Figure 6.5) to yield the complete project cycle. The technical events are often the most significant force driving project length and cost, and they're often the most difficult to manage. For these reasons, we will treat the technical aspect in more detail than the other two aspects. However, this does not mean that the business and budget aspects should be discounted. If the project is to succeed on both financial and technical criteria (the only true definition of success), all three aspects of the project must be skillfully balanced using value as the driver.

The Technical aspect drives the project's length and cost.

SYSTEM ENGINEERING IS VITALLY IMPORTANT TO THE TECHNICAL ASPECT

The technical aspect starts with user needs, which are converted into system functional and performance requirements by adjusting, adding, and eliminating requirements into a set that has the promise of being satisfied. Concept trades are then performed to determine the best value concept to satisfy the system

System engineering is about doing the right thing right the first time.

requirements. The System Concept Baseline is decomposed into the components of the system and the specifications for each entity. These documents systematically define all of the subsystems, assemblies, and parts. They also define the approach for system integration and for the verification and validation that each integration stage, including the final result, meets the user requirements. That is the essence of the system engineering process.

System engineering's role is often confused with that of system design engineering. But system engineering doesn't create the design, rather it creates a description of system parameters, documented in the set of baseline specifications. System engineering is responsible for conducting the trade-offs and creative process which lead to the specifications, starting with the User Requirements Document.

> System engineering defines what is to be done, not how to do it, the latter being a design engineering responsibility.

One of the most important roles of system engineering is the responsibility for the overall system architecture. As Rechtin and Maier[3] noted, "Clearly, if a system is to succeed, it must satisfy a useful purpose at an affordable cost for an acceptable period of time. . . . But of the three criteria, satisfying a useful purpose is predominant. Without it being satisfied, all others are irrelevant. Architecting therefore begins with, and is responsible for maintaining, the integrity of the system's purpose." Stevens et al.[4] said, "Architectural design defines clearly what is to be built. This is potentially the most creative part of the system process, and the point at which the cost of the system is largely fixed."

Examples of system engineering failures illustrate the distinction. In the initial B-1 bomber, the advanced electronic system and counter-attack system interfered with each other—the plane's own electronic countermeasures for jamming enemy systems jammed its own B-1 targeting electronics—yet each system was designed (by design engineers) to meet their individual specifications. On the Blackhawk helicopter, the "fly-by-wire" system failed when exposed to radio broadcast at short range—a test flight crashed when flying over a radio station! On the commercial front (waterfront, that is), a shipping container from a British exporter, for sale in the United States, was discovered to be fully-loaded with hair dryers built only for 50-cycle, 220-volt power. The exporter did not know that the U.S. commercial products ran on 60-cycle, 110-volt power.

The system engineering manager directs the overall process toward achieving the optimum technical solution, including:

- System engineering plans
- Requirements management
- Requirements analysis
- Requirements audit
- Baseline management

- Interface control
- Risk management
- Verification management
- Performance management
- Design audits

The system engineering process progressively decomposes the system requirements and system concept until the lowest level of decomposition (e.g., hardware and/or software units) are specified. Each level of assembly represents one or more entities or Configuration Items (CIs) that make up the system at that level. A Configuration Item typically requires its own:

- Specification (functions, performance, interfaces, design constraints, quality attributes).
- Design reviews.
- Qualification testing and certification.
- Acceptance Reviews (AR).
- Operator and maintenance manuals.

A CI should be selected to facilitate management accountability and replacement capability. For example, a car and a car battery are both CIs to the consumer, because they can be readily replaced. However, the battery's cells are not a CI, because they cannot readily be purchased and replaced by the consumer.

THE VEE MODEL: A TOOL FOR MANAGING THE TECHNICAL ASPECT

Referring to the Vee model illustrated in Chapter 3, System Decomposition and Definition descend down the left side of the Vee (Figure 6.6a).

> The Vee model is a valuable tool for managing the system engineering process and project risk.

Decomposition: The hierarchical functional and physical partitioning of any system into hardware assemblies, software

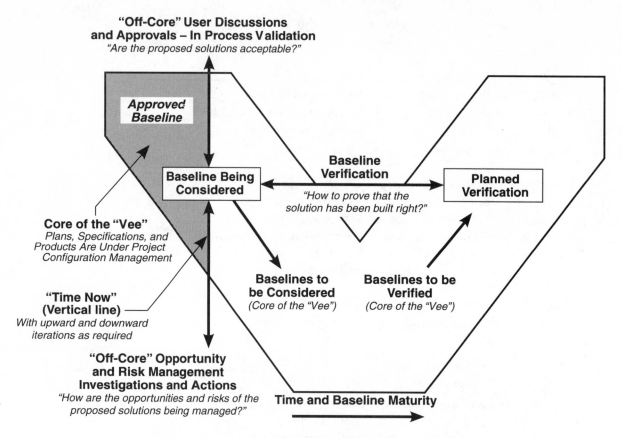

FIGURE 6.6a   Vee model—decomposition and definition.

components, and operator activities that can be scheduled, budgeted, and assigned to a responsible manager.

Definition: The "design to," "build to," and "code to" documentation that defines the functional and physical content of each entity.

Early design and test work should support the decision process and should not be interpreted as out-of-phase project cycle activity.

Unlike most other system engineering models, our Vee model correctly captures the real-world need for exploratory work early in the cycle to identify opportunities and reduce risk. The detailed nature of these essential "off-core" studies is explored in greater depth in Chapter 7, Section 5 (Opportunity and Risk). For example, our project cycle template encourages early hardware and software requirements-understanding models and technical feasibility models. This helps clarify user requirements and ensures that customer requirements are achievable and not impossible as for an antigravity machine. Early involvement of specialty disciplines is an essential part of this risk reduction process.

As the project progresses, requirements flowdown analyses, opportunity and risk identification, and risk reduction modeling continue. This is shown in Figure 6.6a by the vertical off-core activities that descend to the decomposition level necessary to satisfy the concern. For instance, if there is a question about piece part technical feasibility, the downward off-core activity will descend to the piece part level where modeling can prove that ultimate performance is achievable.

While technical feasibility decisions are based on these off-core activities, only the decisions at the core of the Vee are put under configuration management. Off-core analyses, studies, and modeling are performed to substantiate the core decisions. They ensure that opportunities have been identified and are being appropriately managed and risks have been mitigated or determined to be acceptable. The off-core work may not have to be formally controlled and will usually be repeated at the appropriate decomposition level to justify introduction into the baseline definition at that decision gate. As an example, a system concept under consideration may depend on the performance of a critical piece part. Technical feasibility models of the part can be used to prove the part performance, which in turn confirms that the concept is viable, and can be formally baselined. The piece part itself will not be baselined until lower in the Vee decomposition enabling other competitive piece part solutions to be considered up until being baselined at the build-to or Critical Design Review.

The project development process is dynamic. Throughout the project cycle there is iteration at all levels, studying user needs, investigating alternate concepts, performing analyses, building models and conducting evaluations. The Vee model brings order out of what would otherwise appear to be a chaotic situation. The baselines on the core are the anchor for the "time now" iterations shown in Figure 6.6a, but these baselines can be revised through the project change control process. The upward iterations allow evolution of the user requirements, and the downward iterations allow evolution to improved solutions to meet user needs. This iterative, evolutionary process can continue for as long as the project team desires, constrained only by the user's schedule, the customer's budget, and the project's quality objectives. (System-level changes made late in the development process have a high risk that the consequences of the change will not be completely identified and corrected. The cause of the Apollo 13 disaster was traced to just such a late introduction of a change.[5] It took a sequence of five events to trigger the disaster, but the root cause was a change in the design voltage made after the preliminary design review.) At some point the iterations must converge. Late changes are expensive, and without convergence the project will never be complete. There is a rule: "Meeting requirements and walking on water are equally easy—if both are frozen."

System Integration and Verification ascend the right side of the Vee.

> **Integration:** Combining entities to prove performance and compatibility.
> **Verification:** Proving specification satisfaction.
> **Validation:** Proving user satisfaction.

The method of verification to be used at each level on the right Vee leg must be determined as the specifications are developed at the corresponding decomposition level on the left Vee leg.

The critical aspects of the integration and verification process are indicated in Figure 6.6b. Note the overt distinction on the right of the core between verification and validation. Verification is the process of proving that each product meets its specifications. Validation is the process of demonstrating (as opposed to proving) that the product satisfies the user needs, regardless of the specified performance.

As the integration and verification process proceeds up the right leg of the Vee, any problems encountered will involve system engineering in the problem identification, risk assessment, and problem resolution. Issues which cannot be resolved but can be lived with may require a waiver or deviation from the customer. In some environments a deviation (to a specification) is granted before the fact (you don't have to meet the requirement), while a waiver is granted after the fact (the component is built and fails the acceptance test). In many organizations the

---

A complex verification process may over-drive cost and schedule and be the determining factor when considering alternative concepts.

Verification asks: "Building it right?"

Validation asks: "Building the right thing?"

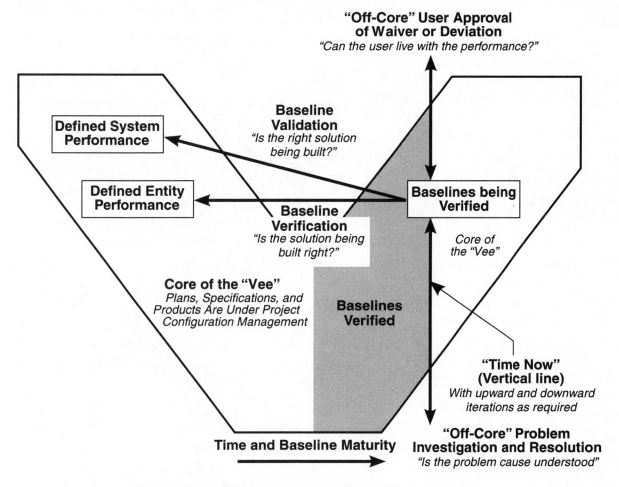

FIGURE 6.6b   Vee model—integration and verification.

terms are used interchangeably, just as concrete and cement in common usage.

Time and project maturity flow from left to right on the Vee, therefore, once a control gate is passed, iteration is not possible backward. However, vertical iteration with user requirements is possible (along the "time now" vertical line in Figure 6.6b) as is the case at every "time now" point as time progresses along the core of the Vee. Increased user requirements introduced after the Preliminary Design Review will impact baselined specifications and may be best held for subsequent versions or releases. If significant changes to user requirements must be made subsequent to the Preliminary Design Review, then the project should be restarted at the position, within the Vee, of the requirement impact. The repeat of much of the sequence may be faster because of previous work and lessons learned, but all affected phases must be repeated in view of the changed requirements.

APPLICATIONS OF THE TECHNICAL ASPECT

Depending on the development approach, the Vee process may be applied multiple times on a single project.

Projects are sometimes initiated with known technology shortfalls, or with areas dependent on emerging technology. Technology development can be done in parallel with the project evolution, shown in Figure 6.7, and inserted as late as the Preliminary Design Review where its performance must be specified. The technology development is represented by a horizontal bar off the core, at the decomposition level (or below) where it will impact the project. It should be managed and statused by the project manager and system engineer as an opportunity critical to the success of the project.

The research and development of the fibrous silica material that ultimately became the space shuttle tile material provides an illustration. The research was driven by the curiosity of the principal investigator, Bob Beasley ("If I could do that, then I could . . .").[6] The four-year research project was finished in 1966, two years before the shuttle concept studies began. The evolution of the research product into a viable, safe component for the shuttle program (and still in use in 2000) was managed by the shuttle project manager, Jack Milton. He recognized that the silica material offered a significant improvement in thermal performance, reliability, and producability compared to any alternate then available. Milton also recognized that the success of his project was based on moving the continued development of the material out of an exploratory research environment and into a focused project-specific technology transfer. This transfer was absolutely essential to the shuttle program success, but it created the basis for four years of antagonism and personal conflict. Both Beasley and Milton had a common goal (one of the key ingredients of teamwork, remember?)—the safe launch and reentry of the

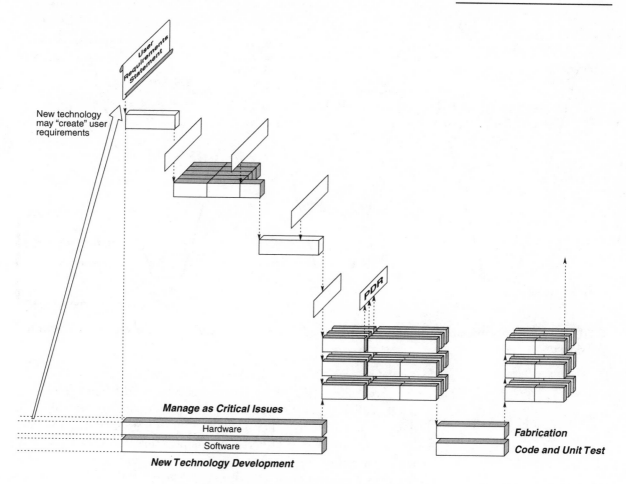

FIGURE 6.7 Technology insertion.

shuttle, and protection of the shuttle crew. It is on the next level that the common goal broke down; each was insistent that he should be in charge. The figures in this book, such as Figure 6.7, are depictions of the real world, and it takes a great deal of work to make projects in the real world function effectively. Without this view of what is going on, the job is even more difficult.

If some user requirements are too vague to permit final specification at the Preliminary Design Review or if the development process itself uncovers unforeseen needs and system applications, an approach is to develop the project in evolutionary releases (like commercial software, see Figure 6.8).

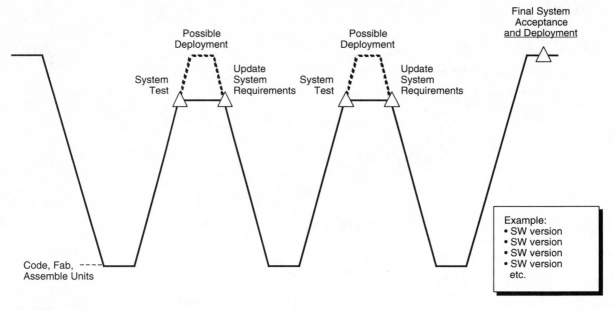

FIGURE 6.8 Evolutionary development: used for incomplete requirements—incremental releases.

Another development strategy can be used when all requirements can be specified up front, but incremental development is desired, resulting in either a single (Figure 6.9) or incremental delivery (Figure 6.10). This development approach is easily visualized using the Vee model.[7] All increments will have a common heritage down to the first Preliminary Design Review. The balance of the project cycle will have a series of displaced and overlapping Vees, one for each incremental release. For the incremental delivery approach, the first release is configured to meet a reduced set of user requirements with subsequent releases providing added functionality and performance.

For incremental releases, the initial version and all subsequent versions are fully functional responses to specified requirements.

BASELINE MANAGEMENT

Effective Baseline Management depends on formal control.

Baselines contain all technical, cost, schedule, and deliverable requirements that are sufficiently mature to be accepted and placed under configuration management, usually at control gates or phase transition reviews. The project team then relies on these

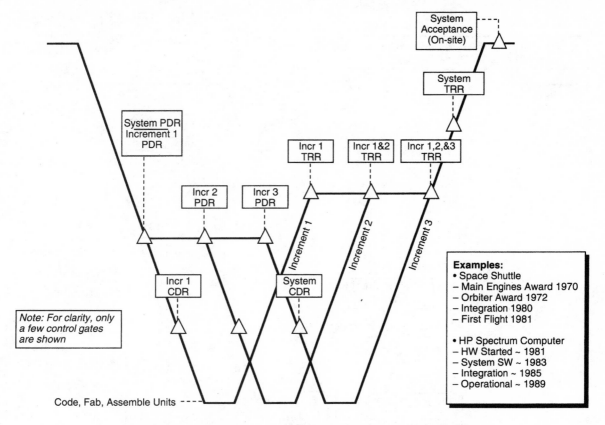

FIGURE 6.9   Incremental development—single delivery.

baselines as the approved state of the project for further development and maturation. It is common to manage to a coordinated business baseline (contract, schedules), budget, and technical baseline (requirements, specification, verification plans, etc.).

Baseline management is performed by configuration management through a formal change control regimen which, for each type of controlled decision document, establishes:

- The event which places that document under change control.
- The method for implementing change.
- The required approvals, usually involving both buyer and seller.

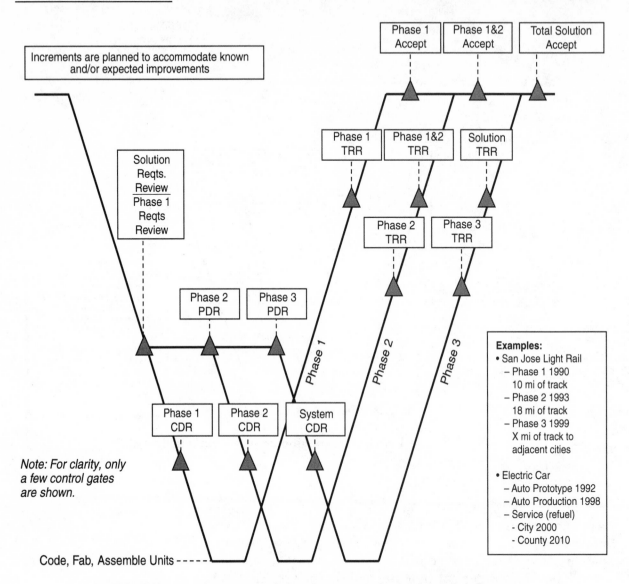

FIGURE 6.10   Incremental development—incremental delivery.

The major purpose of baseline management and change control is to maintain a single knowledge base of the project design maturity. This is necessary for accurate communications with supporting technical, training, sparing, replication, and repair personnel. The change control process, addressed in the next chapter, is initiated by the User Requirements Document—usually the first document to be placed under formal configuration management. As the project cycle progresses, system engineering together with the contributing engineering disciplines, produce a series of technical baselines, proportional to the phases of the project. These are examples of technical baselines:

User Requirements	
System Requirements	As-Replicated (Production Release)
Concept Definition	As-Built
System Specification	As-Tested
"Design-to"	As-Deployed
"Build-to" (Pilot Production)	As-Operated

Changes to the technical or business baselines require joint action (review and approval) by the customer and the provider. In the case of commercial projects, the customer is often represented by the marketing manager or general manager. In this case, the business baseline is established by the initial agreement between executive management and marketing as to the scope, funding, and schedule for the project.

For contractual work for an external customer, the provider's business baseline is the contract. Business baseline changes require contract action, and for federal government contracts funding changes may even require congressional action.

System engineering has to work closely with the business manager (both customer and provider) so that the technical requirements are congruent with business and budget baseline provisions. When there is a reduction of funds, system engineering and the project manager have to ensure there is a commensurate reduction in technical scope.

TAILORING THE PROJECT CYCLE

A project for hosting the Olympics is unlikely to operate well on the technical project cycle tailored for developing a toothbrush that's illustrated in Figure 6.11.

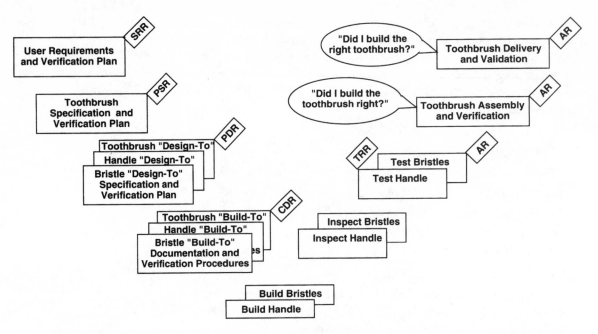

FIGURE 6.11   A technical project cycle tailored for developing a toothbrush.

Each project, or at least each project type, needs a tailored cycle. Major project types which are common to both the government and commercial environments include:

- *System Development*—create new product to meet need. Example: mobile telephone system
- *System Integration*—combine existing designs into functioning system. Example: automated manufacturing facility using commercially available equipment
- *Production*—improve product replication to existing documentation. Example: reduce cost of building computers
- *Research and Development*—discover new approach to solving a problem. Example: use biological models to increase computer capabilities
- *Facilities*—produce a new facility to meet a prescribed need. Example: Airport, hospital, wafer production facility

TABLE 6.1 Project Types Characterized by Driving Force and Risks

Project Type	Driven By	Risk
System development	Performance	Cost, schedule
System development	Cost	Performance, schedule
System integration	Compatibility	Equipment availability
Production	Cost	Performance, cost
Research and development	Technology	Not focused on corporate needs
Facility	Schedule	Performance, cost, building codes

Each type is further characterized by its driving force and risk factors. Table 6.1 is ordered by degree of risk and management complexity, with system development projects at the high end. There are exceptions. A company depending on specialized technology research for the bulk of its income could attribute the highest risk to research projects. Some drug companies fit this category. Likewise, a company that develops very simple and predictable products, such as campaign buttons, but depends on very low cost production, will view manufacturing projects as high risk.

> Most well-known examples of failures and lessons learned come from big projects. That's because failures of small projects get little publicity.

The template developed by your organization needs to be adapted to each project based on the:

> Deviations from the relevant template cycle need to be substantiated with solid rationale.

- Project type, content, scope, and complexity.
- Management environment—customers, contractors, and top management.
- Mandated constraints.
- The management style.
- Balance between project opportunity and risk.

The customer and provider project managers should jointly define their project cycle, the content and conduct of the control gates, and the content of the required control gate documentation.

Tailoring may add or delete project cycle features as shown next:

> The tailoring process is one of the most important aspects of project planning.

Feature Modified	*Example Modification*
Phases	Deactivation phase added.
	Source selection phase deleted.
Control gates	Consent to pour concrete review added.
	Qualification acceptance review deleted.
Products and activities	Field test model added.
	On-site training deleted.

Tailoring requires foresight and good judgment on the part of everyone involved, promoted by the project manager. We recommend these tailoring steps:

Select the phases.

Select the baseline management control gates.

Select the lower level control gates.

Identify control gate products.

Identify all activities.

Review pertinent lessons learned.

Get executive concurrence.

- Phase selection is based on project type (development, research, product integration, production, facilities, service); content (e.g., the hardware/software balance); tactical development and delivery approach (single, incremental, evolutionary); scope and complexity.
- Control gate selection is based on the approach to baseline management. Control gates should always occur at phase transitions and may be beneficial internal to some phases. Add control gates to keep the project sold.
- Lower-level control gates should be chosen to enhance opportunities and to minimize risk. Identify milestones that ensure readiness for the baseline management control gates.
- Identify the products required at the control gates: Documents, Deliverables, Models, and Agreements.
- Identify the activities necessary to produce the products required at each control gate.
- Validate the project cycle against past experience. The critique should include lessons learned from related projects and previous contract information, directly from project officials and on file.
- To obtain approval for your project cycle, be prepared to explain all deviations from the organization's template. Although changes are encouraged, they need to be justified.

Specific internal and external standards may be an explicit feature of your project cycle template. Those standards, as well as those embodied in contracts, need to be critically reviewed as part of the tailoring process. Situations that call for tailoring of standards include:

All requirements and standards should be appropriate to the reliability and risk level of the project.

- Inappropriate application of standards.
- Blanket imposition of standards.
- Under-imposing of standards.
- Implementing a "no-tailoring" policy subsequent to contract award.
- The cost versus benefits of standards implementation is ignored.
- The inappropriate imposition of high reliability or severe environmental standards.
- Standards applied arbitrarily, "just to be safe."
- Extensive and uncontrolled cross-referencing of standards.
- Imposing of obsolete standards.
- Application of government standards where commercial practices are acceptable.

These tailoring techniques apply to standards and other formal documents, especially contract boilerplate:

- Specify exact applicable paragraphs.
- Specify exempted provisions.
- Specify tailored values for referenced standards.
- Expand on referenced standards.
- Specify exact documentation deliverables.
- Extract selected standards and include in contract documentation.
- Allow contractor choices when risk is acceptable.
- Prioritize requirements.

SHORTENING THE PROJECT CYCLE TIME

The increasing challenges imposed by time-to-market demands and technical obsolescence are familiar pressures for shorter schedules. Not only are shorter schedules less expensive, but they free up skilled personnel who may be needed on other projects.

The project cycle is the driver of subordinate project networks and, consequently, the project schedule (Figure 6.12).

Approaches to shorten the schedule should begin at the broadest level—the project cycle. Techniques such as shortening the critical path or running multiple shifts will be addressed in the Planning and Corrective Action sections of Chapter 7.

The best way to ensure the shortest schedule is by applying a strategically and tactically correct project cycle managed by qualified and motivated personnel. You should also consider reducing the technical risks by using previously developed or previously qualified products.

If these approaches aren't appropriate, you can always make a conscious decision to gamble on shortcuts such as skipping phases or indiscriminately eliminating control gates, an extremely risky project tailoring approach that we don't recommend. The GOES (Geostationary Operational Environment Satellite) improved weather satellite project team decided to shorten the project cycle. To reduce the predicted four-year development,

> When you do it right the first time, you get there quicker.

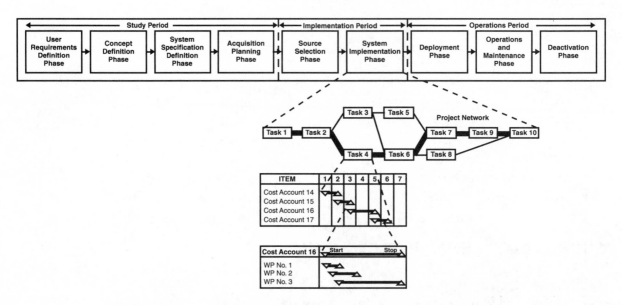

FIGURE 6.12   The project cycle template drives the network.

the study period was deleted. The satellite was delivered nine years later. Technical feasibility development was performed concurrently with on-going system development, driving ultimate costs and schedules to multiples of the original predictions. Properly planned, technology insertion projects have succeeded at NASA and elsewhere.

When exceptional performance is required, the project team should be staffed with experts and co-located to facilitate efficient communications and reduce distractions. This approach is called "Skunk Works" after Kelly Johnson's Lockheed organization that produced quantum leaps in technology in very short time spans.[8] Johnson's team applied project cycle discipline, baseline management, change control, and control gates, but all were applied by the doing team in an informal but effective way.

> A Skunk Works may be appropriate in the case of time-critical missions or emergencies, but there are not enough experts to staff all projects using the Skunk Works model.

The pursuit of better, faster, cheaper has caused teams to discard the discipline of the gated project cycle or to skip selected phases and control gates without due regard for the consequences. This approach has proven to be unacceptably risky and recent failures have confirmed that proven practices were often eliminated in the desire to meet a "better, faster, cheaper" mandate. The key to success is to design a tailored gated cycle that is based on a proven template but that is lean, efficient, and effective. Control gates should add the value of baseline review and approval without stalling on-going progress. In a skunk works environment control gates are usually working sessions but retain the discipline required for ensuring controlled and informed execution. Control gates should not require lengthy and cumbersome processes. A consent-to-pour concrete review should only require an inspection of the layout, forms, steel, and concrete mix, and should not take more than a few minutes. To skip it is irresponsible and can result in a misplaced or poorly structured foundation.

The following are inspiring examples of successful transitions to fast cycle times:

	Implementation Period in Months	
Product	*Original*	*Improved*
HP Computer Printer	54	22
IBM Personal Computer	48	13
Warner Clutch Brake	36	10
Ingersoll-Rand Air Grinder	40	15

PROJECT CYCLE EXERCISE

The objective of this exercise is to provide practice in project cycle design. Performing this exercise may save you considerable money and strife if you ever decide to construct your own custom home.

You and your partner are preparing to build a new fully custom home on a yet to be selected building site. You want to ensure that the entire process goes smoothly and that you remain friends with each other and with all the other stakeholders when it is finally completed (an almost impossible challenge).

To minimize risk, you are to design your preferred sequential project cycle complete with periods, phases, and control gates by formulating the three parallel congruent aspects (business, budget, technical).

For the business aspect, consider the issues of site location; conditions, covenants and restrictions; resale; community trends; school districts; architect selection; engineer selection; contractor selection; whether you will act as general contractor or not; community approval; architectural committee approval; planning permits; building permits; certificate of occupancy; and so on. This is not a complete list. Add to it as necessary to ensure all stakeholders have been considered. Make sure your phases and control gates provide orderly progression and necessary agreements to manage through this minefield.

For the budget aspect, consider the issues of target budgets, should-cost estimates, available assets, loan qualification, loan commitments, progress payments, funds disbursements, management reserve, contractor holdbacks, performance bonuses and penalties, and so on. This is not a complete list. Make sure your phases and control gates provide orderly progression and necessary agreements through this second minefield.

For the technical aspect, consider the issues of zoning; conditions, covenants and restrictions; community or subdivision themes; concept development; detailed design; code compliance; quality control; material control; inspections; and so on. This is not a complete list. Make sure your phases and control gates provide orderly progression and necessary agreements through this third minefield.

Your final product should be a three-row project cycle, one row for each of the three aspects. The rows should be divided into periods and the periods subdivided into phases. As an example, the first period might be the study period with the first phase defined as *User Requirements Definition*. This is the phase in which you and your partner's requirements are established along with the overall budget and schedule for the project, independent of the ultimate site location or building design.

7

THE PROJECT MANAGEMENT ELEMENTS

Principles that are established should be viewed as flexible, capable of adaptation to every need. It is the manager's job to know how to make use of them, which is a difficult art requiring intelligence, experience, decisiveness, and, most important, a sense of proportion.

Henri Fayol,
General and Industrial Management

The orthogonal model, introduced in Chapter 3, depicts the first nine project management elements as the spokes of a wheel (Figure 7.1), held together by its rim, Project Leadership. This model helps to visualize the big project picture and to develop a sense of proportion and intuitive feel for the concept.

"Effectiveness lies in balance," is Stephen Covey's way of expressing the need for a sense of proportion. Too much focus, he quips, ". . . is like a person who runs three or four hours a day, bragging about the extra ten years of life it creates, unaware he's spending it running."[1]

We refer to our set of management principles as the Project Management Elements, consisting of 10 categories of management responsibilities, functions, techniques, and tools that are essential in managing:

The elements should be envisioned as the project's tool chest, with 10 drawers of grouped techniques and tools.

110

- All types of projects.
- All phases of the Project Cycle.
- All organizations participating in the project.

This chapter is organized as 10 major sections, one for each of the management elements. With the big picture in mind, we now focus on the primary techniques and tools that need to be applied to manage a project through its project cycle.

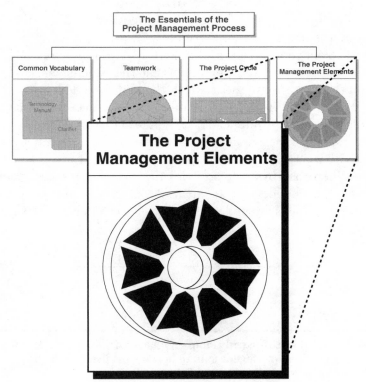

Situationally applied by the project team to manage the project throughout the project cycle.

FIGURE 7.1   The project management elements.

1. PROJECT REQUIREMENTS

**We should have a great many fewer disputes in the world
if words were taken for what they are, the signs of our
ideas only, and not for the things themselves.**

John Locke,
"An Essay Concerning Human Understanding"

A major challenge in expressing project ideas in writing is to choose words that accurately represent the things themselves. Unfortunately, poorly chosen or missing words often create major problems. Figure 7.2 shows an excerpt from the 1907 specification for the Wright brothers' first production contract, which may be the ancestor of one of our most abused requirement cliches, the ubiquitous "user-friendly."[2]

> **Nonessential or overspecified requirements usually result in missing schedule and cost targets.**

Project requirements start with what the user really needs (not what the provider perceives that the user needs) and end when those needs are satisfied. In the end-to-end chain of specifications, there is an ongoing danger of misunderstanding and ambiguity. This often leads to nonessential or over-specified and/or unclear or missing requirements, as illustrated by Figure 7.3—a cartoon familiar to every marketing student.

> **Project requirements end only when the user needs have been satisfied.**

When the customer provides the top-level project requirements, the challenge is to ensure that the requirements and their implications are understood. When the Signal Corps in 1907

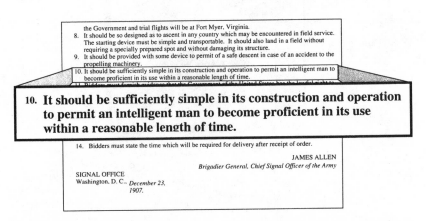

the Government and trial flights will be at Fort Myer, Virginia.

8. It should be so designed as to ascent in any country which may be encountered in field service. The starting device must be simple and transportable. It should also land in a field without requiring a specially prepared spot and without damaging its structure.

9. It should be provided with some device to permit of a safe descent in case of an accident to the propelling machinery.

10. It should be sufficiently simple in its construction and operation to permit an intelligent man to become proficient in its use within a reasonable length of time.

10. It should be sufficiently simple in its construction and operation to permit an intelligent man to become proficient in its use within a reasonable length of time.

14. Bidders must state the time which will be required for delivery after receipt of order.

JAMES ALLEN
Brigadier General, Chief Signal Officer of the Army

SIGNAL OFFICE
Washington, D. C., *December 23, 1907.*

FIGURE 7.2 Wright Brothers' production contract, circa 1907.

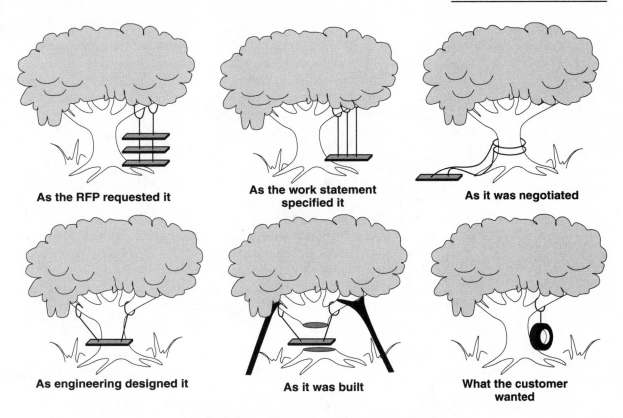

As the RFP requested it

As the work statement specified it

As it was negotiated

As engineering designed it

As it was built

What the customer wanted

FIGURE 7.3   Swings, a classic revisited.

released the invitation to bid on a heavier-than-air flying machine, their overall objective was clear, even though the specification has many unclear details. At that time, however, it was not certain that anyone could build a device to satisfy the requirements. The technical experts of that year argued that "there is not a known flying machine in the world which could fulfill these requirements."[3] Only the Wright brothers knew the project was achievable. In fact, the Army had written the specification around the Wright brothers' claims. The Wright brothers said they had already built machines that proved feasibility of the concepts (but they refused to show anyone until they had a contract in hand). The Army expected one bid. They got 41. There were 40 bidders who had no chance of completing a successful project, because they did not have the expertise to understand the implications of what the customer wanted. However, lack of knowledge didn't slow them down (and this trait hasn't changed much in 93 years). Two contracts were awarded in 1908, and only one contractor delivered.

The challenge of developing the project requirements is even greater when there are thousands to millions of users, as is the case for most commercial products. Recognizing a user need, and having a great idea for solving it, are not enough. Consider, for instance, the typewriter. Since the typewriter was the mainstay of American industry for more than a century, it would seem that when the first typewriter appeared, it would have been an instant success. The user need was clearly there. The idea of a typewriter goes back to 1714, but the first practical office machine, which looks very much like its modern counterpart (with the QWERTY keyboard layout), made its debut in 1874.[4] Acceptance was so slow that its promoters nearly abandoned it as a failure. It took more than a decade for *users* to realize that they needed this machine. In more recent history, the replacement for the typewriter, namely the word processor, had a similar slow beginning. The idea that a word processor was a tool that engineers and managers should use and have available at their workstations was strongly resisted by management in many corporations in the 1970s and 1980s.

Many techniques have been developed to help project champions be more competitive in discovering user needs, and more effective in marketing a solution to meet those needs. One such technique, quality function deployment (QFD), has proven to be very useful and enduring.[5, 6] There are many references that deal with QFD and related topics, so we will not pursue them further, except to note that the end product of these studies is a clear definition of user needs, which then form the starting point to drive project requirements. QFD also defines product quality from the users' perspective, and tells the designers where to put emphasis.

There has been a notable change during the past decade that will impact the timely, competitive development user requirements in the future. In his book, *Business@ the Speed of Thought*, Bill Gates emphasizes the orders of magnitude reduction in time required to gather data on customer interests and customer reactions to fielded products.[7] He discusses how corporations such as Coca Cola and Jiffy Lube have made very effective use of data mining to better profile user interests and needs, and thereby improve their competitiveness. However, the availability of rapid access to data via the Internet does not alter the basic project management process. As noted in Chapter 6, Microsoft follows a project cycle consistent with ours.[8] The vision of the next decades as presented by Gates reemphasizes the need to tailor and streamline our project management processes, as we discussed at the end of Chapter 6.

The project's customer controls the definition of the user requirements. The provider further refines these requirements within the authorized baseline definition. User requirements are usually the first to be placed under configuration management. In practice this could be the Mission Needs Statement (DoD) or the Marketing Requirements Document (commercial) or a specific User Requirements Document embodying one or both of these. When a couple decides to build a house and they each make a list of their individual requirements the combined list is the User's Requirements Document. Paired with this set of requirements is

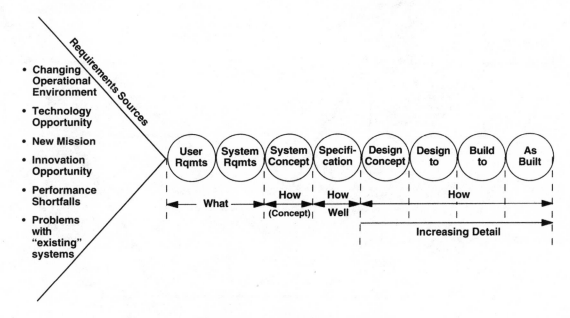

FIGURE 7.4   Document chain.

the Context of Implementation or User Concept of Operations (CONOPS) which describes the project's problem space and environment.[9] For a house, it's the community, climate, and infrastructure associated with the selected building site. These documents will evolve into the full elaboration of project requirements down to piece part and process definitions (Figure 7.4).

REQUIREMENTS MANAGEMENT IS A SITUATIONAL COMPANION TO THE PROJECT CYCLE

Project requirements covers both requirement creation and management. The produced requirements documents are products of the project phases. The sequential facet of requirements creation,

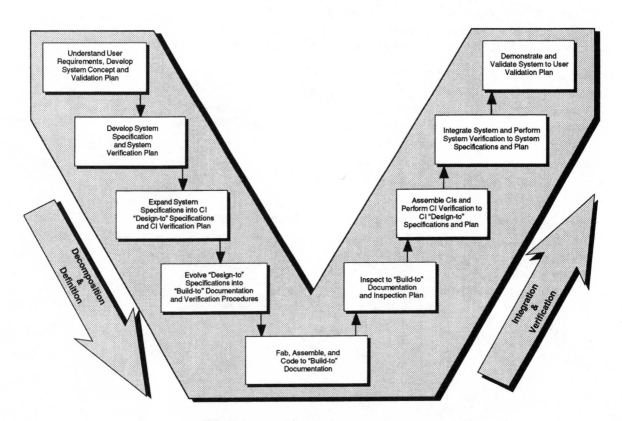

FIGURE 7.5 The basic Vee model.

as represented by the core of the Vee model, is described in Chapter 6 and illustrated in Figure 7.5.

The requirements-management element itself is situational since new requirements can be introduced at almost any point in the project to be managed concurrently with the maturing baselines at lower levels of decomposition. The two subprocesses, orthogonal to the core of the Vee, that we introduced in Chapter 3, are usually repeated many times within a phase proportional to the number of decompositions, integrations, and decisions being made. Note that the process is not the circular depiction often seen, but rather a series of new and original trade-offs to arrive at the hierarchy of decomposed best value solutions (Figure 7.6).

The Decomposition Analysis and Resolution process at each level results in the "Design-to" specifications and verification plans for that level and the requirements for the next lower level.

The Verification Analysis and Resolution process ensures that requirements at each level have been satisfied.

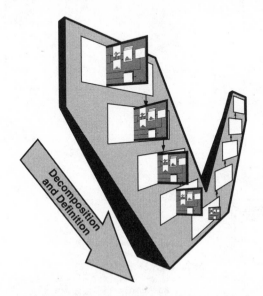

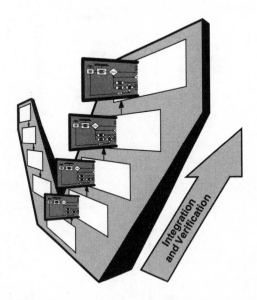

FIGURE 7.6   The Decomposition Analysis and Resolution and Verification Analysis and Resolution subprocesses related to the Vee model.

THE DECOMPOSITION ANALYSIS AND RESOLUTION PROCESS ENSURES USER AND STAKEHOLDER SATISFACTION

The Decomposition Analysis and Resolution Process (DA&R) is the framework for proactive requirements management. It is applied at each level of the Decomposition and Definition sequence and may be applied many times at a level where multiple entities and their associated trade-off decisions are required. This section addresses each of the steps in the management process diagrammed in Figure 7.7.

One author's recent experience in resolving some of the requirements for remodeling his home illustrate the DA&R process. Furthermore, the example demonstrates the benefits of

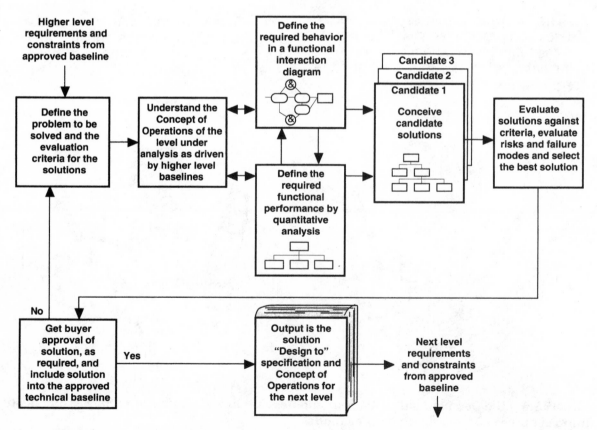

FIGURE 7.7   **The Decomposition Analysis and Resolution process flow chart.**

using such a process—even for simple or familiar projects. In this case, the process is applied to a home-heating system. The "higher level requirements and constraints" include the better half's personal comfort zone (tighter limits than the author's), aesthetics, and the retained house structure. We use the margin notes to relate this example to the DA&R steps that follow.

The Sources and Techniques for Determining Requirements At each level, the DA&R process is driven by higher level requirements, constraints of approved baselines such as the utilities provided to a structure and the influences of users and stakeholders at the system level and at every level of decomposition to the level under consideration.

To ensure all requirements have been extracted, establish a "check and balance" system by using multiple techniques:

Related documentation review	Of best available records. Performed before interviews of stakeholders, if possible.
Interviews	Face-to-face discussions with stakeholders. Best conducted using a checklist. Document and prioritize requirements as they are identified.
Focus groups	Ask open questions. Use to identify issues and establish realistic expectations.
Surveys	Questionnaire to sample users. Quantitative type questions. Often requires statistical analysis. Should be comprehensive and unambiguous.
Comment cards	Provides feedback on an existing product or service.
Observation and confirmation	See if what users say is consistent with what they really do.

Prioritization is perhaps the most significant technique for proactively managing project requirements and is one means for preventing over-specification and unbalanced response. The extent to which proper management discipline can be exercised

The sources for remodeling requirements include contractors and building codes, and most important, the users' comfort. The Context of Implementation is the historical climate of the area, the expected energy loss of the structure, and the constraints of the existing structure.

In our example, fast temperature response, low noise level, minimum dust, and "set it and forget it" operation ranked much higher than cost.

by putting first things first, obviously depends on knowing and understanding priorities. If they aren't explicitly stated in contracts (and they usually are not) they must be understood by the time the user requirements and other requirements baseline documents are placed under change control.

Prioritization is usually done in two forms: *relative* criteria for trade-off among two or more specifications, and *independent* priority levels (at least three grades: Must, Want, and Wish).

Understand the Context of Implementation

The context of the implementation describes the environment within which the project must operate. To understand the context, you need to define the system boundaries and include all operational factors such as reliability, maintainability, availability, human factors, and security. It's often helpful to verify your understanding with a behavioral model, validated by the customer. Use brainstorming sessions to verify your understanding. Ask probing questions and LISTEN.

The contractor in Figure 7.8 had a clear understanding of the requirements, but was a little short on understanding the context.

Defining the Problem to Be Solved and Establishing Weighted Evaluation Criteria

At each level, the problem is defined by the higher level baselined documentation (e.g., user requirements, system requirements, concepts, or entity requirements at each level). Each requirement must have associated evaluation criteria that are priority weighted, and have appropriate scoring methods to determine how well any candidate concept satisfies the criteria.

Before proceeding further, you need to decide the risk philosophy, since the risk philosophy drives risk management. Answers to the following typical questions will help establish the risk philosophy for your project:

- What are the consequences of system failure?
  Cost, schedule, and technical. Include safety.
- What is the maturity of critical technology? Can "off-the-shelf" technology be used?

Sidebar:

For example: San Francisco Bay—mild weather; no freezing, but rapid changes of up to 25 degrees F with fog patterns; maximum outside temperature of about 90° F (32° C) and a minimum of about 32° F (0° C).

The problem to be solved is to maintain a comfortable home temperature under all conditions. Anything less risks marital bliss. The evaluation criteria include a fast reaction time, economical fuel, clean (low dust), low noise, fully automatic operation, and low initial cost.

THE FAR SIDE   By GARY LARSON

Suddenly, a heated exchange took place
between the king and the moat contractor.

**FIGURE 7.8 The FAR SIDE © 1996 FARWORKS, INC/Dist. by
UNIVERSAL PRESS SYNDICATE. Reprinted with permission.
All rights reserved.**

Consequence of delivering a new, but obsolete system,
versus a state-of-the-art system with no logistics infrastructure (e.g., a gas car in 1903, or an electric car in
1998, or a NeXT computer in 1994).

- What are the risks in and from the system? How will they be
managed?
- What are the opportunities of and for the system? How will
they be managed?

What are the future growth expectations?

Risk philosophy is often expressed in terms such as "single thread design," or "no single point failure modes in mission critical functions" or in a reliability number such as 0.9997 reliability. The risk philosophy will drive these risk decisions:

Risk Decision	*Decision Range*
Design for growth	Planned or none
New technology	High use to no use
Expendable margins	High margins to no margin
Reliability	High to low
Part de-rating	Substantial to none
Redundancy	Full to none
Inspection	100% to none
Qualification	Required with high margins to not required
Verification	100% unit verification to none
Certification	Full pedigree proof to no proof
Sparing	Full to none
Cost	Mandatory constraint to desirable target
Schedule	Mandatory constraint to desirable target
Other market applications	Planned to none

Behavior Diagram (Example)

The system behavior is to detect the difference between a temperature setting and current temperature, then to introduce heat until that difference goes to near zero. The performance requires temperature difference detection to two degrees and heater response and makeup to the set point within 5 minutes.

Define the Required Behavior and Performance　The objective is to describe the behavior of the essential system functions, for example, by a flow diagram. When characterizing the behavior, use action verbs such as *detect, trigger, initialize, deliver,* and *cancel.*

This process is not unique. Functions can be grouped in different ways, such as grouping those that are common or in a way that minimizes interfaces.

The two methods for expanding the requirements for lower level decomposition are derivation (analysis) and allocation (past experience and judgment). In the derivation method, the requirements for each succeeding system level are established on the basis of quantitative analysis. Allocated requirements are based on past experience and rules of thumb and, therefore, must be confirmed as the design evolves. Allocated requirements are also provided by object adoption and/or COTS incorporation.

Develop Candidate Physical or Logical Solutions Identify potential solutions that satisfy the functional and performance requirements by brainstorming candidate concepts and developing system discriminators for each viable candidate. Discriminators may be technical, cost, schedule, or risk. Avoid rejecting "obvious misfits" prematurely.

- Identify top level segments for each candidate to further understand each candidate's relative complexity.
- Flow down functional and performance requirements. (Note that the content of the lower level requirements will usually be different for each candidate concept.)
- Identify critical system issues (may require investigation down to hardware part or software unit level).
- Use available performance information or hardware and software feasibility models to determine and/or confirm achievable performance values.

Select the Best Solution By using criteria previously defined, work toward selecting the best solution (Figure 7.9). Evaluate each candidate solution by using the criteria previously defined. This ultimately leads to rational design choices that meet the highest priority requirements.

The techniques for weighting criteria or alternatives include: scoring against a fixed standard; weighting relative to the most important criterion or best alternative; and pair-wise comparison (Analytical Hierarchy Process[10]). The decision criteria may need to include subjective criteria and inputs from many individuals. These can be decided by consensus, voting (permitting multiple votes per individual), or the geometric mean of individual scores. The user should confirm that the decision criteria and weights to be used are appropriate for concept selection. This avoids decisions that are based on incorrect assumptions.

One of the most powerful ways to compare alternatives is to use the decision analysis process developed by Kepner and Tregoe.[11] The weighted comparison matrix shown in Figure 7.10 illustrates the process.

The selection process is not complete until the residual risks have been identified. The highest scoring candidate may not be

---

For this example, the heating candidates are electrical or hydronic baseboard, electrical radiant ceiling, hydronic-in-slab, or forced air heating.

For example, Glycol pipes in slab floors are difficult to repair.

In our example, none of the standard conventional solutions meet all of the criteria. Radiant solutions are too slow; forced air is too noisy and dirty.

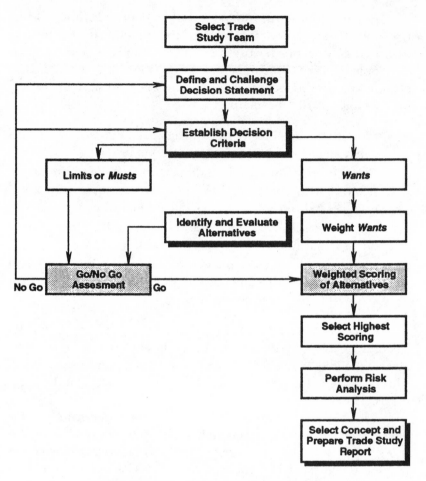

FIGURE 7.9   Selection flow chart.

The process had to be repeated by creating new solutions. Radiant systems were analyzed for decreased response times and no practical solutions were found. Forced air was analyzed for reduced noise and dust. One contractor, brainstorming, recommended

the best choice if the risk is unacceptable. The final step in the trade-off process is to evaluate the risks as follows:

- Assess risks for the highest scoring alternatives:
  —Determine consequences of identified risks.
  —Estimate probability and seriousness.
  —Identify risk mitigation actions.
- Evaluate failure modes and effects for the selected alternative:

Selecting Candidates for Further Consideration

Decision Statement:	Select the best vehicle to meet the needs of the Patrick family. (Mom, dad, and three kids, ages 5 to 16)											
Evaluation Criteria:	**Alternative 1**			**Alternative 2**			**Alternative 3**			**Alternative 4**		
	Mid-Size Domestic Car			Japanese Sports Car			Domestic Mini-Van			Italian Sports Car		
Musts (Go/No-Go):												
• Under $25,000	✗			✗			✗			−		
• Transport 5 people	✗			−			✗			−		
Wants:	Weight	Comments	Score Raw (R)	R*W	Comments	Score Raw (R)	R*W	Comments	Score Raw (R)	R*W	Comments	Score Raw (R)	R*W
• 25 mpg (10.6 kpl)*	8	26.2 mpg avg. (11.2 kpl)	10	80				25.1 mpg avg. (10.7 kpl)	7	56			
• Carry garden supplies	10	Trunk only	2	20				Good capacity	10	100			
• Crash safety	9	Rated high on tests	10	90				Meets min. reqmts	7	63			
• Use on dates (16 yo.)	4	Considered "Cool" by peers	10	40				"Parents" type car	5	20			
Max Score (10xW):	310												
Total Score:				230						239			

* 1 mpg (miles per gallon) = 0.426 kpl (kilometers per liter)

Note: Scores that are within 10% are essentially equal

FIGURE 7.10 Trade Study Process, based on Kepner-Tregoe Decision Analysis Methodology.

—Determine impact on system design.

—Define approach to mitigate effects, for example: requirements for increased reliability, fault tolerance, or fail safe operation.

—Incorporate in the design.

• Adopt risk mitigation actions.

• Rescore candidates with mitigation incorporated.

• Consider effect of remaining risks (residual risk).

The Specification for the Concept Selected Completes the DA&R Process at this Level The approved baseline now includes the specifications and the decision-support documents suspending a forced hot air system in the thermal and sound insulated attic on shock and vibration isolated rods hung from the rafters to minimize noise and to ground residual vibration to the outside walls and foundation. By achieving further isolation with flexible fabric ducting and clean air with an electronic air filter, all criteria could be met with this modified forced air system.

such as trade-off analyses for this decision. Each specification developed must answer the following:

- What is the problem to be solved, and in what context?
- What must the system do? (Functional Analysis)
- How well must the system do it? (Quantitative Performance)
- Within what context and interfaces?
- What level of risk is acceptable (risk philosophy, e.g., redundancy, as detailed previously)?
- How will we know if the system meets the requirements (verification and validation planning)?

This result is now the approved higher level baseline for the next decomposition level.

The DA&R process is repeated until all entities at all levels of decomposition have been baselined. Collaborative design is required where simultaneous decomposition analysis is required at a decomposition level and entity interfaces are mutually interactive. The baselining of any one entity at a level requires close coordination with interfacing entities to assure mutual compatibility.

THE VERIFICATION ANALYSIS AND RESOLUTION PROCESS

The counterpart of the DA&R process is the Verification Analysis and Resolution process (VA&R), an iterative process repeated throughout the integration and verification sequence as new groups of entities are combined to form the system. (Figure 7.11).

The VA&R process is an integral part of requirements management. It provides the framework for verifying each level of integration according to the verification criteria embodied in the requirements documents. Conventional wisdom is that tests are more perceptive than analysis, because tests encompass the "real world" issues that are very hard to model analytically. But beware. Tests can introduce complications of their own, and can mask the actual condition or behavior. In the spring of 1999, an expensive system was in its final system test series. The system incorporated explosive bolts, used to hold a cover in place. The bolts were to fire only on operator command. Analytical studies

---

In our example, "forced hot air" becomes the requirement for lower level decisions like furnace and filter selection, furnace room, ducting design, foundation, wall design, and service locations.

The success of the VA&R process is rooted left Vee planning for right Vee execution.

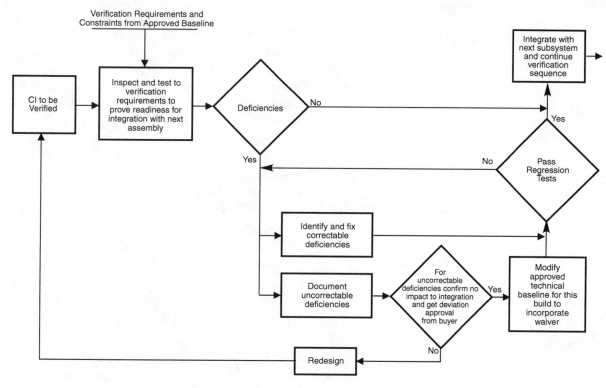

FIGURE 7.11   Verification Analysis and Resolution process flow chart.

predicted that voltage transients at system startup could cause the explosives to fire prematurely, but laboratory tests repeatedly proved the analysis wrong.

The first time the system was put into use, the explosive bolts fired on system startup, just as the analysis predicted. The lab tests used conditioned power, so the system voltage spikes were suppressed. The flawed system test allowed a flawed system to be installed, resulting in the loss of a multimillion dollar system.

Improper setup of a test device allowed the flaw in the Hubble mirror to go undetected for six years, until the telescope was put into orbit and the problem was there for all to see. The unfortunate fact is that the flaw was detected six years prior to launch, but with a less sensitive device. Those troubling data were ignored until it was too late. In college, we often ran lab experiments until we got the right answer, then we quit, ignoring the prior failures. In a project, failures must be explained or you risk finding bad news when it is devastating in its impact.

Verification can be done by analysis, inspection, demonstration, or test. With these cautions in mind, testing is the preferred approach for most situations, supplemented by the other techniques as appropriate. Testing comes in various types and is performed to:

Engineering	Prove feasibility and demonstrate performance to support the design process.
Informal	Demonstrate readiness for formal testing (customer buy-off).
Formal	Produce buy-off verification data. Verifications are witnessed by the customer.
Qualification	Demonstrate that the design will perform in its intended environment *with margin* (temperature, vibration, shock, humidity, transaction overload, unexpected power shutdown and recovery, etc.).
Acceptance	Demonstrate the deliverable is built of sufficient quality to replicate the qualification item performance and will perform in the intended environment.
Environmental	Simulate the operating environment by subjecting the test article to temperature, vibration, humidity, acoustic, shocks, salt spray, radiation, and so on. Can also be used to stress parts to find weaknesses.
Life	Demonstrate system lifetime wear out and failure modes in the expected environment. Accelerated life tests may be used where compression of the time and accelerated exposure does not distort the expected results.
Reliability	Demonstrate system failure rates and failure modes.
First article	Demonstrate quality of first manufactured article.
Nth article	Demonstrate that the quality of any selected unit has not degraded from the first article. Sampling plans may be used when sufficient data have been gathered to provide a reliable statistical basis for doing so.

PROJECT REQUIREMENTS TRACEABILITY AND ACCOUNTABILITY

The identification and management of the proper "parentage" (parent/child relationships) from the highest level system requirements to the lowest level and to verification planning is referred to as Requirements Traceability—a requirements management responsibility. The two methods for defining lower level requirements, derivation and allocation, were discussed earlier.

> In traceability, a child may have many parents.

The flowdown and parentage of software requirements depend on the project type. Where software requirements are primary, such as for information system projects, they can usually be determined at the beginning of the project, and software development usually gets off to a good start. However, in hardware-driven projects, software requirements may depend on hardware needs and often can't be determined until later in the cycle when hardware capability and limitations are understood. Unfortunately, software development in such projects usually gets off to a slow start and will likely pace the project. Such dependencies need to be identified in the study period and provided for in the planning.

Requirements traceability is sufficiently complex to require specialty computer tools to facilitate the mapping and change management. The purpose of requirements accountability is to ensure that all requirements have been responded to and have been verified by test, inspection, demonstration, and, where the foregoing are not possible, analysis. System engineering is responsible for

> Requirements accountability is the proof that all requirements have been satisfied.

DILBERT / Scott Adams

Reprinted by permission of United Feature Syndicate, Inc.

auditing the verification results and certifying that the evidence demonstrates conclusively that the requirements have been achieved. Compliance matrices that present the verification results are often used as customer buy-off evidence for delivery acceptance.

MANAGING TBD AND TBR REQUIREMENTS

It's naive to believe that TBDs and TBRs can be resolved with no impact to cost or schedule.

Unresolved requirements should be viewed as liens against the baseline and should be resolved as early as possible to reduce programmatic risk. The least defined, which cannot be priced or scheduled, are referred to as TBDs (To Be Determined). Once defined, these may be the basis for an engineering change. TBRs (To Be Resolved) can usually be roughly estimated and, when resolved, are subject to engineering change if they're out of predicted range. Formal work-off plans should be developed for both TBDs and TBRs including "must have" delivery dates (Figure 7.12). Failure of the customer to deliver on these negotiated delivery dates may be grounds for a constructive change claim and compensation.

REQUIREMENTS MANAGEMENT TOOLS

From an information systems viewpoint, the handling of requirements data is similar to inventory control. Both involve complex, interrelated tables, cross references, and "where-used" indices. Manual tools such as card files and index tables are readily available.

General purpose database applications, many of them inexpensive desktop products, can be further programmed to address a specific project or even an organization's tailored project template.

Currently, there are a number of specialty requirements management tools available, some with extended capability such as system simulation, behavior analysis, and trade-off analysis capability. Most of these tools are found in the system engineering domain and at system engineering conferences rather than the project management domain.

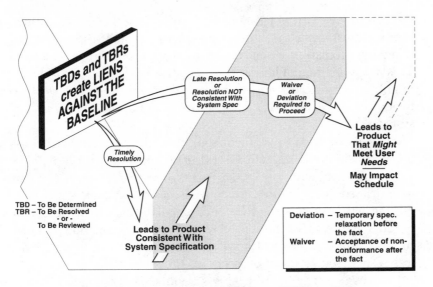

FIGURE 7.12   Resolve TBDs and TBRs early.

THE POTENTIAL FOR LOW-RISK HARDWARE AND SOFTWARE SOLUTIONS

Previously Developed Products (PDP) consist of Commercial-Off-The-Shelf (COTS), Government-Off-The-Shelf (GOTS), and Nondevelopment-Item (NDI) hardware and software products. Because others have already handled the risk of development these products offer potential low-risk solutions to those that can benefit from their reuse. However, they are not risk-free as interface, performance, and technical support problems may override whatever advantages they may appear to have. Thorough investigation is required to examine both the opportunities and associated risks of the intended reuse. As we will discuss in Chapter 9, the push for better, faster, cheaper products in both the commercial and government environments has created added pressure to use COTS and NDI components. In most cases, this is exactly the right thing to do. However, the pressure to shorten schedule, as well as reduce costs, have caused use of these existing components without full understanding of their limitations. Avoiding these problems will be discussed in Chapter 8.

In today's office automation systems and business information systems, there are high percentages of COTS use. In command and control systems, the percentages are markedly lower. This is understandable, recognizing the proliferation of high-quality and reliable business applications and the comparatively nonexistence of commercial multipurpose interactive command systems.

Users of COTS products seek to realize reduced development time and costs and to achieve known and predictable performance. Users also hope to be able to rely on long-term technical support. While these advantages are attractive the user may actually experience substandard performance, difficulty in producing integration code, rights to data issues, and no technical support due to modification of the product or later version releases superseding the used product.

In evaluating COTS products, requirements should be prioritized to facilitate selection between candidate COTS products, none of which may satisfy all requirements. Therefore, a best of the group choice may have to suffice.

The following checklist of lessons learned regarding the use of COTS or other PDP products is an alert to potential problems:

1. COTS may be more or less capable than needed.
2. Required features may be dropped by vendor in later upgrades.
3. Bugs in present version may never be fixed.
4. Upward compatibility may not be assured.
5. Interface hardware and software is often required.
6. COTS rarely has hooks for integration and integrated performance is often difficult to predict.
7. Source code may be required and difficult to get. May have to hold in escrow account.
8. Difficult to get capability certifications.
9. Alteration usually voids any warranty.
10. Vendor may abandon product.
11. Training may not be available.
12. Life-cycle costs dependent on supplier behavior with new releases.

There are a growing number of computer-based tools specifically designed for management of project requirements. The tools provide assistance from the initial documentation of user requirements, through the evolution of the function and performance requirements determined through behavior analysis, to the final executable specifications and verification plans and procedures. Some tools only provide requirements management while others are much more capable adding system simulation, behavior analysis, and decision support capability.

Other computer-based tools are available to handle the mechanics of weighting, scoring, and evaluating alternative concepts and designs to arrive at a best value solution. An excellent source for current information on system engineering tools is the web site for International Council On System Engineering (INCOSE) (www.INCOSE.org). The main menu will lead you to the tool evaluation page.

REQUIREMENTS ELEMENT EXERCISE

The objective of this exercise is to provide experience in developing and stating requirements using a method of musts, wants, and priorities.

You have decided to purchase a new vehicle. You have not yet decided on the model or brand and want to make certain that you find the best solution for your needs. You are to make a list of your "musts" (will not buy without them being satisfied), your "wants" (not mandatory, but desirable), and you will weight the wants according to their importance to you.

The musts must be strictly quantitative such as "must cost less than $35,000" or "must have four or more doors." Statements like "must be low maintenance" are qualitative and do not qualify for the must category and are relegated to the want column. It is perfectly acceptable to have an issue in both categories. For instance "must stop from 70 mph in 170 feet" can be a must and "short braking distance" can be a want to give points to those that pass the must for consideration and are then better than others at braking.

Once you have listed all of your musts and wants, prioritize the wants by selecting the most important want and assigning it a weight of 10. Then compare the importance of each of the other wants to the importance of that standard and give it an appropriate weight. If you judge two or more wants to be of equal importance, they will have equal weights. Your final list with weights provides you with the evaluation criteria against which you can score the alternatives you will consider. The alternative that best satisfies a want is scored a 10. The other alternatives are compared to the best relative to that want and are scored appropriately. Again, equal scores are acceptable. Multiplying the criteria weight by the alternative score results in a weighted score. Sum the scores for each alternative. A comparison of the sum of the weighted scores will lead you to the alternative that best satisfies your criteria.

2. ORGANIZATION OPTIONS

Confusion is a word we have invented for an order which is not understood.

Henry Miller,
Tropic of Capricorn

Organization: A structure through which individuals cooperate systematically to conduct business.

A great deal has been written about organizational theory—a favorite topic of industrial psychologists. The variations on form and order are limitless, as are the behavioral implications. Experience reveals that the point of confusion usually occurs when the order, though rationally structured by management, is not adequately explained to those who must operate by it—team members and others who participate in the project. This confusion is largely eliminated when individual, as well as organizational, roles and relationships are determined by a defined process. Preferably the structure itself implies much of this order, for example, the logical path to problem solving, conflict resolution, and, information. But even so, these need to be explicitly defined in the organization charter and reinforced by the project manager.

Each project manager faces the task of changing the organization structure to suit the changing phases of the project cycle. While effective management, leadership, and teamwork are more important success factors than structural details, the optimum organization can contribute significantly to project performance and efficiency. In most organizations the project manager does not have freedom to reshape the external reporting relationships of the project unless the project is the major part of the corporation. For instance you usually do not have the freedom to choose a projectized structure in a matrix-oriented corporation. If you are in a well-established, traditional hierarchical organization, then trying to convert to a matrix or trying to introduce cross-functional project teams can be a major and distracting challenge.[12] However, understanding the organization strengths and weaknesses of various options will allow you to work more effectively within your constraints, and to push for change when there is a high return in doing so. The following section covers the Project Team, the associated management element focused on building a working organization.

The organization's design should promote the team's dominant interfaces and communication channels. Its purpose is to ensure that project requirements are met, hence the importance of designing the organization after the requirements of the project are established and understood. As a practical matter, the core team (initially consisting of the project manager, systems engineering manager, and other lead positions) is probably involved during the study period.

> The organization design should respond to what it will take to satisfy the requirements.

Most projects are best served by some form of matrix organization combined with elements that are pure functional and others that are pure project, each addressing specific project or environmental needs. We will address the primary reasons for selecting each form after reviewing their relative strengths and weaknesses.

FUNCTIONAL ORGANIZATIONS

The functional organization is the traditional business structure. It has prevailed throughout the manufacturing-driven, industrial era. The functional organization has proved its effectiveness, with a few exceptions, for single-technology companies having these characteristics:

- One high-volume product line serving a common market, with
- A common manufacturing process, and/or

- A business segment with relatively slow or predictable technical changes.

One notable exception is a company serving a broad common market, but also having one large customer with special requirements that requires the focused attention of a project manager. A semiconductor company, for example, supplying standard parts might benefit from a separate product or project organization to serve customers requiring ruggedized versions of the same products.

Pure Support (Functional)—Skill Centers

Strengths	Weaknesses
+ Skill Development	− Customer interface unclear
+ Technology Development	− Project priority unclear
+ Technology transfer	− Confused communications
+ Low talent duplication	− Schedule/cost controls are difficult
+ High personnel loyalty	

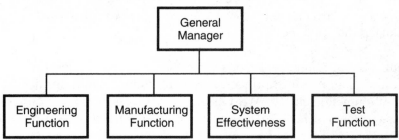

As organizations grow to multiple project/product environments with multiple markets/customers, the pure functional organization often proves ineffective. For example, one of our clients was trying to manage some 50 project/product lines through a traditional functional organization. When a customer called the salesman to find out how their project was doing, the following scenario often occurred. The salesman would refer the customer to one of the functional departments, such as engineering or production. The functional managers would pass the inquirer along to others or respond inappropriately, being aware only of the status of their project portion. For projects that were in the design or production phase the customer might end up talking to an engineering manager or to production control who would give partial or misleading information, or avoid blame by revealing internal problems with other departments. This resulted in the customer calling the president for better service. The president would then raise that customer's priority to #1 causing all the other projects to suffer as the priorities in design or on the shop floor shifted. Priorities would change daily as the #1 position was given to the latest squeaky wheel!

This confusion in managing priorities and determining status usually leads to setting up product centers or divisions.

Pure Support (Functional)—Product Centers

Strengths	Weaknesses
+ Product development	− Customer interface unclear
+ Technology development	− Technology transfer difficult
+ High personnel loyalty	− Project priorities unclear
	− Communications confused
	− Schedule/cost controls are difficult

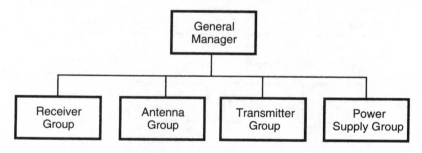

THE PURE PROJECT ORGANIZATION

The pure project organization, shown below, is composed of separate autonomous units, each being one project. They often evolve from functional or support organizations with the success of a high-priority task force as a model. Since the project manager has full line (hire and fire) authority over the team for the project's duration, project organizations maximize the project manager's control and the clarity of the customer interface. Unfortunately, the dramatic success of a single, high-priority task force is not easily replicated when multiple projects are competing for key company resources and priority.

Pure Project Organization

Strengths	Weaknesses
+Accountability clear	−Talent duplication
+Customer interface clear	−Technology awareness
+Controls strong	−Technical sharing
+Communications strong	−Career development
+Balances technical, cost, and schedule	−Hire/fire
	−Staffing irregular workloads

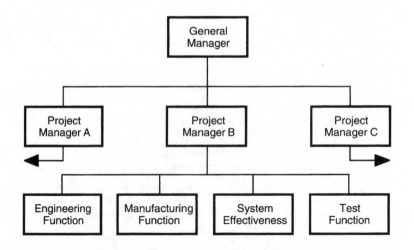

Project organizations are relatively costly because of the inability to share part-time resources and they may cause isolation of personnel from the company's strategy and technology focus. Also there is a natural tendency for team members to be kept on the project well beyond the date that is justified. Team members are typically dedicated full-time—another contributor to the inefficiency of this organization. This is one of the reasons that some functions such as Personnel (Human Resources) and Finance are often maintained as central support departments, with specific people assigned to project organizations on an as-needed basis.

THE CONVENTIONAL MATRIX ORGANIZATION

Most organizations are a blend of Functional and Project structures in the form of a matrix with solid (hire/fire management) vertical lines and dotted (task assignment or borrow/return) horizontal lines. The most common form of matrix has the team members connected to project managers by dotted lines and connected to their functional managers by solid lines as shown in the Conventional Matrix below. These structures combine the best aspects of both pure forms, as demonstrated by their relative strength.

An effective matrix structure is perhaps the strongest of all project management organizational options. The key word is "effective." To succeed, all participants have to understand their roles and responsibilities. The project team member has two bosses, but this should cause no conflict to the project team member if it is clear that the project manager defines only what is to be done, and the functional manager defines how to do it. All three authors worked for decades in highly efficient matrix environments. As consultants we have also witnessed very poorly implemented matrix organizations. In fact, in the large-scale mergers that have occurred in the 1990s many organizations have lost the key and their current matrix structures are staffed with unhappy team members. A well-functioning matrix organization is like a bicycle—it is dynamically stable but statically unstable.

Those of you familiar with military resource deployment have seen a similar battlefield evolution brought about largely by technology. Traditional, vertically organized, functional branches (Army, Air Force, and Navy) are rapidly being "matrixed" into battle units or task groups. This counterpart to the business task force consists of tightly coordinated resources under the direction of perhaps a tank commander, for the period of one engagement. The infantry, armor, aircraft, and even ships form a team, coupled more by computer communications than by voice. These task groups, after having carried out their mission, return to their permanent units available for other deployments.

> The strengths of a matrix organization can usually be increased by effective leadership.

> The military matrix in the field is analogous to the Conventional Matrix on the business battlefield.

Conventional Matrix Organization

Strengths	*Weaknesses*
+ Single point accountability	− High management skill level required
+ Customer interface clear	− Competition for resources
+ Rapid reaction	− Lack of employee recognition
+ Duplication reduced	− Management cooperation required
+ Technology development	
+ Career development	
+ Disbanded easily	

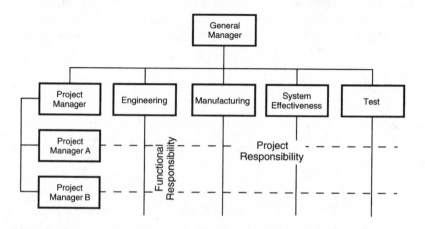

Functional organizations that have evolved to product centers may transition to a matrix organization based on those product centers. While this structure does offer some of the advantages of the Conventional Matrix, it combines the disadvantages of both the matrix and the product-centered functional organization. It tends to inhibit both technology and career development and requires greater integration skills. We will therefore focus on variations of the Conventional Matrix which have proved to be effective.

Conventional Matrix organizations operate in two ways. In the first, the project manager borrows people from the support managers and provides daily supervision and funding. In the second form, the project manager "subcontracts" the work to the support manager, providing a task statement and funding. For example, a key technology development may require the combined talents and synergy of a team of specialists working in close proximity. This need may best be met by technical specialists meeting periodically without disrupting their on-going technical focus and the teamwork within their specialty.

THE COMPOUND OR COLLOCATED MATRIX ORGANIZATION

Some environments may benefit from variants of the Conventional Matrix form. To compensate for structural and/or personnel short-comings, most large projects will introduce pure functional and/or pure project sections to form a compound matrix. For example, critical resources (either administrative or technical) may report directly (solid line) to the project manager or, alternatively, be collocated with the project office. The latter, known as the Collocated Matrix, is shown next.

The Compound and Collocated Matrix forms offer effective compromises between the Project and Conventional Matrix structures.

The Collocated Matrix

Strengths	*Weaknesses*
+ Single point accountability	− Technology awareness
+ Clear customer interface	− Management support
+ Good control	− Technical sharing
+ Single location	− Staffing irregular workloads
+ High personnel loyalty	− Personnel evaluation (by functional manager)
+ Career development	

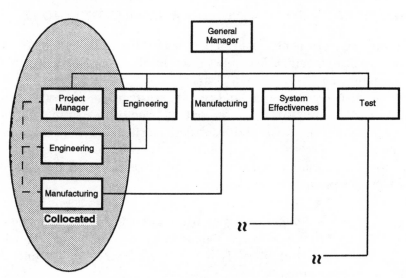

It provides for maximum focus on project objectives with a corresponding disadvantage: isolating the project team members from the company's overall strategic operations.

In some project intensive environments, such as the aerospace industry and in geographically dispersed companies, the relationships are sometimes reversed. In the Hybrid Matrix, the team members are connected to the project manager for the duration of the project by solid lines approaching a pure project organization. In this case, the functional departments are small core staffs responsible for long-term strategic technology and concept development—perhaps even common component or subsystem development. For example, the corporate engineering manager typically looks for means to avoid duplication, share technology, and provide for professional development. He or she may have line/budget authority for proprietary technology development projects—some or all of which may be performed by direct reports. Another variation shares a common (typically high-tech) manufacturing operation, but assigns the Production Engineering function, usually part of the manufacturing function, to the project.

For further details of organizational theory and how the matrix organization evolved to meet the needs of projects refer to the list of references on pages 334–336.

DESIGNING AND MAINTAINING A RELEVANT STRUCTURE

A single government agency or company will often simultaneously use several organization options for project management. Furthermore, each project will typically experience several structures during its life cycle and the project manager and customer can significantly influence the option selected. Deciding on the initial structure involves both subjective criteria, such as prior organizational experience, and objective criteria, such as the availability and location of resources. The guidelines that follow are for simple projects or subprojects:

- *Pure functional* organization is the best match for a single project that is relatively independent in interface or technology. Pure functional is not preferred for management of multiple projects.

The Hybrid Matrix retains the focus and most advantages of the pure Project while improving efficiency.

All decision criteria should be prioritized.

- *Pure project* is a good choice for projects for which schedule and/or product performance is paramount and development cost is relatively unimportant.
- *Conventional matrix* works well if the project manager has authority to manage the funds and has business relationships with supporting managers, including formal work commitments and participation in project planning. The matrix fails when the project manager is seen as only a coordinator and the support managers operate on a "best effort" basis.
- *Collocated matrix* should be considered for very high priority projects dependent on critical resources and/or technologies and when on-going involvement with company strategy and long-term business goals are secondary.

INTEGRATED PROJECT TEAMS AND INTEGRATED PRODUCT TEAMS

There are many ways to develop an organizational structure. Some managers begin by assuming a starting form, say a conventional matrix, and then they modify it to resolve staffing barriers. We prefer a process that matches the organization to the requirements (as segmented into major work packages by the Work Breakdown Structure). In this process, the total project is viewed as a set of simple projects, defined by the nature of their deliverables and/or resource requirements (Figure 7.13). The terminology for this approach is Integrated Product Teams.

Matrix refinements, such as Integrated Project Teams and Integrated Product Teams, have solved product responsibility issues; however, these forms bring a new set of issues regarding system integration and responsibility for the perpetuation of the enterprise, such as technology development and technology sharing.[13] The role of system engineering, always important, becomes crucial when integrating a system developed by multiple product teams.

As Peter Drucker commiserates, ". . . at best an organizational structure will not cause trouble."[14]

When defining the original structure, you need to plan responses to the inevitable project cycle dynamics. Without anticipating changes, you may find yourself evaluating the symptoms below and thrashing through crisis-driven reorganizations. While

Integrated Project Teams and Integrated Product Teams instill responsibility and accountability.

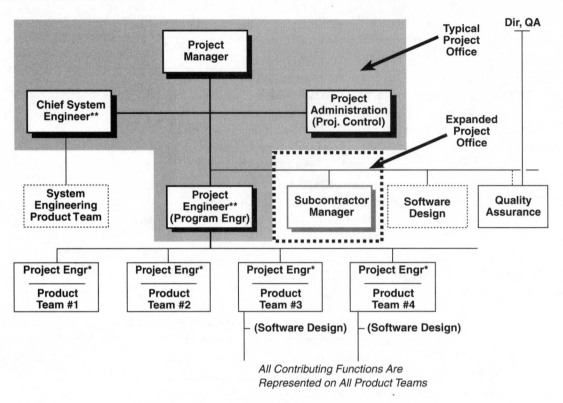

FIGURE 7.13   Typical project team organization.

no organization is expected to be perfect, some may be flawed to the extent that project success is at risk. Before reorganizing, be sure it is justified. The authors of *Dynamic Project Management*[15] offer these symptoms of an inappropriate organization to watch for:

> Is there a [lack of] product pride and ownership among the team members?
>
> Is too much attention typically given to one particular technical function, to the neglect of other technical components?
>
> Does a great deal of finger-pointing exist across technical groups?
>
> Is slippage common, while customer responsiveness is negligible?
>
> Do project participants appear unsure of their responsibilities or of the mission or objective(s) of the project?

Are projects experiencing considerable cost overruns as a result of duplication of effort or unclear delegation of responsibilities?

Do project participants complain of a lack of job satisfaction, rewards, or recognition for project efforts?

The authors observe that "Unfortunately, when symptoms of inadequate organizing appear, some companies typically respond by applying more time, money, or resources to the already weakened and inadequate project organization. If the problem truly is an inappropriately structured project organization, simply addressing the symptoms while ignoring the basic problem itself may leave the organization and its people frustrated and demoralized, as projects continue to slip and conflict continues to grow."

On the other hand, each of these symptoms, taken separately, could have little to do with the organization and a lot to do with leadership, or the lack thereof. One has to look closely at the combinations and patterns to conclude that a reorganization is indeed needed.

The single biggest error in organization design is over-complexity or redundancy leading to confused responsibility. We've defined several complex configurations and suggested others in an effort to define the problem and provide choices. However, some configurations such as the Hybrid Matrix are suitable for only the very largest projects or for an entire multidivisional corporation.

> Complex projects should not always lead to complex structures.

ORGANIZATION OPTIONS EXERCISE

The objective of this exercise is to provide experience in judging the adequacy of an organizational structure for a particular project.

You've been appointed the project manager for a new project. The project will last nine months, of which the first three months will involve design work. Four months have been estimated to actually develop the product and the remaining two months set aside for testing and delivery. The design work will require four highly skilled experts. The development involves a large number of technicians working in four separate locations, one of which is overseas. Test and integration and final delivery are to be done at the main facility located 30 miles away from your present location. Your company uses matrix management and all resources are available from within the company, however, other major projects frequently compete for key resources. You can either select staff by name or obtain services from other departments, but you've got to decide which mode of operation best suits your needs. You know that a project of particular significance is about to be launched and will probably need resources similar to yours for its start up activities.

Since you've not been given the alternative of using other than matrix management, list the advantages and shortcomings of matrix management in this context. Once you've identified the potential problem areas, define actions you will take to minimize the potential problems.

Define an organizational structure that might be better given the context of the project.

3. THE PROJECT TEAM

> **The meeting of two personalities is like the contact of two chemical substances: if there is any reaction, both are transformed.**
>
> **Carl G. Jung**

Forming the team starts with selecting the right people and defining their roles.

In Chapter 5, we focused on instilling teamwork, a perpetual property of projects and the second Essential to successful project management. We now look at team formation, a situational process, ongoing throughout the project cycle as each phase requires a different mix of talented individuals. As Lewis comments in his book, *Team-Based Project Management*, "Teams don't just happen—they must be *built*."[16]

Forming the team requires:

1. Defining the project manager's roles, responsibilities, and authority.
2. Selecting the project manager.
3. Chartering the project and confirming the project manager's authority.
4. Staffing the team.

    5. Managing the organization's interfaces and interrelationships.

The Project Team element goes beyond the traditional staffing function and includes management of the interfaces with supporting organizations, with contractors, with upper management, and with the customer (which may be the internal marketing/sales department) (Figure 7.14).

DEFINING THE PROJECT MANAGER'S ROLES, RESPONSIBILITIES, AND AUTHORITY

The project manager's roles are broad—like those of general managers—going from administration to technical to leadership.[17]

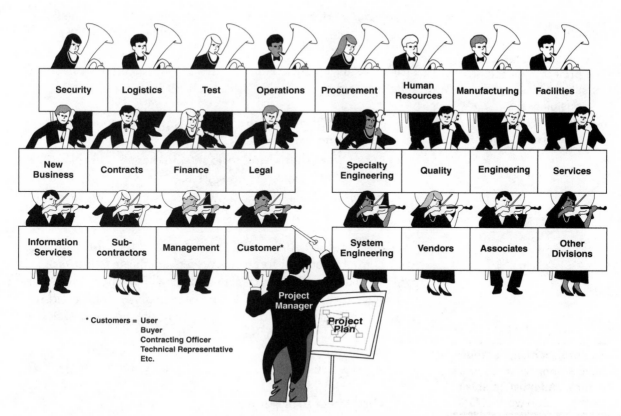

FIGURE 7.14　The project team.

But the focus is shorter range than that of a line manager who must manage the long-term strength of the organization. By contrast, the project manager should be correctly focused on the relatively short-term results of the project. In many environments the project manager is viewed as the general manager for the project.

Roles	*Complications*
Manage the project to the Project Cycle.	Meet an aggressive schedule.
Balance technical, schedule, and cost performance.	Implement state-of-the-art technology.
Solve problems expeditiously as they arise.	Perform within the budget by using limited funds and resources.
Inspire and motivate the entire team.	Optimize the mix of dedicated, shared, and contract personnel.

> A major challenge is to make both the customer and the organization successful by leading the project team.

Project management challenges are often exacerbated by an imbalance among:

- *Responsibility*—the duty or obligation to complete a specific act or assignment.
- *Authority*—the power to exact obedience and make decisions to fulfill specific obligations.
- *Accountability*—the acknowledged state of being answerable for success or failure.

> The project manager must have total project responsibility and accountability, yet often has too little authority.

Broad responsibilities increase the need for information and work contribution and force the project manager to cut cross organizational lines, like a general manager. But without the general manager's formal authority, the project manager (equipped with implied authority) must often depend on interpersonal skills and negotiating abilities to influence others.

While the range of the project manager's authority varies greatly, effective project management policy should require that:

- The project manager have financial control.
- The support managers view the project manager as their customer.

> The project manager must have authority for resource control and must be able to start and stop work.

- A culture of "make a promise—keep a promise" exists.
- Delineation of responsibilities is understood and agreed to.

Before selecting the project manager, the responsibilities need to be determined. They should include responsibility for:

- Establishing the project vocabulary;
- Establishing the team and teamwork environment;
- Inspiring and motivating the team;
- Ensuring all project requirements are defined and that they flow down to the lowest level;
- Leading the planning and managing to the plan;
- Pursuing opportunities and managing risk;
- Ensuring controls are in place and effective;
- Controlling the evolving baseline through a change control system;
- Ensuring that visibility techniques are in place and are effective;
- Determining the content, frequency, and the detail of project status reviews; and
- Executing timely corrective action to correct variances from the plan.

SELECTING THE PROJECT MANAGER

There are many sources for ideas for a new project. When an idea seems promising enough to pursue, a project champion is either appointed or he or she seizes the opportunity to aggressively develop understanding of the opportunity (the users needs and potential return from meeting them) and to estimate the resources required to pursue the opportunity. The champion will also evaluate the risks inherent in satisfying the user (and other stakeholders). Even on projects that ultimately involve billions of dollars, the project champion at the very beginning usually works alone, with occasional input from various experts, to create the first estimate of the project plan. If it is decided that a study team is warranted, the project champion may be the appropriate one to lead the effort in the early, or even the entire study period. At the end of the study period the project requirements are clearly

In the beginning . . . there is a project champion. As the project matures, the implementation project manager should be selected . . . *after* the project challenge is understood, but *before* other team members are selected.

understood and the project manager for the implementation period must be selected. It is unusual for the project champion to fill this role.

Selecting the key person on the team, namely the project manager for the implementation period, is a critical matchmaking task for executive management. In too many cases, the project manager is selected before the requirements and the organizational form of the project are determined. This is backward, and often leads to a bad match of project manager skills with the challenge of the job.

Selecting the right project manager is critical to project success, and for this reason must be carefully done. The project manager must fulfill the requirements of the customer or user, must answer to senior management by generating a fair return on investment, and must provide a stimulating, positive work environment for the project team, while at the same time satisfying personal family obligations and goals.

Peters and Waterman[18] report a high correlation between project success and the leadership qualities and/or authority level of the project manager. In many types of projects, leadership qualities are more important than authority level. But this should never be taken for granted. It is essential that the project manager operate as a manager/leader rather than just as a coordinator/monitor. He or she must have well-defined, business interrelationships with the support managers participating in the project.

When selecting any team member, it is important to have an objective basis for evaluating the most important competency factors for the specific project. The example competency model (Table 7.1) illustrates the contractual skills portion.

The base structure for most projects is some form of matrix, designed to take advantage of critical technical demands, to accommodate unique management strengths and weaknesses, and to balance short-term project priorities with the long-term priorities of the company and/or functional organizations. They are all characterized by complex interpersonal relationships requiring that the project manager be selected more on the basis of behavioral (e.g., negotiating and leadership) skills than on technical skills. However, the project manager should be "conversant" in the project domain and knowledgeable of the system engineering process. The person selected for this challenging assignment must have the right

The project manager has roles in three different arenas, the customer's, executive management's, and the project team's.

Our experience shows that strong leadership can compensate for a lower authority level.

TABLE 7.1   Example Competency Model

Rating Factor	Basic	Score	Advanced	Score	Expert	Score
Project Management Training	Has had some project management training		Has had the company's or equivalent project management training		Has had the company's, PMI[1], or equivalent certification in project management	
Project Management Experience	Has served as a deputy or assistant project manager		Has been a successful project manager		Has managed several successful projects	
Contracting and Negotiating	Is knowledgeable of types and applications of the relevant contract types		Has participated in developing contract negotiation strategies		Has considerable experience in contract negotiation strategy and participating in negotiations.	
Sub-contracting	Is knowledgeable in the difference between purchasing and subcontracting		Has participated in the selection and award of subcontracts		Has successfully managed subcontractors	
Decision Analysis	Is aware of the importance and practice of Analytical Decision Analysis[2]		Has been trained in Analytical Decision Analysis[2]		Has been trained and routinely practices Analytical Decision Analysis[2]	

[1] PMI (Project Management Institute) certification as a Project Management Professional is based on a comprehensive eight-hour examination.
[2] Analytical Decision Analysis was originated by Kepner Tregoe Associates (Princeton, NJ).

combination of attributes and qualifications. ". . . the ideal project manager would probably have doctorates in engineering, business, and psychology, and experience with ten different companies in a variety of project positions, [yet] be about twenty-five years old."[19] In addition to the skills identified, the project manager should exhibit the following capabilities:

- Leadership and team building.
- Entrepreneurial and business acumen.

- Balance between technical and business capabilities (generalist).
- Planning, organizing, and administration abilities.

CHARTERING THE PROJECT AND CONFIRMING THE PROJECT MANAGER'S AUTHORITY

The first step in gaining recognition for a new project and team is to formally charter the project manager and project office. High-level authorizing of the project's charter mitigates the historical handicap mentioned earlier: project management responsibility without commensurate authority. Harold Kerzner[20] offers this sage advice: "Generally speaking, a project manager should have more authority than his responsibility calls for, the exact amount of authority usually depending upon the amount of risk that the project manager must take. The greater the risk, the greater the amount of authority."

The project manager's authority should be documented when the project is chartered. The project's charter represented by the sample letter in Figure 7.15, performs several key functions:

- Identifies the project and its importance to the organization.
- Appoints the project manager and other key personnel.
- Establishes top level responsibilities and authority.
- Positions the support organizations and their authority.
- Places subcontractors in a service relationship.
- Acknowledges the project team.
- Establishes the funding control.
- Confirms that the cognizant executive started the project and chose the manager.

Figure 7.15 sets the tone for teamwork by accepting personal accountability for the proposal made by the team. This may seem like an obvious gesture, but even though accountability, unlike authority, can never be delegated, not all senior managers publicly acknowledge their accountability for the team's efforts. Publicizing such memoranda is useful.

The project manager's authority needs to be confirmed and maintained on a daily basis. Authority is a way of thinking that

Document the charter and get your management to sign it.

The organization's culture should view the project manager as the customer.

MEMORANDUM

Date:

To: All Functional Managers; President's Office; List

From: Vice President, Special Projects

Re: Establishment of the Advanced Systems
                Development Project

I'm pleased to announce that, after tough competition, we have been selected by the customer as the prime contractor for the Advanced System Development. We have pursued this prestigious opportunity aggressively and we are now committed to providing this state-of-the-art system.

To carry out this critical project, I am establishing the ASD Project Office with Fred Jones as Project Manger, reporting directly to me. I have delegated to Mr. Jones the authority to manage all activities necessary to fulfill our contractual obligations by working directly with our key subcontractors. Mr. Jones will be held fully responsible and accountable for the technical, schedule, and financial success of this project.

Others with key responsibilities for the ASD project are: Joan Wait as System Engineering Manager, Jim Wu as Business Manager, and Mary Fay as Contract Administrator.

The Program Implementation Review will be held 30 days from today with the primary objective of executive approval of the total Project Plan. At that time, I expect to approve the necessary funding, under Mr. Jones's control, for the next period of the project.

Congratulations to all of you who contributed to this important win! I am asking for your full support for Mr. Jones and his team in this most important business opportunity.

Our customer is counting on us to perform and, in turn, I am counting on you to deliver as we have promised in our proposal.

/signed/
Vice President,
Special Projects

FIGURE 7.15   The project team charter.

starts by delegation at the top, to be accepted and seized by the project manager. Continuing authority is based on acknowledgment by the organization's culture and should be reinforced by executive management in daily decisions and demonstrated by the project manager's consistent actions. As Kerzner[21] observes,

> Authority can be delegated from one's superiors. [Personal] power, on the other hand, is granted to an individual by his subordinates and is a measure of their respect for him. A manager's authority is a combination of his power and influence such that subordinates, peers, and associates willingly accept his judgment.

> In the traditional structure, the power spectrum is realized through the hierarchy, whereas in the project structure, power comes from credibility, expertise, or being a sound decision-maker.

While the proper chartering is necessary for establishing the project manager's authority, it is far from sufficient.

STAFFING THE TEAM

The stages of staffing correspond to the project phases and funding milestones, beginning with selection of the core team. We frequently refer to just the project manager when discussing management responsibilities, authority, and accountabilities, but there are three distinct roles which comprise the project office (Figure 7.16).

For small projects, two or three roles of the triad may be performed by the project manager.

The *system engineer/manager*—second only to the project manager in responsibility and accountability—is responsible for the technical integrity of the project while meeting the cost and performance objectives of project requirements. The system engineer is a key participant in the planning process and provides technical management of the system engineering process directed at achieving the optimum technical solution. To ensure the appropriate balance between technical and business factors, it is highly desirable to have a system engineering manager specifically responsible for the technical integrity of the project:

- Requirements management, analysis, and audit.
- Orchestrating technical players in timing and intensity.
- Baseline, risk, performance, and verification management.
- Interface control.

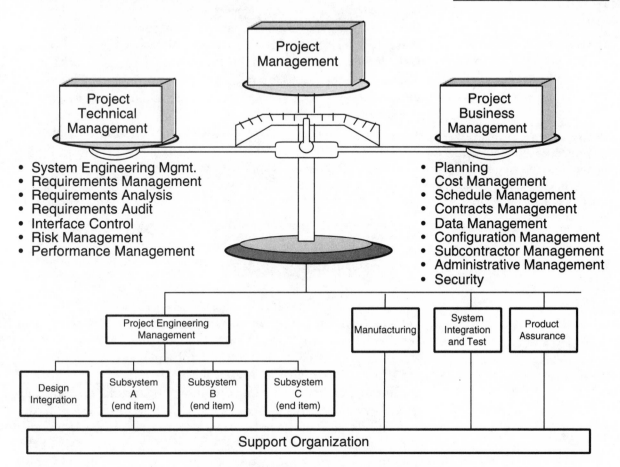

- System Engineering Mgmt.
- Requirements Management
- Requirements Analysis
- Requirements Audit
- Interface Control
- Risk Management
- Performance Management

- Planning
- Cost Management
- Schedule Management
- Contracts Management
- Data Management
- Configuration Management
- Subcontractor Management
- Administrative Management
- Security

FIGURE 7.16   The project office triad.

- Design audits.
- Alerting the project manager to technical risk and required risk management.

The *business manager* is responsible for all business aspects of the project including planning, scheduling, contractual matters, as well as legal, moral, and ethics issues. The business manager also assists the project manager in implementing planning, control, visibility, statusing, and corrective action systems.

Before selections occur, the required functions and related skills should be determined. The nature of the project will dictate the core team, for which the project manager should prepare formal job descriptions. Most job descriptions can be based on the task descriptions provided by the Work Breakdown Structure. These job descriptions are not only important in the selection process, but they are also a vital tool for successful negotiations with the support managers.

Staff selection for the independent project environment is influenced more by personal attitudes than functional positions that normally require less teamwork. There are three selection categories that need to be consciously balanced:

> People who are attracted by project assignments are generally motivated by intangible factors such as the work itself, rather than position or title.

- Functional skills required by the project.
- Skill inventory of the candidate.
- Personal attributes of the candidate.

Those who thrive in the project environment will typically be adaptable and interdependent as well as independent and results-driven. To paraphrase Stephen Covey,[22] independent thinking alone is not suited to the interdependent project reality. "Independent people who do not have the maturity to think and act interdependently may be good individual producers, but they won't be good leaders or team players."

While all team members are selected on the basis of both skills and personal attributes, it is particularly important that the core team have previous project experience, preferably at the task and project management level.

As each member is added to the team, it is a wise, proactive practice for new members to define their roles and to have these roles acknowledged by the rest of the team, beginning with the project manager. Doing this early affords the opportunity to make adjustments to create synergy and minimize discord. Until the detailed planning is done, roles and responsibilities may have to be defined in general terms with later refinement consistent with the planning results.

Outsourcing is an increasingly popular alternative to staffing. Subcontractors, vendors, and consultants can be a very cost effective way to obtain a critical skill or fulfill a specific project requirement outside the organization's functional repertoire. However, you should be just as diligent in selecting an outside source as you are in selecting a staff member, including reference checks, facility tours, and key person contract clauses.

THE IMPORTANCE OF CONCURRENT ENGINEERING

The project team needs to include and consider, *from the outset,* all elements of the product life cycle. This extended breadth of the team to involve all stakeholders in the development process is known as Concurrent Engineering (Figure 7.17). For example, airline pilots should participate in the concept definition of a new plane to properly influence the operational aspects of the system. Likewise, the baggage handlers should influence that part of the system design pertinent to their operations. Similarly, recent generations of computer architecture have benefited greatly from having software engineers involved in the hardware design. Concurrent Engineering also promotes simultaneous product and process development.

> Concurrent Engineering is the concept that all stakeholders need to be considered throughout the project cycle in order to produce the best product.

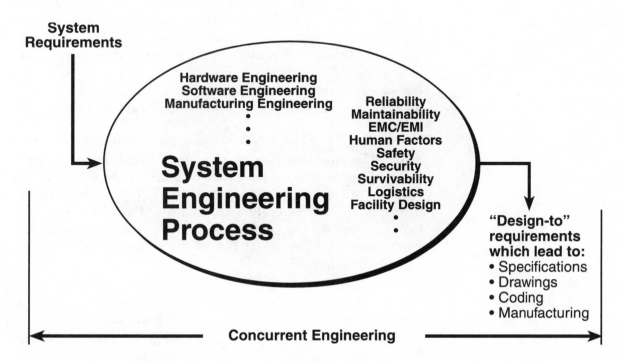

FIGURE 7.17   Concurrent engineering is a system engineering technique.

System engineering must ensure the timely involvement of all disciplines.

System engineering is responsible for involving the key personnel (to address human factors, safety, producibility, inspectibility, reliability, maintainability, logistics, etc.) at each step, starting with early risk analyses and feasibility studies in the Concept Definition Phase. This does not require a dedicated team of specialists. However, it does require a proactive system engineer who can ensure that appropriate expert advice and detailed assistance is applied to manage project risk.

MANAGING THE MAJOR INTERFACES AND INTERRELATIONSHIPS

The authors of *Dynamic Project Management*[23] have likened matrix interactions to those of a marketplace. "Negotiations concerning assignments, priorities, equipment, facilities, and people are constant. Matrix team members often complain of the continuous meetings, but it is through such meetings that the characteristic decentralized decision making occurs."

The complex relationships and confusing lines of authority in the project/functional lattice demands thoughtful planning. As illustrated in Figure 7.18, the project manager identifies what is to be done, primarily by means of work authorizing agreements or MBOs derived from the requirements. The functional organizations are responsible for defining and negotiating with the project manager how the tasks are to be performed and then implementing them.

Both project and support management responsibilities are assigned by executive management. The project manager ensures that project objectives are achieved on schedule and at the lowest cost compatible with user/contractual requirements. The support managers ensure the performance of specific project requirements as defined and authorized by the project manager. In addition as the advocate for technical excellence, each support manager is responsible to:

- Perform for executive management in support of all projects.
- Perform as agreed with each project manager.
- Maintain personnel expertise at the leading edge of technology.
- Recommend creative ways to meet project objectives.

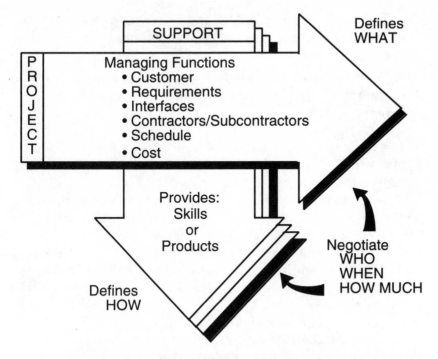

FIGURE 7.18   Matrix functions chart.

- Provide that function's cost, schedule, and technical risk assessment.
- Assign skilled personnel to support projects.
- Actively participate in problem solving and conflict resolution.

One of the most significant techniques for minimizing confusion and avoiding excessive interaction is to clarify roles and responsibilities where conflict in authority and function are likely to take place. The critical areas of potential conflict that should be resolved are:

- Project direction, objectives, priorities, planning, reviews, status, and controls.
- Assuring project effectiveness and customer commitments.
- Proposal preparation, contract negotiations, and contract management status.

- Technical, schedule, budget, and make versus buy decisions.
- Assignment of key personnel and establishment of employee objectives.
- Communications, correspondence, and data requirements.
- Point of contact for customer, upper management, and support interfaces.

A technique for managing any form of matrix organization is the Project Work Authorizing Agreement or an equivalent method for authorizing work. The PWAA is a contract between the project office and the supporting organizations. As illustrated in the next section on Planning, it contains task definition, budget, schedule, performer's commitment, and project office authorization. Companies or organizations which have a formal, quantified, and measurable Management By Objectives (MBO) program can make use of that system to supplement, or in the case of simple projects, substitute for the more formal PWAA. These methods are addressed in the sections on planning and statusing.

These are common expectations of executive management, the customer, and the team members:

- *Timely, accurate information*—for teams to work well, information and ideas have to flow smoothly.
- *No surprises*—for cooperation to grow, communication must be complete and candid. There is no place on a project team for a problem withholder.
- *Credit given where credit deserved*—the rewards must match the risks and recognition given for both individual and team efforts.

Matrix operations depend on their project manager being viewed as a buyer of services provided by the support managers (Figure 7.19).

PROJECT TEAM EXERCISE

The objective of this exercise is to provide experience is thinking through the actions required of a project manager to staff a project.

> Teams rarely go wrong by themselves—more often they suffer from lack of direction and false assumptions.

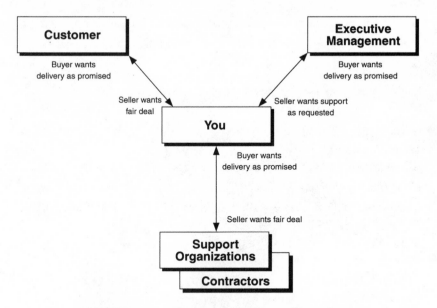

FIGURE 7.19   The buyer/seller viewpoints.

You've been given the opportunity you've been waiting for. You've just been named the project manager for that project on which your company is bidding. Successful performance will position your company for the growth opportunity it's been seeking. Unfortunately, the last project your company won of a similar nature was poorly staffed and the resulting product required extensive rework before being accepted by the client. The expense and delay hurt reputations in the marketplace and management is very concerned about repeating the problem.

You've been asked to prepare a staffing plan for review with your boss. The project is to last 18 months and will require the equivalent of 10 full-time people for that period although actual head count will vary, beginning with just a few key designers, expanding to a large staff of development people, testers, and so on and then tailing off to a few key staff needed for sustaining engineering during final testing and delivery to the client. All staff will report to you for the duration of the project and all will be collocated in a single facility. What type of information will you collect in order to be able to present a plan to your boss? Prepare a list of the issues and considerations that should go into structuring the plan.

PROJECT TEAM EXERCISE ANSWER

What authority do you think you will need to be able to effectively manage?

What types of managers and other task leaders will you need to help manage this effort?

What authority will those managers working for you need in order to effectively manage their portions of the work?

What types and levels of technical and managerial skills are going to be necessary to deliver the product?

What staff resources are available from within the organization?

What limitations exist for hiring from the outside?

How will you know if the technical and managerial skill levels of the staff you choose (or are given) match the required skill levels?

What resources do you have for training those not at acceptable skills levels?

4. PROJECT PLANNING

> **"Would you tell me please, which way I ought to go from here?"**
>
> **"That depends a good deal on where you want to get to,"
> said the cat.**
>
> **"I don't much care where—," said Alice.**
>
> **"Then it doesn't matter which way you go," said the cat.**
>
> **Lewis Carroll's,
> *Alice's Adventures in Wonderland***

Planning is performed in each project cycle phase to prepare for the subsequent phases.

PLAN THE WORK AND WORK THE PLAN

We define planning as the process which determines beforehand the activities necessary to complete the project. Planning evolves as the project progresses sequentially through the phases of the project cycle. A plan contains at least:

- *What* is to be done.
- *When* it should be done.
- *Who* is responsible for doing it.

At the highest, total-project level, planning is performed in each project cycle phase to prepare for the subsequent phases. The lowest level of iteration occurs within each step—such as iterating through network development and task schedules to determine and shorten the critical path. While the emphasis, level of detail, and risk factors change from one phase to the next, the process defined here is relevant to each project phase. Some aspects will require only minor updates as a new phase is entered.

The project plan (Figure 7.20) is usually composed of a set of specialty plans. Some plans, such as the Acquisition Plan and the Source Selection Plan may not be required for all projects. The Implementation Plan is common to all projects and will be used to illustrate the overall planning process.

> Project planning is an iterative process on several levels, as well as an ongoing one.

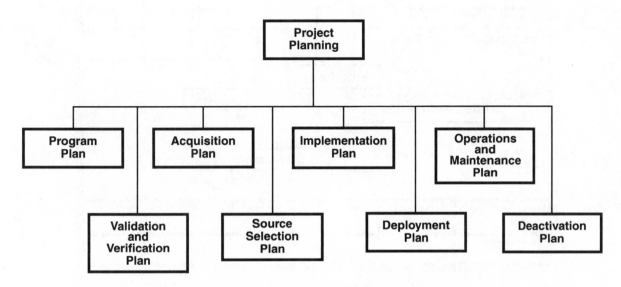

FIGURE 7.20   The total project plan evolves from several plans.

IMPLEMENTATION PLANNING IS TURNING THE REQUIREMENTS INTO ORDERLY WORK

We define implementation planning as the process of converting all project requirements into a logically sequenced set of negotiated work authorizing agreements, as illustrated by Figure 7.21, and subcontracts.

Project Work Authorizing Agreements are internal contracts containing:

- Task description.
- Schedule for deliverables.
- Time-phased budgets.
- Agreement by the implementer.
- Agreement by the project manager.

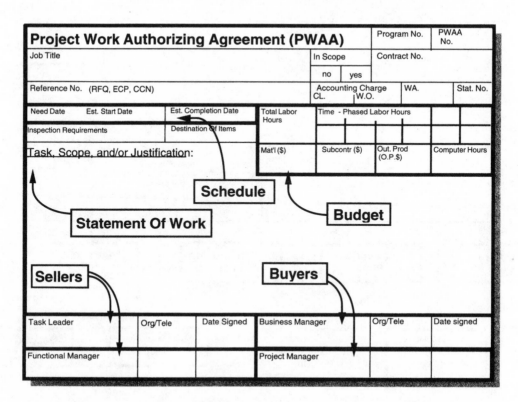

FIGURE 7.21   The project work authorizing agreement (PWAA).

Subcontracts are external contracts containing all of the above plus:

- Contract terms and conditions.
- Legal authority to perform.
- Conditions for default.

THE PLANNING PROCESS IS SIMULATING THE PROJECT

An overview of the plan development objectives and process is depicted in Figure 7.22. It highlights the role of the project manager in integrating the customer objectives with those of the management, and it emphasizes a major reason projects fail: lack of team interaction. Productive interaction helps motivate and commit the team. But it has to be a true interactive process. The most difficult project objectives offer the best team brainstorming opportunities. When the team members resolve strategies to achieve the objectives and impact the plan, their investment skyrockets—they're committed to attaining success.

A significant contributor to planning failures is lack of a systematic and structured process. As emphasized in Chapter 2, to

> Implementation planning is driven by the objectives and the need to communicate and to obtain agreements and commitments.

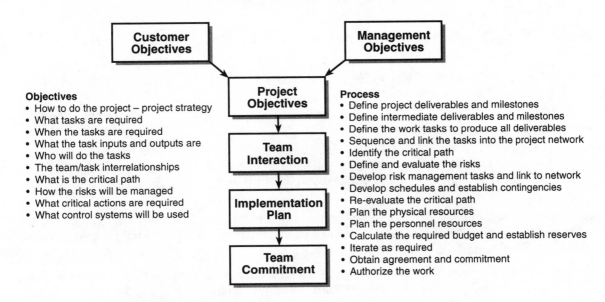

Objectives
- How to do the project – project strategy
- What tasks are required
- When the tasks are required
- What the task inputs and outputs are
- Who will do the tasks
- The team/task interrelationships
- What is the critical path
- How the risks will be managed
- What critical actions are required
- What control systems will be used

Customer Objectives → **Project Objectives** ← **Management Objectives**

Project Objectives → Team Interaction → Implementation Plan → Team Commitment

Process
- Define project deliverables and milestones
- Define intermediate deliverables and milestones
- Define the work tasks to produce all deliverables
- Sequence and link the tasks into the project network
- Identify the critical path
- Define and evaluate the risks
- Develop risk management tasks and link to network
- Develop schedules and establish contingencies
- Re-evaluate the critical path
- Plan the physical resources
- Plan the personnel resources
- Calculate the required budget and establish reserves
- Iterate as required
- Obtain agreement and commitment
- Authorize the work

FIGURE 7.22 Planning objectives, process, and drivers.

test for a sensible plan, it is important to be able to envision it—to be able to decompose it into deliverables and then simulate the work flow in a visual walk-through. Our planning process steps converge on a Cards-on-the-Wall (COW) networking technique that provides this visualization. The main process elements are listed in Table 7.2.

TABLE 7.2 The Planning Process: Major Elements and Techniques

Key Element	Process	Primary Technique
Products	*Decomposing* the deliverables into their hierarchical structure—all the way from the project requirements down to the lowest level internal and external deliverables.	Project Product List and Fact Sheets
Development Strategy	*Determining* the development strategy such as incremental or evolutionary with either single or multiple deliveries.	Application of the "Vee Model"
Risk Strategy	*Identifying* opportunities and associated risks and the customer-compatible opportunity and risk strategy with preventive, causative, and contingent plans.	Lessons Learned
Tasks	*Defining* the tasks needed to complete each deliverable.	Work Breakdown Structure
Network	*Logically arranging* the required tasks to portray the best delivery approach.	Cards-on-the-Wall network, followed by a computerized network and critical path determination.
Schedules	*Scheduling* each task then refining and shortening the project's overall critical path through iterative steps.	Scheduling software
Resources	*Establishing* resources (personnel, equipment, finances) needed to accomplish each task on schedule.	Spread sheets and cost estimating models
Commitments	*Committing* the necessary resources and funds for each task as determined from the schedule and task definition.	Project Work Authorizing Agreements

These planning techniques, as flowcharted in Figure 7.23, offer a systematic way to transform the project activities into a baseline plan suitable for both proactive and reactive management. In the remainder of the planning section, we will address each flowchart element in detail.

The goal of planning parrots the project goal: ensuring that all commitments to the customer are met. To get there, we start the planning with the project requirements which include the Statement of Work (SOW), the milestone schedule (Master Schedule), cost targets, and definition of all deliverables. The Master Schedule identifies the overall start and stop dates and all major milestones.

> The project manager reviews the project requirements to eliminate any fuzziness, ambiguity, or inconsistency with the project objectives.

DETERMINING THE PROJECT DELIVERABLES

One of the first planning steps is to determine all of the project deliverables and to provide a narrative description of each. The Project Products List (PPL) is derived from system decomposition and definition and is a list of all contract deliverables and internal deliverables, in all forms produced, with the quantities required. Examples of the different forms of products that could be produced are:

> The Project Products List and Fact Sheets are techniques that facilitate this step.

- Drafts.
- Simulations.
- Models (user requirements understanding, technical feasibility, physical fit, field test, preproduction. etc.).
- Qualification units.
- Deliverables.
- Spares.

An example of a hardware PPL and a software PPL are shown in Figure 7.24. Other PPLs would include support equipment, documentation, and services.

A Project Product List Fact Sheet should accompany each PPL (Figure 7.25). Its purpose is to provide a description and use for each item. It is usually written by the most knowledgeable expert available, whether they are to work on the project or not. The

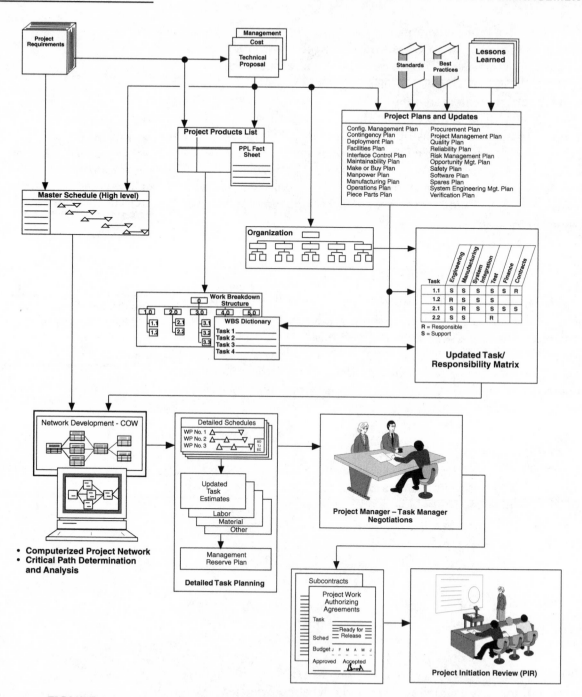

FIGURE 7.23   The planning process: From problem solving to commitment.

Project Products List

Title: **Propulsion System Dual Tank Configuration (WBS 11.01.02)**
Project Office Approval
Organ No.   Name:

Legend — Status: N = New, M = Modified, E = Existing

"Category": TF – Technical Feasibility Model; PF – Physical Fit Model; TS – Thermal Simulation Model; SI – System Integration Model; FT – Field Test Model; Q – Qualification Unit; DV – Development Vehicle; F – Flight; S – Spares

Date   Revision   Page 1   Of 2

Item no	Nomenclature and WBS Number	Drawing Number (or similar to)	Make or buy	Des	Hdwe	TF	PF	TS	SI	FT	Q	DV	F	S	Remarks
1	Propulsion Module (10.01.02 .19)		M	N	N							1	2		Assemble, Install & Test
2	Propellant Tank (10.01.02.07)	8160485 - X (2P64002)	B	M	N				2	1		2	4	1	Spherical Version Of 2P64002 (cylindrical)
3	Reaction Engine Module (10.01.02.06)	8160481 -X (2P64000 - 13)	B	M	N			14	16	1	2	2	32	2	RRC Intelsat V 0.5 LBF Thruster Mounted In Pairs On An REM
4	Latching Solenoid Valve (11.01.02.11)	2P60481 - 3 or equivalent	B	E	N				4	1		4	8	1	
5	Service Valve (11.01.02.11)	2P60483 - X	B	E	N				3			3	6	1	
6	PR XDucer (11.01.02.15)	8111210 - X	B	M	N	1			4	1	1	4	8	1	Modify To Increase Shielding For New Radiation Environment
7	Filter (11.01.02.10)	8103465 - 15	B	E	N				4			4	8	1	

Also software
Also support equipment
Also documentation
Also services

PROJECT PRODUCTS LIST — Software

LEGEND
STATUS: N - New, M - Modified, E - Existing
PRODUCT LEVEL: CSCI – Computer Software Configuration Item; CSC – Computer Software Component

WBS NO. 1.3.7.1
SUBSYSTEM Data Compression
WORK PKG NO. 1.3.7.1.0
Date June 12   Revision 1.2   Page 1

NOMENCLATURE	MNEMONIC	CI	CSC	User Rqmt's Model	Technical Feasibility Mdl	-01	-02	MAKE (M) OR BUY (B)	SOFTW. DESIGN	PROGR. CODING	EST. LINES OF CODE	SECURITY CLASSIF.	REMARKS
Data Base Core	RDMS	X		X	X	X		M	M	N	125K	Uncl	Convert to Ada
Report Writer	WRIT		X	X		X		M	N	N	87K	Uncl	
Graphics	GRAF		X			X		B	N	N	42K	Uncl	
Dictionary	DICT		X				X	M	N	N	65K	Uncl	

FIGURE 7.24 Project product list (PPL) examples.

Item:	Pressure transducer
Part No:	8111210 - 503
Source:	Electromech, Inc.
WBS No:	11.01.02.15
Description:	This transducer is identical electrically to existing part no. 8111210-501. The envelope is to be modified to increase heat survivability. The shield concept must be proven by tests of the development model. The shielding design must be qualified by selected qualification tests per the test plan.

FIGURE 7.25   PPL fact sheet example.

fact sheets are used by project participants to plan and estimate each deliverable.

DEFINING THE WORK BREAKDOWN STRUCTURE AND THE TASKS

As the keystone of the plan, the WBS depicts the project decomposition and associated tasks.

The Work Breakdown Structure (WBS) is used to depict the system by assemblies, subassemblies, and components rather than by discipline or functional organization (such as engineering, manufacturing, testing, etc.). The WBS is represented graphically or in an indented list (Figure 7.26), and illustrates the way the project will be integrated, assigned, and statused. The WBS is mandatory for project planning because it is the basis for work assignments, budgeting, scheduling, risk assessment, cost collection, and performance statusing.

Figure 7.27 illustrates how the Work Breakdown Structure relates the work to produce the individual components (from the Product Breakdown Structure) to the work to integrate those components into the system.

The WBS has been successfully employed by government agencies such as the DoD and NASA, and is fast becoming an important planning technique for commercial projects as well.

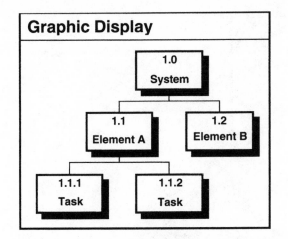

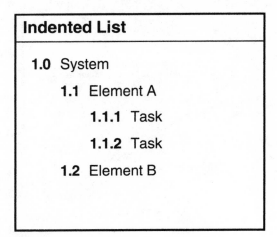

FIGURE 7.26 The work breakdown structure (WBS).

For government projects, the Request for Proposal usually provides a top level WBS to which the project WBS must interface. MIL-STD-881A (government WBS standard) embodies WBS requirements as well as examples. It provides a system management structure for:

- System decomposition.
- Specifications and drawings.
- Configuration management.
- Budgeting.
- Scheduling.
- Responsibility.

The following guidelines (Figure 7.28) refer to the WBS examples of hardware and software subprojects, and reflect our experience in refining this planning technique:

- Structure the WBS by product and elements of the product.
- Include all authorized tasks.
- Cost collection is usually one level below budget performance reporting to facilitate problem cause identification.
- Identifiers for like tasks should be similar.
- All tasks for an element should be collected with the element identifier.
- WBS depth (number of levels) depends on the risk to be managed and reported.

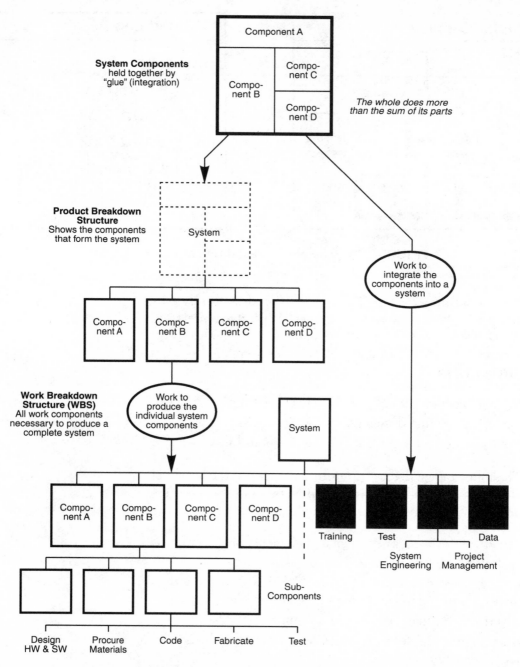

FIGURE 7.27　The work breakdown structure related to system and products. (From the NASA Systems Engineering Handbook, page 31.)[24]

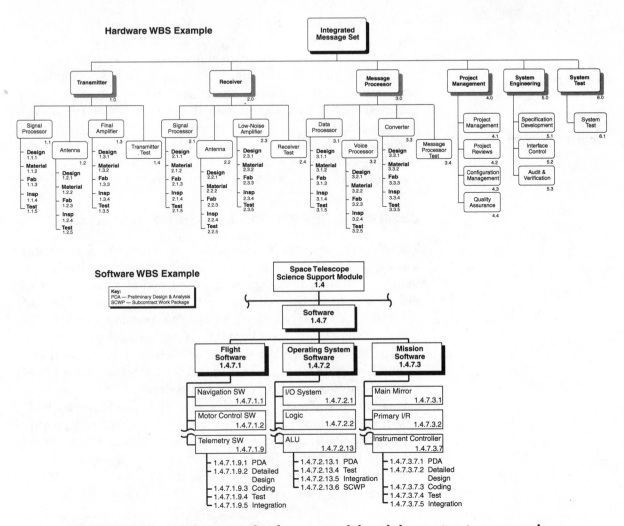

FIGURE 7.28 Hardware and software work breakdown structure example.

- Level-of-effort tasks are usually at the second level, which may include project management, system engineering, system integration, and system-level testing.
- The task level should employ verbs such as *design, fabricate, code, assemble,* and *test.*

The WBS is supported by the *WBS Dictionary,* which links the WBS elements to the final technique in the task definition—

work packages. As Figure 7.29 shows, the *WBS Dictionary* is a narrative description of each work task identified in the WBS. This document drives task estimating and supports task assignment.

The work package contains a complete task description, including what, when, how, by whom, and the budget and schedule requirements. It may incorporate the *WBS Dictionary* entry or reference it. The work package represents another important link in the planning—the connection between the WBS and the functional organization or contractor assigned to the task, which is accomplished by the Work Authorization Agreement.

DEVELOPING THE PROJECT NETWORK AND SCHEDULES

There are three types of schedules to resolve: performance, personnel, and budget. This section deals primarily with performance schedules, bounded by the start and stop dates for each task. They form the basis for the other schedules. Personnel schedules identify the timing for specific personnel involvement and facilitate resource planning. Cost schedules define the planned allocation and spending for each task as a function of time. Their primary purpose is to facilitate funding management.

Scheduling usually involves more iterations than any other stage in the planning process. This is partially due to the tradeoffs which must be made among the constraints of time, cost, technical requirements, available personnel, and risk. Another complicating factor is that all task interdependencies may not be obvious when scheduling is performed only at the task level.

The WBS tasks are the foundation for the project network and schedule as shown in Figure 7.30.

> **Component Test**
>
> This task consists of preparing test procedures, test facility, test personnel, and test conduct including documentation and resolution of all test discrepancies. The output from the task is a satisfactorily completed test, resolution of all test anomalies, and the final test report.

FIGURE 7.29 Work breakdown structure dictionary excerpt.

A work package is prepared for each element at its lowest level in the WBS.

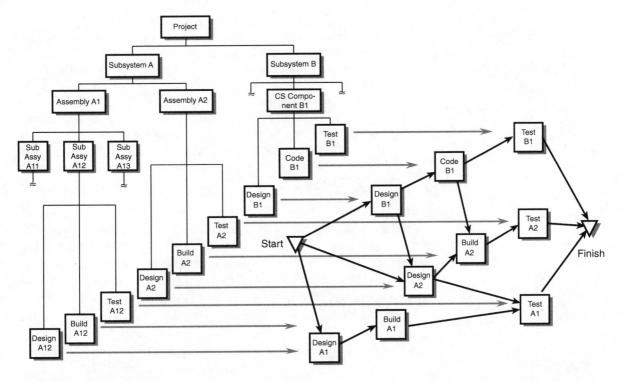

FIGURE 7.30 The work breakdown structure tasks are the foundation for the project network and schedule.

The scheduling process iterates through these steps:

- Combine the tasks to form a project network.
- Define and evaluate the risks.
- Develop risk mitigation actions and add to the network.
- Factor in task duration time.
- Determine the critical path.
- Shorten the critical path.
- Commit to performing the task schedules.

Historically, there have been two principal methods for constructing network diagrams, the Program Evaluation and Review Technique (PERT) and the Critical Path Method (CPM). In their very basic but easy-to-use book,[25] the Bakers characterize these methods as follows:

PERT and CPM emerged in different ways in the late 1950s. PERT was developed by Lockheed and Booz, Allen, and Hamilton for the U.S. Navy Special Projects Office. The CPM was developed at about the same time by Morgan Walker and James Kelly for E.I. Du Pont.... (The primary difference is in the way the two techniques treat time estimates for tasks.) ... the networks are largely the same in terms of sequencing possibilities. In CPM, one time estimate is used for creating the schedule; PERT uses a more complex system based on three time estimates that are used to determine the most probable time for completion.

The distinction, then, useful from a risk assessment perspective, is that the PERT network allows a three-point estimate for the duration of each task (nominal, earliest completion, and latest completion). With the three-point estimates one can perform Monte Carlo simulations for the entire network and determine the nominally expected completion date (the output of the Critical Path Method), the probability of achieving that date, and the date for 95% or 99% probability of completion. The widespread availability of high speed, high capacity desktop computers makes this process readily available and potentially useful to the project team.

Technically, the Cards-on-the-Wall result is similar to PERT/CPM, but the process is much more visual and interactive, leading to more reliable schedules.

PERT or CPM afford very limited opportunity for team interaction during network construction. Computer-based network construction, regardless of the specific software, is usually built from work packages and input by a single person working alone at the keyboard and viewing the resulting network on the computer screen. The problem with using a computer at this early stage is that the team is not building the network. We prefer a more interactive network diagramming technique that begins with a method we have dubbed Cards-on-the-Wall. In this method, the team literally hangs each work package on the wall, by project phase, and interconnects them to reflect the interdependencies (Figure 7.31). We prefer the wall as a work space because it allows the team to cluster around the evolving network to discuss its logic. We use "wetware" (the brains of the team) for creating the network, and software for capturing that network and computing the critical path. We've devised a form for creating the network, as shown on a section of the network wall in Figure 7.31.

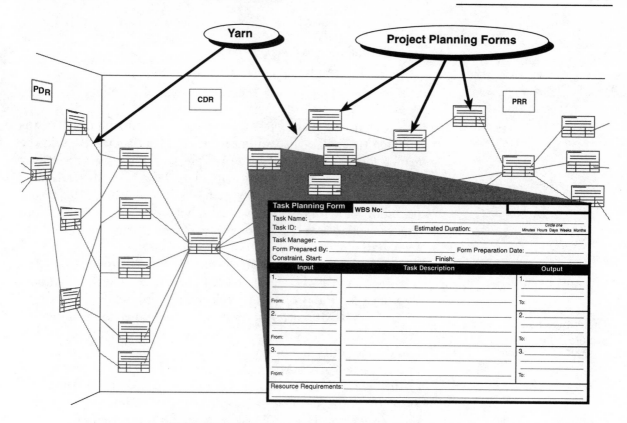

FIGURE 7.31   The cards-on-the-wall method.

Our Cards-on-the Wall process uses:

- A 5″ × 8″ project planning form for each task,
- Yarn or string for interconnecting the cards, and
- Ample walls to hang and arrange the cards.

The Cards-on-the-Wall method consists of interconnecting the tasks (cards) to reflect the optimum order of events and the interdependencies. Among the benefits of this interactive, visual procedure are:

- Participative decision making.
- Fewer "I forgots."

- Shared risks.
- Shared concessions.
- Quality results.
- *And most important:* team ownership of the plan.

In a recent planning session, someone commented that it was a shame that the walls weren't magnetic. "But they are," said the leader, looking at the cluster of people over at the wall discussing how to shorten a link in a critical path, "they attract human flesh." We've never seen people crowd around a computer terminal talking about how to move tasks, but we've seen lots of groups cluster around a wall draped with cards and yarn, moving "logic" around to make a tight schedule work.

Schedules at the task level usually employ a linear format or bar chart such as the Gantt chart. Figure 7.32 shows the relationship between the project network and the task schedules.

The critical path paces the project schedule.

The next step after network construction is determining the critical path—the task sequence that paces the project. When asked to identify his project's critical path, one rather defensive project manager we encountered asserted, "This project has no critical path, if it does, we will eliminate it." We define the Critical Path as the sequence of project activities for which there is minimum or zero slack. The critical path for vacation preparation is shown in bold in Figure 7.33. For convenience, we talk of "the" critical path. In fact, there may be several critical paths, and there are frequently many other "near-critical" paths. The following discussion applies to all of these situations.

After adding contingency spans and risk management tasks, the critical path needs to be re-evaluated. Analyzing resource requirements for concurrent activities and using the critical path as the time scale, will usually reveal sub-optimal lumping of personnel resources. At the same time, these tasks are considered for resource leveling or smoothing, the following actions to reduce the critical path should be considered:

- Eliminate or shorten tasks on the critical path.
- Re-plan serial paths to be parallel.
- Overlap sequential tasks.
- Increase the number of work days or work hours.

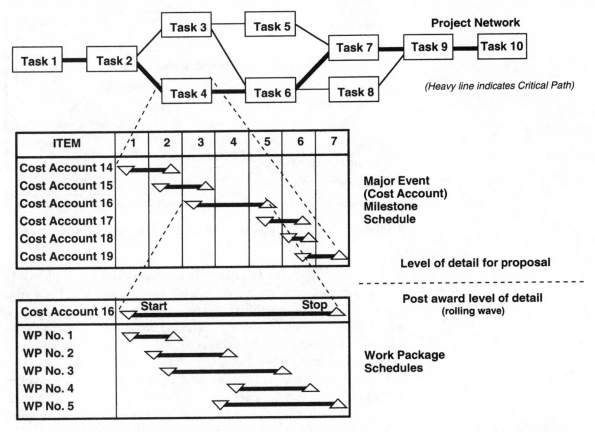

FIGURE 7.32   The relationship between the project network and the task schedules.

- Shorten tasks; the best candidates are those:
  —That are long or easy to speed up.
  —For which you have available resources.
  —That cost the least to speed up.
  —That your own organization controls.

Actions taken to shorten the critical path usually have other impacts. Using the vacation preparation example (Figure 7.33), the critical path could be shortened by having the hitch installed while the car is being fixed, or you could rent a car to pick up supplies while the car is being repaired. In the first case, if the car is having the fuel injection system repaired, the mechanic may not

> Each action to shorten the critical path should be justified.

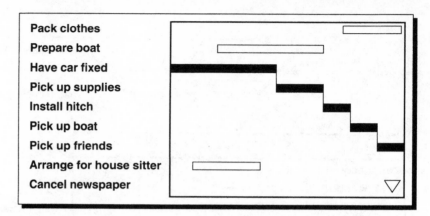

Pack clothes	
Prepare boat	
Have car fixed	
Pick up supplies	
Install hitch	
Pick up boat	
Pick up friends	
Arrange for house sitter	
Cancel newspaper	

FIGURE 7.33   Critical path example: Vacation preparation.

have the skill to install the hitch, hence a risk would be added. In the second case, renting a car adds cost. You could also have your friends pick up the supplies (add project resources) or, as one student proposed, you could go on vacation without your friends (change requirements). In each case you must ask yourself, "Is it worth it to shorten the schedule?"

Sometimes risk reductions and critical path reductions are synergistic. You can expect to move lower risk tasks off the critical path, which can contribute needed resources to the higher risk tasks, thereby reducing the critical path and/or the risk. The optimum balance is achieved when both sets of tasks end up on the new, shorter critical path.

Next, resource leveling and optimization can be performed. These steps can be performed with the help of computers, once the network is constructed. However, resource restrictions or problems are usually localized and good judgment and common sense will produce meaningful results. Reducing the critical path and optimizing resource allocation can significantly affect a task's cost as illustrated graphically. Shortening a task schedule below the optimum point can lead to an increase in its cost (Figure 7.34). On the other hand, optimization at the network level may consist of offsetting a relatively small increase in task cost with a significant savings at the project level. For example, the incremental cost associated with compressing one task may result in equivalent burn rate savings for the total project.

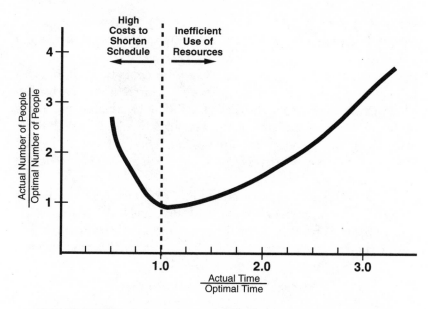

FIGURE 7.34 Schedule compression/expansion effects.

PLANNING THE RESOURCES

While this section focuses on the two limiting resources in most projects, personnel and funds, a unique physical resource can also impact the schedule. Take nothing for granted. Just when you need a special piece of test equipment that hasn't been used for six months, you can be sure Murphy will need it too. And Murphy's team reserved the equipment when they planned their project. Another property issue to plan for in government projects is the use of government furnished equipment, services, and material (generally called GFE). First, contractual commitments must be made for the delivery dates for the needed GFE. Second, permission must be granted by the government agency that owns the equipment (or services or material) that authorizes use of the material on your project. In one instance one of the authors won a contract that involved manufacturing of components on special equipment owned by the U.S. Army, although prior permission for the use of the equipment had not been obtained. When asked for permission to use the machinery, the Army project office said, "Of course. What is the Army project number?" Answer: "It is a U.S. Air Force contract." Response: "Air Force?

What air force? We don't have an air force. Permission denied." Incomplete planning and preparation almost always leads to a bad outcome.

To illustrate the time-phased requirements for task, personnel category, and total project levels, Gantt charts are useful. They are derived from the PERT/CPM network, but are more easily understood by the team. Having already adjusted some tasks to smooth resource requirements or reduce risks and/or the critical path, the next step is to return to the task level and define the personnel schedules in more detail.

The WBS is the basis for identifying task responsibilities (Figure 7.35). As a checklist, the Task Responsibility Matrix (Figure 7.36) is useful in summarizing who and which organizations have been assigned primary and support responsibilities for each

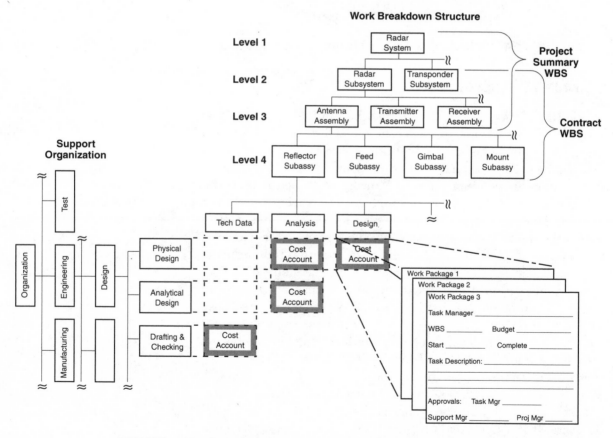

FIGURE 7.35 Relationship between WBS and organization.

Task	Engineering	Manufacturing	System Integration	Test	Finance	Contracts
1	S	S	S	S	S	R
2	R	S	S	S		
3	S	R	S	S	S	S
4	S	S		R		

R = Responsible
S = Support

FIGURE 7.36   Individual task responsibility matrix.

task, and who will participate in the Cards-on-the-Wall process. Figure 7.37 is an example of a planning form that extracts the monthly personnel needs from the task Gantt chart at the functional organization level and combines that with other resource requirements.

OBTAINING THE COMMITMENTS AND INITIATING THE WORK

The payoff for all of the detailed planning and scheduling is in securing full support and commitment on the part of the team, functional organizations, subcontractors, general management, and the customer or user. The key negotiations, made easier by detailed scheduling, are those with the functional managers. The resulting agreement should be documented in the form of a Project Work Authorizing Agreement (PWAA) shown earlier. The PWAA contains task definition, budget, schedule, performer's commitment, and project office authorization. Subcontracts add terms and conditions clauses. The approved PWAA results from having:

Authorization Agreements and Subcontracts authorize the project work and, collectively, represent and authorize the Implementation Plan.

- Open and direct negotiations.
- Tasks understood.
- Milestones agreed to.
- Budgets accepted.
- Contingencies identified.
- Caveats documented.

Our project cycle template includes a Project Initiation Review. The objectives are to secure executive management approval of the implementation plan and to obtain corporate commitment of resources. The items to review include: contractual statement of work, deliverables, and incentives; project strategy; project plan; opportunities, risks, and actions; functional organization commitments; and resources required.

KEEPING THE PLAN CURRENT

The harder it is to plan, the more you need to plan!

The project manager is responsible for:

- Assuring that all plans are consistent with current strategy, constraints, and project environment.
- Establishing the methods, tools, and techniques used in planning.
- Using the tools and techniques to update the plan.

Organization Task Estimate	MFG No.	Contract	CCN No.	Doing Org. Name	No.
	Date Of RFP	Program		Responsible Org. Name	No.
WBS No:	Subject/Title of Task				
Work Package No:	Time - Phased Labor Hours				

Yr	Jan	Feb	Mar	Apr	May	Jun	Jul	Aug	Sep	Oct	Nov	Dec

Material description	$	Computer HRS	Other
Task description		Skill Mix	
		Basis of Estimate	

Prepared By	Doing Org. Manager's Signature	Responsible Org. Manager's Signature	Control
	Date	Date	17633

FIGURE 7.37 Resource planning form.

The techniques and tools, especially software applications, that support these responsibilities are constantly improving. Before committing to a new software tool which may come up short as the project grows, you may do well to heed the following precautions:

- Beware of nonstandard data input and output formats.
- Some products are conceived and promoted as a full management tool, but only provide a scheduling algorithm.
- Test run the software.
- Use implementation tools. There are many computer-based tools available to mechanize the planning process and capture the project's data. These tools facilitate the planning process all the way from product decomposition through network development, critical path analysis, and schedule definition. They also provide for cost estimation, budget development, personnel planning and resource leveling. Most tools will facilitate status recording and associated rebaselining, if necessary.
- Talk to users who manage projects similar to yours.
- Set up operating procedures and standards.
- Insist that the standards be used.

PLANNING ELEMENT EXERCISE

The objective of this exercise is to provide experience in developing a project network and in identifying and calculating the critical path for a simple but relevant project.

Scenario: You are to develop a precedence network and the critical path for the turn-around of a commercial 140 passenger jet airliner from final approach to take-off clearance.

A WBS for the airplane turn-around follows:

WBS for the Aircraft Turn-Around Project
1.0 Passengers and crew
    1.1 Passengers
        1.1.1 Unload arriving passengers
        1.1.2 Load "Pre-board" passengers

          1.1.3 Load terminal-area passengers
          1.1.4 Load commuter plane passengers
          1.1.5 Obtain head count
     1.2 Flight crew
          1.2.1 Unload arriving crew (if required)
          1.2.2 Load departing crew

2.0 Baggage
     2.1 Unload arriving baggage
     2.2 Load baggage from terminal
     2.3 Load baggage from commuter plane
     2.4 Misroute baggage for nasty passengers

3.0 Cabin service
     3.1 Food
          3.1.1 Unload empty food carts
          3.1.2 Load new meals and beverages
     3.2 Cleaning
          3.2.1 Pick up trash
          3.2.2 Vacuum or sweep cabin
     3.3 Sanitation
          3.3.1 Clean lavatories
          3.3.2 Empty toilet sump tanks

4.0 Fuel
     4.1 Determine fuel load required
     4.2 Load fuel
     4.3 Verify fuel on-board

5.0 Operations Integration
     5.1 Landing control
          5.1.1 Obtain permission to land
          5.1.2 Land aircraft
     5.2 Take off control
          5.2.1 Obtain permission to take off
          5.2.2 Take off
     5.3 Taxi control
          5.3.1 Obtain permission to taxi after landing
          5.3.2 Taxi to gate
          5.3.3 Obtain permission to taxi prior to take off
          5.3.4 Taxi to take off holding point

5.4 Gate control

    5.4.1 Obtain permission to open door

        Ensures that the exit ramp is in place before opening the door.

    5.4.2 Open cabin door

    5.4.3 Obtain permission to close door

        Ensures that all ticketed passengers in gate area are on board, and that all maintenance and service personnel have completed their tasks and have left the plane. The pilot and ticket agent must both concur plane is ready.

    5.4.4 Close cabin door

5.5 De-icing application if required

        The de-icing operation is done after all passengers are on board and the cabin door is closed. De-icing can be done at the gate or on the taxiway near the terminal. It must be completed within 15 minutes of actual take off.

    5.5.1 Apply de-icing if required

    5.5.2 Verify de-icing application is within time limit

6.0 Project management

  6.1 Data management

    6.1.1 Gather turn-around time statistics

    6.1.2 Report performance

  6.2 Manage "Turn-Around Improvement Project"

The following functions should be provided for:

Air Traffic Control

Ground Control

Passenger and Crew Management

Food Management

All operational tasks in the WBS shall be timed (Example: clean airplane—12 minutes), and then linked into the serial/parallel relationships that will satisfy a turn-around time schedule of 40 minutes. Plan the events from aircraft touchdown to aircraft lift-off. You must budget 3 minutes from touchdown to arrival at gate and 3 minutes for departure from gate to lift off, and to allow 2 minutes additional for de-icing in winter.

Your result should be an understanding of the critical path and what tasks would have to be attacked to shorten the turn-around time.

5. OPPORTUNITIES AND RISKS

Problems are only opportunities in work clothes.

Henry J. Kaiser,
Maxim

When management tells you to *take risk,* they really mean *pursue opportunity.*

Opportunities are defined as chances for progress or advancement. In project management, opportunities are the chances of improving the value of the project results.

Risks are defined as chances of injury, damage, or loss. In project management, risks are the chances of not achieving the results as planned.

Opportunity and risk management are essential to, and performed concurrently with, the planning process, but require the application of separate and unique techniques justifying it as a unique management element.

Whenever we pursue opportunity we normally incur risk. The opportunity to experience the thrill of an exciting sport like hang gliding, or scuba diving, brings with it the attendant risks. Many instinctively make the trade that the thrill is worth the risks.

When we pursue the opportunity to arrive at a destination early by speeding down the highway, we accept the risk of being caught and receiving an expensive ticket and higher insurance rates. When speeding, our accelerator foot stabilizes at the exact speed where the probability and benefit of arriving early is exactly equal to the probability and consequences of getting caught. We instinctively make this trade and automatically balance the expected outcomes with our accelerator foot for this combination of opportunity and risk.

In project management, there are two categories of opportunities and risks. Since a project is the pursuit of an opportunity, the first category, the macro opportunity, is the project opportunity itself. The approach to achieving the project opportunity and the mitigation of associated risks are structured into the strategy and tactics of the project cycle, the selected control gates, the teaming arrangements, personnel skills, and so on.

The second category includes those opportunities and risks within the project itself that become apparent at lower levels of decomposition and as project cycle phases are planned and experienced. This group includes the approaches to satisfying the project details as new and possibly risky technology tempts the team. It also includes the temptation to shortcut proven practices in order to achieve better, faster, cheaper.

Opportunities and risks are endemic to the project environment. However well-planned a project may be, there will always be risk elements. Projects without risk are like ships in a harbor— they're safe. But that's not what ships are built for. Ships are built to pursue opportunities.

In the heat of project battle, it is easy for opportunities and risks to slip in (or by) inadvertently. It is the project manager's responsibility to maintain a high level of awareness among all project participants, especially during:

- Project definition.
- Detailed planning.
- Concept trade-offs.
- Development of system documentation.
- Manufacturing preparation.
- Supplier selection.
- Coding preparation.
- Test preparation.
- Shipping/Handling.
- Deployment.
- Change evaluation.

Regarding the career-limiting effect of under-estimating future risks, March and Shapira[26] have articulated this management dichotomy: "Society values risk taking but not gambling, and what is meant by gambling is risk taking that turns out badly . . . Thus, risky choices that turn out badly are seen, after the fact, to have

If you don't identify opportunities, they won't be in your field of view.

If you don't actively attack risks, the risks will actively attack you.

been mistakes. The warning signs that were ignored seem clearer than they were; the courses that were followed seem unambiguously misguided."

This section is about maximizing opportunities and dealing directly with the inevitability of risks—the foreseeable ones as well as the "unknown unknowns" that occur throughout the project.

Ours is a value driven approach to managing both opportunities and risks, meaning that the relative merits of exploiting each opportunity and mitigating each risk is carefully evaluated. You make that kind of evaluation in your personal life every time you decide what insurance to carry and what level of deductible. And while most car manufacturers and consumers don't question the relative value of carrying a spare tire, we seldom carry other spares, such as certain wear-prone engine parts, because of the space required and the expertise or special tools needed to replace them. The latter is given by one motor home manufacturer as the reason for pricing a spare tire as an option.

We define opportunity and risk management to be the methodical process used to enhance the opportunities and reduce the risks by:

- *Identifying* potential opportunities and their risks.
- *Assessing* associated probabilities of occurrence and the impact (benefit or consequence) of the occurrence.
- *Deciding* to:

Do nothing	*OR*	Take causative action for opportunity, preventive action for risk	*OR*	Take contingent action later based on an identified trigger

Opportunity management objectives are driven by the desire to excel while risk management objectives are driven by the desire to not fail. The major driving forces for each are shown in Figures 7.38 and 7.39.

Opportunity and risk management depends on a solid foundation of planning and proactive project management to manage the plan:

Our personal insurance policies and the spare tires we carry in our cars are everyday examples of risk management.

- Develop (and use) an Implementation Plan:
  —Developed by and committed to by the project team.
  —Kept current.
- Use proven processes tailored to your project:
  —System engineering methodology.
  —Software development methodology.
  —Hardware development methodology.
  —Reliability and quality methodology.
- Manage the business and technical baselines:
  —Keep participants informed of the evolving baseline.

The project team may feel they have already "managed" the risks by creating the initial risk-management plan. But risk

Since many opportunities and risks are discovered in the decomposition process, it is impossible to identify all risks up front.

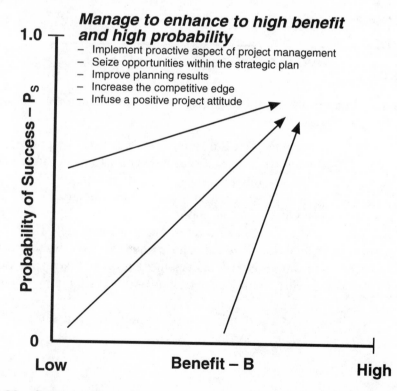

FIGURE 7.38 Opportunity management objectives—driven by the desire to excel.

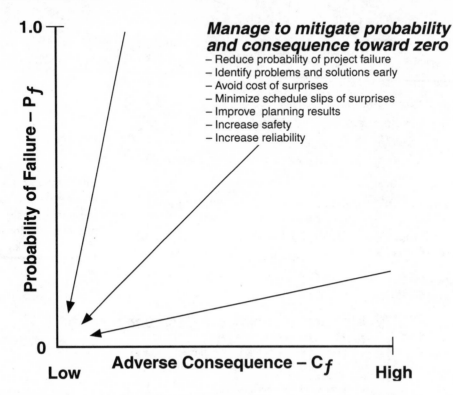

FIGURE 7.39   Risk management objectives—driven by the desire to succeed.

management is ongoing—it evolves as the project proceeds. Plans need to be updated as new opportunities and risks are identified and the impacts are evaluated.

Opportunities and risks are interrelated as the risks must be justified by the opportunity pursued. We have structured a process which separates the uncertainties themselves and their analysis, from the management actions and decisions. This opportunity and risk management process takes specific steps to make overt, conscious decisions with justifiable rationale:

> Each opportunity or risk needs to be evaluated as a whole, taking into account relative probabilities and offsetting benefits and consequences.

1. Identify the opportunities and risks:
    —What opportunities are available? What benefits?
    —What are the risks? What consequences?
    —Describe with "If . . . , Then . . ." statement.
    —Group by like categories.

2. Assess both probability and impact. Forecast the expected outcome.

3. Prioritize using expected outcome.

4. Develop candidate management actions to enhance opportunities and mitigate risks.

5. Estimate the cost of proposed immediate and contingent actions.

6. Compare resultant changes to expected outcome against action costs.

7. Decide on actions required, and obtain concurrence.

8. Document and incorporate decisions in all planning.

Some project managers and executives make a distinction between eliminating versus insuring against a risk (such as liability insurance), or deciding on an action versus planning a contingency. In our view, these are simply alternative cases of opportunity and risk management and need to be evaluated as such. For example, we consider insurance as one possible mitigating action for product liability risks. The examples that follow demonstrate techniques that are unique to opportunity and risk management.

IDENTIFY THE OPPORTUNITIES AND RISKS

One of the biggest problems a project manager faces is motivating team members to identify risks. You want to make everyone risk conscious. However, there is often that hesitancy to surface risks, lest one be labeled a worrier or negative thinker. It's partly a problem that messengers are in fact often punished or at least put down by their management (the problem with a risk being identified is that you have to do something about it) and partly a failure to realize the real value of risk identification (you can't mitigate it if you don't know it's there so it's better to anticipate a lot of problems, some of which won't happen, than too few and miss the "project-killers"). It's easier with opportunities because everyone wants to be a hero and find ways to do it better, faster, cheaper and that suggests some strategies. The simplest is to reward risk identifiers. The best (and cheapest) one we've seen is a listing outside a manager's door of all the risks anybody had identified on her project together with the name of the identifier. A brief statement of what actions were to be taken (or if no action was to be taken, why not), and who had the action. The listing had powerful effects:

- It showed that the manager wasn't afraid to identity risks.
- It rewarded risk identifiers (printed recognition is an effective, inexpensive reward).
- It stimulated others to think of other risks.
- It precluded people from submitting the same risk.
- It prompted others to offer suggestions for how to mitigate identified risks.

The manager wasn't concerned with who got the credit as long as the project succeeded—a good leadership and teamwork technique as well.

It can be helpful to subdivide the myriad of possible opportunities and risks into categories. Opportunity categories are strategic and tactical like deciding what business to be in (strategic) and pursuing the business (tactical). Figure 7.40 illustrates examples in each category. Using emerging technology or new development tools would be a tactical opportunity.

Risk categories are implementation and product, such as lack of sufficient funding (implementation) and using dangerous toxins (product). Figure 7.41 illustrates examples in each category. This is only a representative list—all relevant areas must be considered.

Identify the opportunities and risks for each project cycle phase by systematically applying the appropriate techniques based on analysis, planning, and history.

Techniques based on analysis include:

- Opportunity and risk checklists (the categories and lists in Figures 7.40 and 7.41 offer a beginning checklist).
- Rules of thumb/standards of performance.
- System decomposition and critical items (off-core studies).
- Hazard analysis.
- Failure modes analysis.
- Interviews with experts.

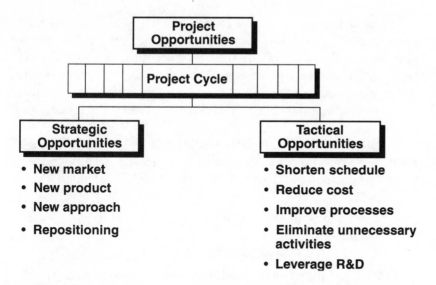

FIGURE 7.40   The two categories of project opportunities.

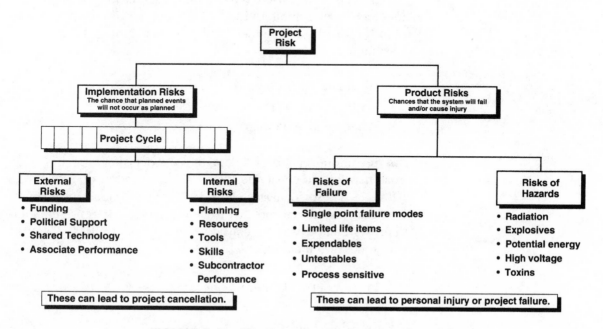

FIGURE 7.41   The two categories of project risk.

Hazard analysis is used to ensure all system hazards have been identified and anticipated. Once identified, all hazards to personnel and to the system are either accepted, reduced by design, or contained by design. For example, a high pressure gas hazard could be reduced by designing with a large safety factor or contained by placing sand bags between the hazard and personnel.

Failure Modes and Effects Analysis (FMEA) is a risk management technique used to ensure all failure modes have been identified and planned for. This tool employs the following method:

- Select a ranking technique for project failure modes concern and attention.
- Identify all single point failure modes and rank them.
- Analyze failure modes and the resultant operational effect.
- Determine those requiring correction: redundancy and/or increased reliability.
- Implement the corrective action decision.

A technique based on planning—scenario planning—is a "low-tech" technique for visualizing opportunities or risks, is useful in the realms of judgment and project planning. It consists of querying:

- What if . . . ? followed by . . . then what?
- What opportunities might be considered?
- What could go wrong?

This technique can be used to build a decision tree based on broad market and economic trends: If the economy does this, I do that . . . . These scenarios can often identify important assumptions that traditional forecasting tends to miss. It represents another systematic way to consider future possibilities. Planning techniques also include:

- Project network interactions.
- Critical Path.
- Schedule slack.

Techniques based on history are the most natural to apply. They include:

- Similar efforts and lessons learned.
- Technical surveys.
- Development test results.

Generalized historical templates can work well in some industries. For example, construction projects are highly repetitive, compared with research and development. Since the work patterns of one project may be similar to selected ones from the past, the same types of risks are likely to occur.

On the other hand, misperceptions or misinterpretations about prior projects will sometimes lead project teams to overestimate their ability to control future risks or to exploit future opportunities. It has often been left up to project leaders to identify risk based on their own experiences and perception of the situation. Such projects were at the mercy of whatever their experiences and perceptions were. As one engineer put it, "The alligator that was the closest to you was the one you worried about the most. You didn't look at the other 'gators in the swamp, even though they were bigger and meaner." A common misperception is that successful experiences with simpler projects scale to complex ones. Every new project has to be analyzed in detail to understand those unique properties which distinguish it from its predecessors. This needs to be an ongoing team effort and rely heavily on lessons learned.

> Not only is each project unique, but the uniqueness is often related to its risk.

ASSESS BOTH PROBABILITY AND IMPACT

A goal of identifying and anticipating all opportunities and risks would usually be doomed to failure. The result of anticipating every possible opportunity and risk could bury the team in questionable information and turn the project into a hand-wringing exercise. This dramatizes the importance of prioritization.

There are a number of sophisticated and powerful tools available for opportunity and risk analysis, such as decision trees and Monte Carlo simulations. These tools and others are described in texts such as Clemen's book, *Making Hard Decisions.*[27]

For most decisions we face in a project environment, however, a much simpler tool (called Expected Outcome) can be used, and it is described in the following paragraphs.

The Expected Outcome (EO), sometimes called weighted value, is a technique for quantitatively comparing both opportunities and risks. It provides the project manager with a measure for sizing management reserves for investment and protection. The Expected Outcome of opportunity and risk is equal to the probability of occurrence multiplied by the impact, for example:

Probability of occurrence of an opportunity = 0.6

Benefit of the opportunity = $720,000 if it does occur

Therefore: EO = (0.6) × ($720,000)

= $432,000

Expected Outcome provides a tool for quantitatively comparing both opportunities and risks. The primary use of Expected Outcome is to prioritize actions. When applying EO, be sure to use consistent units. For the purposes of prioritizing, "burn rate" (usually expressed as daily expense rate) may be used to measure schedule impact in dollars. The following is an example of prioritization of two risks.

When applying Expected Outcome, common sense and good judgment are required since the calculations, usually based on subjective information, have low precision.

Risk 1 Expected Outcome

(0.8) × ($100,000) = $80,000

Risk 2 Expected Outcome

(0.4) × ($60,000) + (0.4) × (45-day slip) = $24,000 (cost) plus 18-days (schedule)

Assuming a $2000/day burn rate, a 45-day slip would cost $90,000.

Expected Outcome, on a cost basis, = $24,000 + (0.4) × ($90,000) = $60,000.

On the basis of this analysis, Risk 1 should be of higher priority than Risk 2. Risk and opportunity can be managed by influencing the *probability* of occurrence and/or the *impact* of the outcome.

A complete listing of the possible influencing activities with their associated costs should be developed (Figure 7.42). From

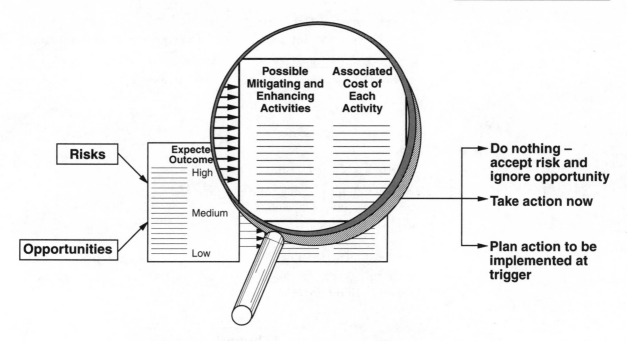

FIGURE 7.42   Management of opportunity and risk actions.

this, you can decide on the appropriate actions. There are basically two types of actions to consider: causative/preventive and contingent. Contingent actions are the same as causative/preventive actions, except no action is taken other than preparation, until a predetermined trigger applies the action.

Examples of Causative/ Preventive Actions:

Redundancy to eliminate single point failure modes

Higher quality to increase reliability

Increased margins to improve safety

Examples of Contingencies:

Red line limits in test procedures (terminate test if exceeded)

Establish thresholds for variance analysis and corrective action (triggers focused review)

Planned strategies contingent on competitor's performance

Examples of Causative/ Preventive Actions:	*Examples of Contingencies:*
Enforced use of common software language and standards across subcontractor and prime team.	Unsolicited proposal based on associate's poor performance.
Expert review to ensure best approach.	
Overtime to shorten critical path.	
Over-design for possible future growth (pre-planned product improvement).	

The cost effectiveness of candidate actions can be evaluated using mitigation leverage (ML) or enhancement leverage (EL) factors defined as follows:

$$ML = \frac{EO\ before - EO\ after}{Risk\ mitigation\ cost}$$

$$EL = \frac{EO\ after - EO\ before}{Benefit\ enhancement\ cost}$$

The leverage values can be used for comparison and as an aid in the selection process.

DECIDE ON ACTIONS REQUIRED AND INCORPORATE THEM IN THE PLAN

The value of the opportunity must justify the incurred risks.

It is often impractical to accurately estimate the probabilities of occurrence and impacts of potential events. In these cases, decisions may be based on a qualitative assessment for both the probability of occurrence and the benefit or consequence. In the sample risk decision matrix in Figure 7.43, based on qualitative assessments, carrying a spare ignition key for your car in your wallet or purse is a high-impact, low probability instance (for some, a high-probability instance).

All opportunity and risk management actions must be incorporated into the project plan and kept current (Figure 7.44). Carrying a spare key for the car you sold two years ago is an example

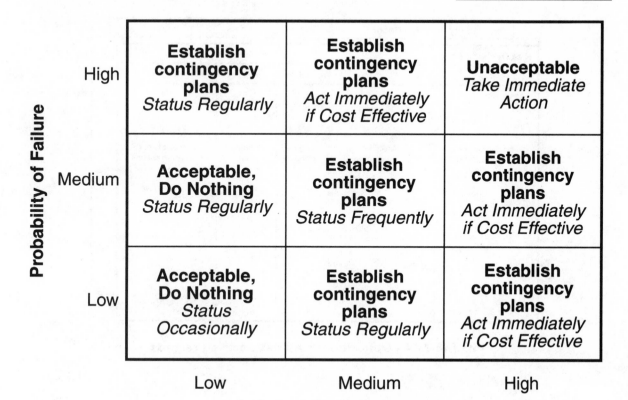

FIGURE 7.43 Sample risk decision matrix.

of a good risk management decision that, through neglect, turned bad (what's worse, you believe you're secure until that first time you discover you have the wrong key).

On cost reimbursable contracts, get customer concurrence with opportunity and risk management actions, since the customer is likely to be paying for them.

To be effective, this management process should occur throughout the project and at all levels in the system decomposition. The management actions must:

- Result from overt, conscious decisions;
- Have justifiable rationale;

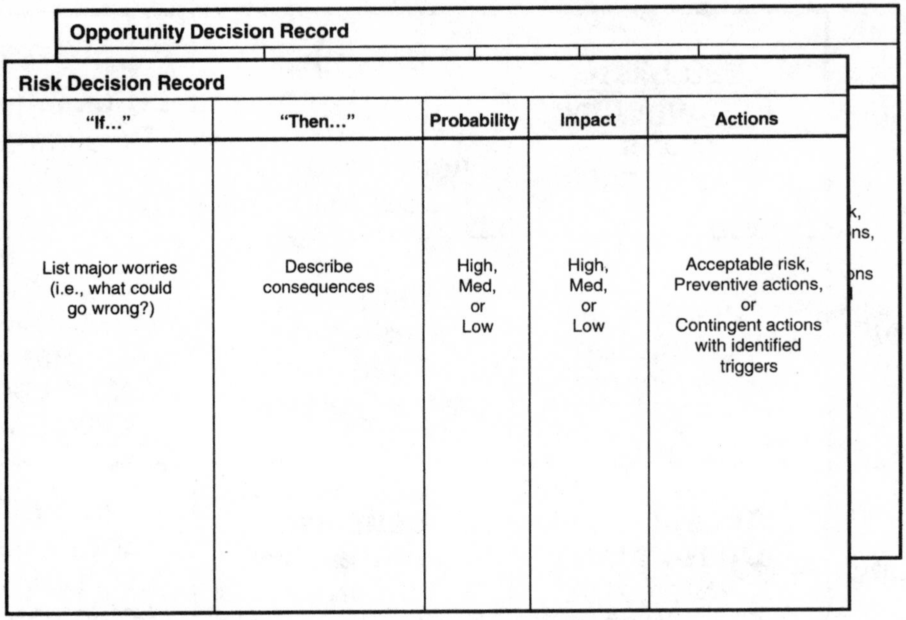

Opportunity Decision Record				
Risk Decision Record				
"If..."	"Then..."	Probability	Impact	Actions
List major worries (i.e., what could go wrong?)	Describe consequences	High, Med, or Low	High, Med, or Low	Acceptable risk, Preventive actions, or Contingent actions with identified triggers

FIGURE 7.44   Opportunity and risk decision records.

- Be incorporated in the plan; and
- Be implemented through work authorizations and subcontracts.

RELATING OPPORTUNITIES AND RISKS TO THE PROJECT CYCLE

As we emphasized earlier, risk management is ongoing—it evolves as the project evolves. Perhaps one of the greatest project risks is in not following the (updated, as necessary) project plan. Not following the plan is the direct cause of the fatal, tragic end of Rob Hall's Mt. Everest expedition in 1996.[28]

The sources and nature of opportunities and risks vary from period to period and from phase to phase. For example, the major risks during the study period may be the instability of the requirements, lack of understanding of the user problem, and at risk project funding, whereas, training, logistics, and supplier quality may loom as the largest risks during the implementation period.

The Vee model[29] of the technical aspect provides a visual basis for identifying and managing opportunities and risks during system decomposition and definition. We used Figure 6.6a in Chapter 6 to introduce the idea of using off-core activities for opportunity and risk management. Figure 7.45 lists critical issues to be studied off-core during the user requirements understanding phase, since users (or the organization representing the users) often do not have a clear understanding of their needs. This diagram details the first part of the core of the Vee, starting with the statement of user need. Until concepts, and even lower level details are defined, the user requirements statement may continue

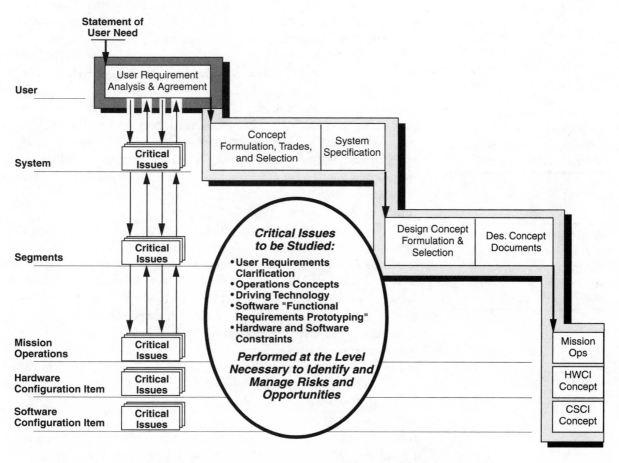

FIGURE 7.45   Critical issues for user requirements phase.

to evolve. Off-core studies provide the opportunity for user requirements clarification and understanding.

Opportunities may include innovations that extend the product useful life through planned technology upgrades or value enhancements which reduce the cost and/or broaden the market. An example of the latter occurred several years ago on a client's project to develop a new calculator for the U.S. financial community. As part of the off-core user's requirements clarification, a meeting was held with a group of financial analysts. The users requested that a button be added to the keyboard which divided the current display by 365, the U.S. standard for interest-bearing days. This feature was an opportunity for a competitive edge and was adopted. Still another opportunity occurred soon thereafter which more than doubled the market. A development team member suggested reconfiguring the keyboard to accommodate the 360-day European standard. The change was easily accomplished at this early stage, but would have had a major impact after coding or manufacturing had started.

Off-core studies usually begin early in the project cycle and may be very simple explorations requiring only a few hours to explore opportunities and to ensure that risks are acceptable. However, if the solution is challenging the state of the art, the studies themselves can be very involved projects requiring years of effort (the Reagan-era "Star Wars" space defense initiative is an opportunity exploration example).

The studies may be analytical in nature, or they may require development of a software or hardware model to resolve system capabilities, constraints, and technology or integration issues. These models may need to go to the lowest level of detail in selected areas. For example, creating a software algorithm to prove that a data search of a large, distributed database can be performed within a specified period. The authors were involved in developing a database management system that could perform a complex search of six-million entries in three seconds. The off-core feasibility studies focused on functionality rather than performance, resulting in an algorithm that was successfully tested on 100,000 entries. Unfortunately, the project failed when the fully-implemented system required up to one minute to perform a complete search (even though the typical search met the three-second limit).

Off-core studies do not seek a final solution, but rather a demonstration that at least one is feasible.

Projects that fall short of user expectations, even though they surpass the state of the art, are not likely to succeed.

The core of the Vee extends to the lowest level of hardware parts and processes and computer software units. Figure 7.46 illustrates a six-level hierarchy. The number of levels on a given project depends on the system complexity and the system integration approach.

In the development of the Boeing 777 a new and lightweight material offered the opportunity of weight savings, fuel economy, and increased payload. However, perfectly good metal could have cosmetic cracks that would require explanation to the 777 airline customers. Boeing decided the downside risk of having to explain cracked metal was not worth the benefits to be achieved. Boeing's competitors probably would have had a field day with "Boeing builds with cracked metal."

> Upward iteration with the user is often needed to get buy-in to the opportunities and to manage the risks in the continuous process of user requirements clarification.

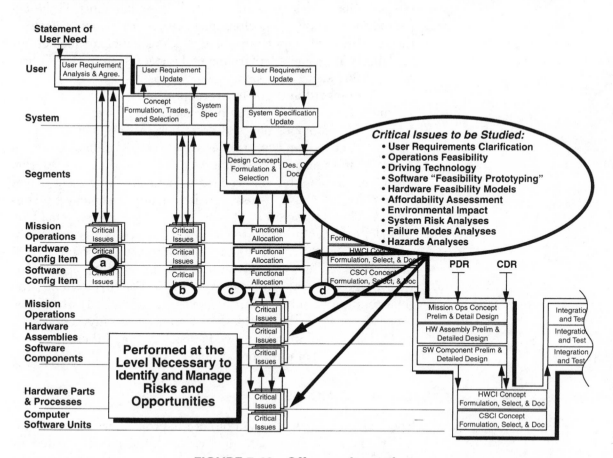

FIGURE 7.46   Off-core alternatives.

After completion of early project phases, it is often necessary to revisit the decisions as external events change, or as new insights are discovered through off-core studies in lower level detail. In our model calendar time and design maturity move from left to right, so the revisiting process does not occur by going back up the core of the Vee, but rather, by moving vertically to the system specification update, concept update, or user requirements update, as shown.

The functionality that the user expects must be flowed down to components within the system. In order to complete those components, piece parts and lines of code must be provided. At each of the subtier levels there may be critical issues that should be explored to minimize the risk that, when these details are finally designed and verified, they fall short of the expected functionality or performance. Other critical issues include the expansion of opportunity and risk evaluation to include affordability assessment, environmental impact, system risk, failure modes, and hazard analysis.

The upward and downward opportunity and risk iterations continue through the preliminary and critical design reviews. During the decomposition and definition process major areas of risk are identified and approaches are developed to manage them. As shown in Figure 7.46, it is not necessary that the same solution to a given problem be followed throughout. As the project moves from phase to phase, a new and better approach may be conceived. Thus the solution at step (b) in the diagram could be superior to the solution at step (a). In fact, step (a) may be a hardware solution, while step (b) may be a software solution. Furthermore, steps (b) and (c) may represent widely varying approaches with no evolutionary path between them. For this example, the final configuration item must be developed at step (d) which may evolve from (c) or be distinctly different. The only necessity is that a feasible solution be proved at each step and then baselined at its level of decomposition within the Vee [step (d)].

THE SPIRAL MODEL

The Vee is one view (abstraction) of the project environment. Another commonly discussed view is the spiral model created by Barry Boehm.[30] Many software organizations use the spiral model in their development. Microsoft, for instance, uses a process that is ". . . similar to the risk-driven, incremental 'spiral' life cycle model."[31] Some attendees in our classes have told us that they cannot use the Vee, because their organization uses "the Spiral." They are, of course, misinformed, because the spiral is simply another view of the project environment. It emphasizes the repetitive need for risk analysis and software "prototyping." While the spiral is basically a sound model, it obscures the need for continuous

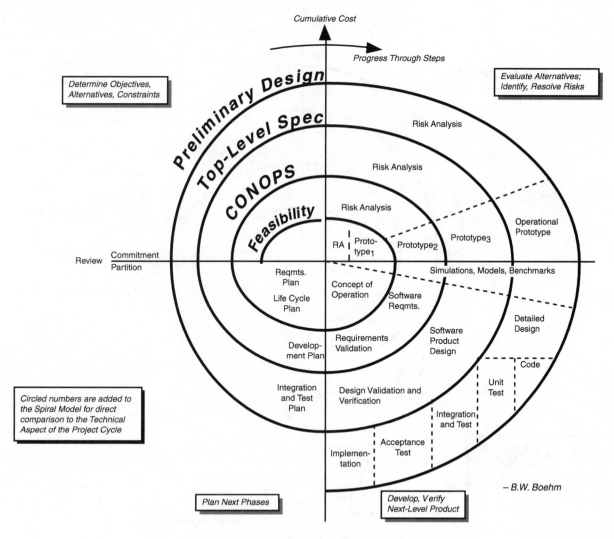

FIGURE 7.47 Spiral model.

attention to opportunity and risk management, rather than just in one quadrant. In fact the spiral and the Vee are two views of the same process. Figure 7.47 shows the spiral as Boehm created it. Figure 7.48 adds numbers along the spiral for reference. Figure 7.49 shows the spiral overlaid on the Vee, which emphasizes their similarity.

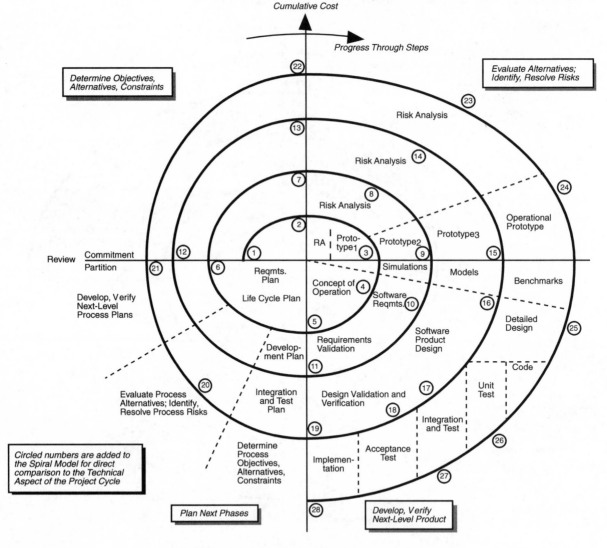

FIGURE 7.48   Spiral model—annotated.

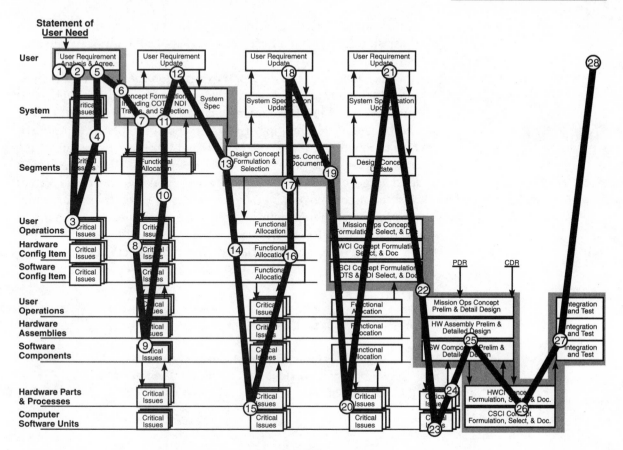

FIGURE 7.49   Spiral model overlaid on the "Vee."

OPPORTUNITY AND RISK ELEMENT EXERCISE

The objective of this exercise is to provide experience in relating risk to opportunity and in illustrating how risk tolerance drives risk mitigation decisions.

Make a list of all the risk mitigation actions that you practice in the normal conduct of your life. Categories for consideration are: insurance (life, homeowners, liability, collision, comprehensive, umbrella, etc.), insurance deductible provisions, security (alarm systems, motion detector lights, alertness, etc.), personal safety (life vests, seat belts, roll bars, hard hats, etc.), and there are many others. For each of these mitigation actions, identify the opportunity that you embraced that forced you to incur the risk, the risk mitigation, and the residual risk following your selected mitigation.

For instance, the desire to experience the thrill of a bungee jump incurred the risk mitigation of being instructed and checked out by a qualified technician, but you incur the residual risk of the bungee cord breaking. However, the thrill of the jump justified proceeding in spite of the residual risk. People that desire to live in California accept the risk of earthquakes and the associated large deductible amounts (20 percent of the home value) now common on earthquake insurance. With these large deductibles and high premiums, many don't carry earthquake insurance and chose to self-insure.

Residual risks must be justified by the opportunity being pursued.

6. PROJECT CONTROL

A good system of control helps prevent undesirable surprises; it provides for turning the "lemon" into lemonade.

Henri Fayol,
General and Industrial Management

Fayol goes on to say, "Control activities provide an opportunity for people to take the initiative in planning against deviations (proactive), to head off forces that might cause a deviation, to make corrections very quickly (reactive) when a deviation does occur, and finally, to redirect the firm to capitalize on a deviation when correction is less feasible." Fayol referred to the final alternative as "making lemonade." Note that even Henry Fayol, in 1916, recognized that project control is both proactive and reactive.

PROJECT CONTROL IS PROCESS CONTROL

A tracking function is not a control function and can lead to project failure by giving the false impression that project controls are in place.

Most project management texts describe project control as comparing actuals to plan (status). While monitoring and tracking of cost and schedule data is one step toward reactive control, it is hardly project control without corrective action.

We define project control as both proactive and reactive process control, a dual system designed and implemented to reduce risk:

- Proactive baseline control,
- Reactive performance control.
- Proactive control of the Project Plan and changes to the plan.
- Reactive control of variances in performance to the project plan.
- Management techniques that help ensure that results happen as planned, and that results not planned do not happen.
- Corrective action taken when unplanned results do happen.

> Project control needs to be proactive and reactive and seldom inactive. Contrary to popular opinion reactive management is essential in managing projects.

This section deals with the functions of *defining* and *establishing* the five essential elements common to all control systems (Figure 7.50). They are:

1. *Things to be controlled.* The function that must be controlled to a standard of performance.
2. *Control standard.* The approved standard of performance.
3. *Control authority.* The person or organization authorized to impose the standard and grant exceptions.

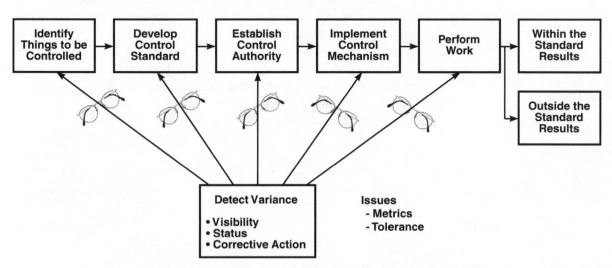

FIGURE 7.50   Project control is process control.

4. *Control mechanism.* The forum or technique that measures compliance to the standard.
5. *Variance indication.* The identification of flaws in the control process or violations of the standard.

Typical factors to be controlled:

Project baselines, business, cost, and technical	Reliability
Environment	Safety, both product and personnel
Funding	Security
Hardware development process	Software development environment
Manufacturing process	Software development process
Materials	Test
Parts	Time recording
Personnel conduct	Time recording
Quality	Work standards

Control systems are designed to control achievement of the project as planned. Of high importance are those controls required to manage risk and process sensitive methods. Mature, well-established processes should be periodically improved to achieve even higher consistency of results. New processes may require frequent inspection to ascertain that both the process and the results are as expected. As the processes mature and are proven to be reliable the inspections can be reduced and possibly eliminated.

Examples of control functions are:

Function to Be Controlled	Control Standard	Control Authority	Control Technique	Variance Indication
Wiring	Electrical Code	Building Department	Inspection	Deficiency notice
Project work	Contract	Contract Administrator	Work authorizations	Out of scope work
Schedule	Master schedule	Business Manager	Work authorization	Off plan
Security	Need to know list	Security Manager	Guard	Unauthorized access

Variance control (Figure 7.51) is designed to detect practices or performance considered substandard. Variances can result from flawed implementation of standards or deviations from the standards. This corrective action system relies on the management elements of Visibility, Status, and Corrective Action to close the reactive process control loop. We address each of these elements in separate sections.

Process controls are needed to manage important project functions and to control risk. Without appropriate process controls, details may get lost or overlooked. Smaller projects are often vulnerable due to overconfidence that the details can be informally "kept in mind."

- Large projects have complex communication paths—details get lost or overlooked.
- Geographically dispersed projects have informal communication paths—details get lost or overlooked.
- High reliability projects must be built to exacting standards—details get lost or overlooked.

> Control examples within the business baseline include schedule, funding, changes, personnel quality, headcount level, key personnel, work practices, ethical conduct.

> Personnel safety control examples include high pressure, radiation, toxins, high voltage, slippery surfaces, sharp edges, overhead clearance, stair risers, air quality.

	Activity +	Visibility +	Project Plan =	Status +	Corrective Action =	Reactive Project Control
Case 1: No Visibility	?	No	?	No	No	No
Case 2: No Plan	Yes	Yes	No	No	No	No
Case 3: No Corrective Action	Yes	Yes	Yes	Yes	No	No
Case 4: Desired Approach	Yes	Yes	Yes	Yes	Yes	Yes

FIGURE 7.51   Reactive control of variances.

- Long duration projects have personnel turnover—details get lost or overlooked.
- Projects with subcontractors have complex communications paths—details get lost or overlooked.

It follows that large, long, high-reliability projects using sub-contractors need the ultimate system of process control. Analysis of failed projects often reveals the circumvention of an existing system. In short, projects with inadequate process controls usually fail. Projects having the appropriate process controls have a good chance for success. But what is the "appropriate" level of control?

TOWARD ACHIEVING THE APPROPRIATE LEVEL OF CONTROL

The appropriate level of control is achieved by pursuing the optimal balance between formality and discretionary freedom. It reflects and accommodates the need for change by managing those changes with formal, trackable procedures. Configuration management, discussed below, is perhaps the best example of an optimally-designed control procedure.

As Leonard Kazmier[32] observes:

> Ultimately, the success of a control system is determined by its effectiveness in getting people to make the necessary modifications in their own performance. Although the classical approach to control systems assumes that people will automatically act to correct their own behavior when directed to do so, this does not necessarily happen. Individuals may resist formal control systems for a variety of reasons, some of which are discussed below.

Stated another way:

- Controls disrupt a person's self-image (they highlight things a person has done poorly).
- People tend to avoid unpleasant involvement (such as behavioral changes).
- Goals of the control system may not have been universally accepted.

- Standards of expected performance are too high.
- The controls seem irrelevant or lack completeness.
- An outside staff is administering the controls.
- Informal team norms may conflict with, or violate, company norms.

One of the most pervasive reasons for resistance to controls is the equating of project controls with a lack of freedom. Controls therefore should never be arbitrary—they should make sense. But even the most logical controls may encounter resistance. We are increasingly scripted in a "zero sum" concept of personal freedom and control—the more we're controlled, the less we are free. Enlightened managers know, however, that appropriate controls enhance rather than inhibit creativity. Such controls free the project team to be creative in finding solutions, rather than being distracted by the day-to-day confusion of deciding what the project activity should be or how things should be done. Since this may not be the initial perception, particularly for inexperienced team members, it is the responsibility of the senior team members to gain general acceptance for the process control system. To accomplish this, the team needs to be intimately involved in: process control definition and implementation; the reasons for the controls, the control activities and decisions; and access to relevant information at all organizational levels.

Some team members may still have to be sold on the potential benefits to gain their acceptance and to maintain a high level of teamwork. In this regard, the productivity and quality improvements that accrue from designing, selecting, and tuning the controls through team consensus, can be particularly convincing.

Peter Drucker[33] stresses the importance of *congruency:*

Meaningful control systems . . . are discernible and appropriate for the complexity of the tasks being assessed and the size of the project effort. They are timely, simple to employ, and congruent with the events being measured.

In summary, both proactive and reactive process controls should be:

- *Relevant.* Controls should never be arbitrary. Their purpose, rationale, and benefits should be clear. The controls should be designed and selected to match the risk of the project. In general, the more visible and larger the commitment of resources and the greater the human risk, the greater the requirement for controls.
- *Efficient.* While designing the controls, determine the minimum required to assure performance. Avoid the tendency to measure and report information just because it's available (such data tend to mask and divert attention from more important items). Tailor the information to the needs of the team members who need the data to take action. Summarize and use graphics wherever possible.
- *Simple.* Keep the controls as simple as possible.
- *Timely.* Controls need to be in place and tested before they're actually needed. The process should produce timely information to facilitate corrective action. This means determining the proper "sampling rate" to avoid obscured visibility at one extreme and information overload at the other.

To be effective, project control systems must be tailored to the nature, complexity, and risk of the situation and must be in place by the time the control is needed. As relayed below, one of the author's recent experiences demonstrates just how important the appropriate controls are and how critical the timing can be.

The incident occurred on vacation while I was driving a 24-foot motor home, towing a two-ton jeep. The primary control to slow the vehicle down is the brakes, but in mountainous country another even more powerful control is the compression of the engine. By shifting to a lower gear, a safe vehicle speed can be maintained on a steep incline. On the highway between Flaming Gorge in Southern Wyoming to the town of Vernal, Utah, there is a 20-mile stretch of an 8 percent grade, with accompanying precipitous cliffs along the roadside. Going down this hill I used the primary or standard control (brakes). The car ahead of me was proceeding rather slowly, and judging by the tail lights, was using the brakes frequently. In fact, we could actually smell the overheated brakes. I had to use my brakes fairly frequently since it was a no-passing zone, and I decided to stop to take some photographs to put some distance between us and the slow vehicle. After I started downhill again, I tried to use the brakes to slow the vehicle at about 30 mph. But due to brake failure caused by excessive heat destroying the brake shoes, the brake pedal went to the floor with no effect on the vehicle speed. I immediately shifted to low gear but the vehicle would not slow down because the automatic transmission would not downshift from second to first at speeds above 25 mph. We continued to accelerate. A hairpin turn loomed ominously less than a half-mile ahead, with a drop of considerable depth very close to the road. Rather than go over the 300 foot-cliff, I chose to run the motor home and jeep straight up a rocky embankment on the right just before the hairpin turn. The impact slowed the vehicle to a stop with less than 100 feet to spare to the cliff edge. Miraculously, there was no damage as a result of the impact.

Because of the failed brakes, the motor home could not be driven, and was towed by truck with exactly the same engine and brakes as the motor home down the same steep grade of 8 percent. This journey was made without incident because the tow truck driver started in low gear and the engine compression kept the speed of the vehicles at a safe 20 mph.

The significance of this story is that powerful control processes are available to us, but are ineffective if they are not engaged at the proper time. The entire journey down the steep grade from Flaming Gorge to Vernal could have been made in low gear without requiring use of the brakes, but only if the choice was made before the descent was begun. The same thing is true in a project environment. There are many powerful controls such as configuration management or earned value performance measurement, that can be very effective if implemented at an appropriate time. It is also important to recognize that there are situations when these tools are not appropriate. There are low risk projects for which more simple tools are entirely adequate, and the more sophisticated approaches are not needed. In driving a car down a steep incline, it is appropriate to use low gear as the primary control, but even the most ardent controls enthusiast would not advocate driving all the way across the United States using low gear. That ardent control enthusiast would, however, have at least suspected that the strong hot brake smell could be coming from the motor home brakes rather than the vehicle in front, and would have responded promptly to the warning signs.

GENERAL CONTROL TECHNIQUES

Guidelines
General

One person should be placed in charge of specific areas, for example:

—Project Manager: Overall project requirements.

—Chief System Engineer: Technical requirements and technical baseline.

—Business Manager: Contracts and business baseline.

Approved documents must be readily accessible. This is best accomplished by establishing a project information center with a responsible information manager. This subject is addressed in the section on Visibility.

Technical

One person must control each task.

There must be a controlled work release system.

There must be an audit for compliance with project requirements.

Variances must be negotiated with the project manager.

Cost

Team leaders must control to their budget.

Variances must be negotiated with the project manager.

Schedule

All team leaders must sign off on the integrated schedule and Project Work Authorizing Agreements and control to them.

Variances must be negotiated with the project manager.

Contract Control   The buyer controls sellers to standards set by contract types and incentives.

Type	Application	Control Provided
Fixed Price	Reliable prior cost experience	Technical, cost, and schedule
Cost Reimbursement	Research or development with advancing technology	Pursuit of a solution
Cost Sharing	Seller shares cost in return for use of technology	Pursuit of a shared result
Time and Material	Not possible to estimate the task beforehand	Labor and material rates
Labor Hour	Like Time and Material, but labor only	Labor rates
Indefinite Quantity	Establishes price when quantity and schedule are uncertain	Per item price
Letter	Limited project start without completed negotiations	Initial spend rate

Data Control   A data manager should control all contract data and approved baseline data. Typical tools include a project library and a computer-based document management system.

Self-Control   Operates at the most personal level. This kind of control is infectious.

"Setting a good example" includes:
- —Being on time to work and to meetings.
- —Demonstrating high personal standards.
- —Reacting appropriately to stress.

and controlling the pen by:
- —Authoring strawman documents.
- —Proposing agendas.
- —Recording Action items.
- —Reviewing and signing letters.

Management by Objectives Can supplement, or in some cases substitute for, the Project Work Authorizing Agreements (PWAA) introduced earlier as planning techniques to control work authorization. Conversely, managing with definitive PWAAs can be thought of as MBO in its most effective form. In either approach, the corporate accounting system must provide cost accounting down to the task level in order to measure cost performance against the PWAA/MBO commitment and to provide early, in-process warning of potential problems.

In the absence of a WBS/PWAA system, a rigorous MBO system can accomplish many of their control functions. MBO is also a useful supplement to WBS/PWAA at a more detailed and shorter range, that is, the level of detail associated with monthly schedules and/or the first and second levels of the organization.

Many companies and government organizations have developed comprehensive MBO systems. Among their primary benefits, MBOs align individual contributions with the broadening objectives at each level of the organizational hierarchy, starting with the top strategic goals. In that environment, project teams can benefit substantially by using the same MBO structure to align project team goals with functional unit goals and with individual team member goals as well.

For an MBO system to be effective and self-motivating for the user, objectives need to be thoroughly documented (typically on a quarterly schedule) and reviewed/revised regularly (usually weekly) and in detail. An effective system is characterized by objectives that are:

- Specific, clear, and unambiguous.
- Realistic, measurable, and verifiable.
- Consistent with available resources.
- Consistent with company policies.

The best results are usually obtained by starting at the top levels. Every manager and all individual contributors draft their own objectives to fit with the level above while adding more detail and assumptions to represent their specific contributions. Each objective needs to include assumptions, measurement means, and verification methods. Joint commitments should be

---

A loosely managed MBO system is worse than none at all. It will demotivate employees.

negotiated among the parties to arrive at identical objective statements. Team objectives are best negotiated with the team leader in a joint session resulting in consensus.

CONFIGURATION MANAGEMENT AND CHANGE CONTROL

As illustrated in Figure 7.52, Configuration Management is used to maintain the project baselines after their approval. A vital element of configuration management, the Change Control Board, controls changes to the baselines. Configuration management recognizes the inevitability of changes in the configuration of hardware and software. It assures that changes are adequately accounted for as they reverberate through the baselines, impacting technical performance, budgets, schedules, and so on. Each time the project successfully passes a major milestone (a point of consensus between seller and buyer—a control gate), the approved baselines which result are subject to formal control.

> Change control is intended to manage changes—not to prevent them.

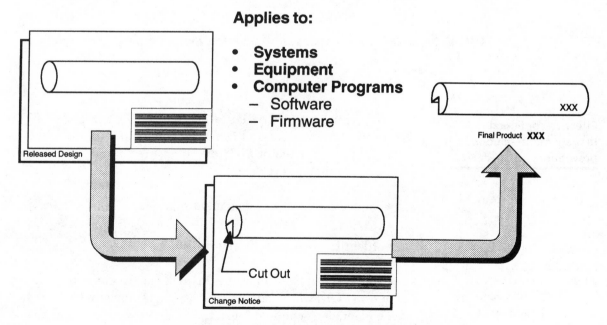

Applies to:

- **Systems**
- **Equipment**
- **Computer Programs**
  - Software
  - Firmware

Released Design

Cut Out

Change Notice

Final Product **XXX**

XXX

FIGURE 7.52   Configuration management.

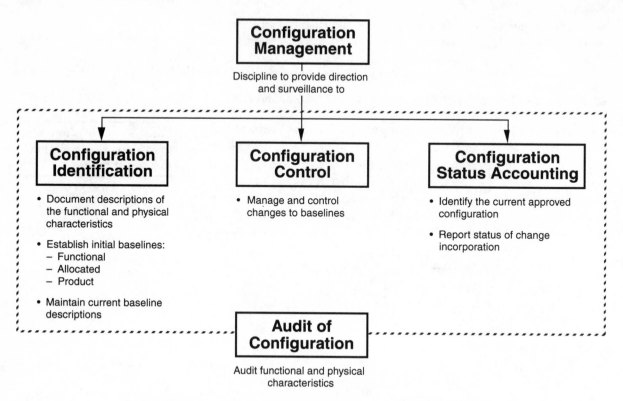

FIGURE 7.53   Key elements of configuration management.

Effective configuration management—an ounce of prevention.

The purpose of Configuration Management (Figure 7.53) is to control the physical and functional characteristics of the system and the elements of a system to ensure that total system integrity is maintained through:

- Management of physical and functional characteristics.
- Control of changes.
- Identification and communication of changes.

Augustine's Law—No change is a small change—drives the need for change control.

The change process usually begins with an Engineering Change Request (ECR) which documents the change including the technical, budget, and schedule impact. The ECR precipitates a Change Control Board (CCB) review (Figure 7.54). The participants

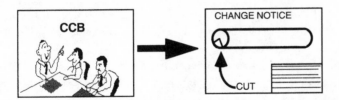

FIGURE 7.54   The change control board.

include the managers of each affected organization. The project manager chairs the CCB and is responsible for ensuring that:

- The decision is informed and objective.
- Each change is logged for traceability to the work package level of the WBS.
- All affected parties are notified of baseline changes.
- Upper management and the customer are officially informed of all baseline changes.
- Changes requiring customer approval are forwarded to the customer change board.

The CCB Agenda needs to include the following issues which must be thoroughly understood before an informed decision can be made:

- The details of the change and the need for it.
- What is the impact of the change on the performance, design, cost, schedule, support equipment, spares, contract, customer, project team?
- What is the impact of making the change versus not making the change?
- What is the change effectivity (e.g., date, versions and units affected)?
- What documentation is affected by the change?
- What is the customer's position?

The project manager needs to factor the customer's situation into the decision process. Likewise, secondary impacts on the project team need to be accounted for in schedules. For example,

> Usually the impact on people is the trickiest to assess objectively. For this reason, the customer impact and customer position are two different items.

the disruption resulting from redesigns are often underestimated. Conversely, a substitution or alternative approach could eliminate a source of conflict or risk.

Affected work authorizations must be revised to effect a change. Recognizing that a large project requires many PWAAs, rapid action is required to avoid having people working to an incorrect project plan. Figure 7.55 is an example of a major failure caused by a poorly implemented change. Use telephones or e-mail to notify all affected parties that a change is forthcoming.

QUALITY CONTROLS AND TECHNIQUES

We define "Quality" as conformance to the project's requirements. Quality is ultimately judged by the customer, not the project manager or other provider personnel. In this case the "customer" may be any person or organization in the complete provider-customer chain extending from those internal to the project to the intended user.

It is the final user who determines product or service quality, that is, fitness for use. That viewpoint encompasses ease of learning, usability, serviceability, reliability, durability, and documentation effectiveness.

NASA, Intelsat Discuss Shuttle Rescue Of Satellite Stranded In Useless Orbit

NASA and Intelsat have begun planning a space shuttle rescue mission to either retrieve or reconfigure the $157-million Intelsat 6 spacecraft that was stranded in a useless orbit Mar. 14 by a malfunction in its Titan 3 booster.

Martin Marietta has traced the failure to a design error in the wiring associated with the separation electronics on its Commercial Titan...

When the core vehicle of the Titan's second stage shut down after a normal launch from a propulsion point of view, the vehicle's computer sent a spacecraft separation command. But the mismatch between the software and the wiring resulted in a signal being sent to the wrong wiring position, and the satellite stayed locked atop the booster.

According to Martin Marietta managers, the hardware engineers were supposed to go through a formal engineering change procedure to communicate any hardware changes to the software engineers.

"The hardware guys thought they had communicated that change to the software side of the house," a Martin Marietta official said. But the communication breakdown occurred because an established change procedure was not used, the official said.

The same communications breakdown allowed the same wiring mistake to occur on the next Titan being prepared for an Intelsat launch. That vehicle is being rewired.

— *Aviation Week & Space Technology; March 26, 1990*

FIGURE 7.55   Ineffective change control.

Traditional Quality Assurance   The traditional approach to controlling quality (Figure 7.56) focuses on the results of manufacturing operations where quality is most visible. For example, product Quality Assurance consists of an organization that screens the product (perhaps at several points in the manufacturing process) for adherence to its specifications (Figure 7.57). Faulty material is rejected and dispositioned for scrap or rework—whichever is the least costly. Eventually, most design or process defects are recognized and corrected by the change control process.

A sensible and enduring standard for all industries is illustrated in Figure 7.57. Current ISO quality standards are based on these same sound concepts.

Total Quality Management (TQM)   The need to improve profitability and respond to increasing global competition

> The basic quality challenge is to produce specifications that result in a product that satisfies the customer's desires.

> In many industries, quality is considered the top competitive success factor.

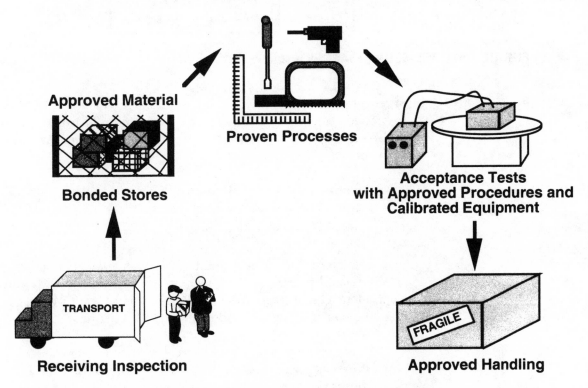

Approved Material

Bonded Stores

Proven Processes

**Acceptance Tests
with Approved Procedures and
Calibrated Equipment**

TRANSPORT

Receiving Inspection

FRAGILE

Approved Handling

FIGURE 7.56   Traditional quality assurance.

Provisions:

There should be a quality organization.

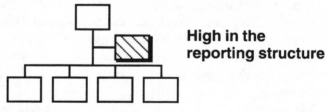

High in the reporting structure

Quality's functions should include:
- Quality Engineering
- Standards Control
- Process Control

- Inspection
- Audits

There should be a system for handling discrepancies.

Use as is

Scrap

Rework

FIGURE 7.57   MIL-STD-9858A: Still a sensible standard for all industries.

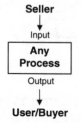

Seller

↓

Input

Any Process

Output

↓

User/Buyer

in recent years has motivated both product and service industries to broaden the scope of Quality Assurance in order to reach the entire organization at all stages of the process. Total Quality Management is:

- Required from project initiation to completion.
- Required of everyone.
- Applied to every process and transaction.

The quest for higher quality has been embodied in two closely-related practices: Total Quality Management (TQM) and Continuous Quality Improvement (CQI). Total Quality Management is a concept that is founded on the following fundamentals:

1. Everything that people can do can be described as a process which can constantly be improved. This concept, known as Continuous Quality Improvement (CQI),

emphasizes the process—the *system* for doing things—rather than the results themselves.

2. To produce satisfactory results, each individual must have clearly defined expectations.

3. The person you deliver your output to is your customer and deserves to be satisfied. Every customer has the right to reject any unsatisfactory deliverable.

Most people are unaware of their own process and therefore do not consciously attempt to improve it for the customer's benefit, as well as for their own. Creating this awareness and motivation is part of the leadership responsibility of both the project manager and the system engineering manager.

Attention to TQM principles can enhance other control techniques, notably Management By Objectives (MBO). The two concepts are complementary in the sense that TQM/CQI stresses the process while MBO stresses results.

> To the extent that the project team is aware of and accepts these fundamentals and conscientiously applies them:
>
> • Project output rises.
> • Failure rates decline.
> • Efficiency improves.

Software Quality Assurance   The Software Quality Assurance (SQA) function is responsible for auditing software development for compliance to the SQA plan. The availability of an audit trail, from automatically generated software configurations, enhances the efficiency of this audit which:

- Assures that prescribed development environment standards, procedures, and methods are being adhered to.
- Verifies process adequacy.
- Alerts the project manager to deficiencies.

TECHNICAL CONTROLS AND TECHNIQUES

The following controls expand on the basic control techniques described above. The major selection criterion for these controls is the risk associated with each technical area, regardless of the proportion of project resources it represents. In general, the value of each technique depends on the project type, the risk associated with the technologies involved, and the project complexity.

Controls Unique to Software Software-intensive projects have historically been poorly managed. We hear excuses like "I didn't change that section, so there's no need to test it." (invariably, "that section" fails because of a change in another section that was tested independently.) Worse yet is the assurance, "I only changed a few lines of code, so it was easy to verify manually."

An incident that received national attention in June 1991 provides a graphic example of the consequences of such "leaky" manual controls. The telephone service in Los Angeles and Pittsburgh was temporarily shut down. The reason turned out to be faulty software change and verification controls. A computer programmer, not understanding the potential consequences of his action, changed a few lines of code. Since only a few lines were changed, performance verification tests required by the company policy were omitted. The thirteen changed lines of software inadvertently caused the program to generate a repetitive message saying that the system required maintenance. Soon the system was swamped with such messages, blocking all calls.

Part of the problem is the intangibility of software until the code is highly functional. Other factors include the rapid change in development tools and technology, coupled with the explosive growth in size and complexity of software products. Although details of the conventions, techniques, and controls needed to manage the design process is beyond the scope of this book, the following techniques are common to most software development projects, regardless of size.

Before development is started, choices must be made among the myriad software development environments. False starts can sometimes be avoided by having this environment evaluated by an experienced expert. A Computer Resources Working Group is a name given to a panel established to judge the adequacy of the software development environment before it is implemented and at major conversions or ports.

Two major areas requiring improvement in software change controls are integration and automation. Integration refers to the combination of all source, executables, objects, graphics, documents, and other applications that are related. The Software Development Library is a controlled collection of software, documentation, test data, and associated tools that include global resources common to the entire project as well as product

> Having the development environment evaluated by an expert can avoid expensive false starts.

modules. By adding automatic generation capability, the development system supports the regeneration of any level or version. This level of automation is capable of facilitating an automated audit trail as well, fulfilling an important Quality Assurance audit requirement.

The Software Engineering Institute's Capability Maturity Model (CMM) can be used for internal and external evaluation of your software process, or that of your software suppliers. The CMM appraises the software process maturity of an organization against criteria for five escalating levels. This is discussed in more detail in Chapter 8.

Design Controls and Design Drawing Controls   Design drawings can best be formally controlled through a subprocess of baseline controls whereby all affected disciplines approve initial releases and design changes. It is also vital that affected disciplines be involved in the design process itself. Known as concurrent engineering, this process was discussed in the section on the project team.

Design must be controlled to both technical requirements and development standards. Design controls occur at several organizational levels with commensurate formality. Supervisors, being familiar with the designer, the standards, and the design interface on a daily basis can adjust review depth and frequency to match the risk. Formal design reviews are addressed in the section on control gates.

Peer reviews vary in rate and formality, from informal walk-throughs and chalk talks, to formal peer group presentations. Peer reviews can be highly effective and they can provide the additional benefit of cross training. A review board of a recent 60 million dollar project failure identified lack of effective peer review during the design evolution as a significant contributing cause.

> We strongly recommend peer review on everything of significance, even short memos.

Expert reviews usually draw on objective experts outside the project—often outside the organization. They occur less frequently than peer reviews and require considerable preparation on the part of both reviewers and the reviewed. The customer may also conduct expert reviews. The government often contracts for independent technical experts to perform on-going reviews of risky development projects.

THE CONDUCT AND RESOLUTION OF
CONTROL GATE REVIEWS

We defined Control Gates in Chapter 6 and discussed their role in managing the project cycle. Their primary control objective is to ensure that the project team has completed and has baselined all required deliverables so as to avoid progressing to a phase for which the team is unprepared.

Control Gate conduct should lead to confidence in the project's progress by being:

Honest	Constructive in challenges
Open and interactive	Mutually beneficial
Helpful and supportive	Synergistic

Control Gates – Attitudes

Adversarial　　Constructive　　Authoritative/
　　　　　　　Challenge　　　Condescending

It's easy to slip off of the best behavior.

Each control gate should be defined to the following criteria:

Purpose of the control gate	Agenda and how conducted
Host and chairperson	Evidence that is evaluated
Attendees	Actions
Location	Closure method

The control gate decision options are:

- *Acceptable*—proceed with project.
- *Acceptable with reservations*—proceed and respond to identified action items.
- *Unacceptable*—do not proceed; repeat the review.
- *Unsalvageable*—terminate the project.

Upon successful completion of a control gate review, the appropriate agreements (usually in the form of documents, products of a project cycle phase) will be added to the baseline and put under configuration control.

PROJECT CONTROL ELEMENT EXERCISE

The objective of this exercise is to provide experience in understanding proactive and reactive project control.

Most texts on project management portray project control as what to do when the project is off plan, the reactive type of control. Since it is preferable that projects be kept out of trouble, this exercise concentrates on the proactive aspects of project control.

Since controls are used to ensure responsiveness to predetermined standards they permeate all aspects of projects. Some controls are only proactive while others are both proactive and reactive. Examples are: The tachometer in your car is proactive in that it has been installed before hand and alerts you to when you are nearing the red line limit (the control standard). More modern systems now include ignition cutout to prevent violation of the red line limit, a completely proactive and reactive control system. A traffic light is only proactive while a building sprinkler system is designed to be both proactive and reactive.

Make a list of control systems that you can think of. Identify if they are only proactive or both proactive and reactive.

7. PROJECT VISIBILITY

Not only is there but one way of doing things rightly, but there is only one way of seeing them, and that is, seeing the whole of them.

John Ruskin,
The Two Paths

The lack of total visibility is obscurity, referred to by Robert A. Heinlein as the "refuge of incompetence" and by Vauve-Nargues as the "realm of error." In the project environment it is both, and consequently, a major cause of project failure.

Project visibility, as diagrammed in Figure 7.58, is the means by which project personnel and management are made aware of project activity to facilitate timely statusing and effective corrective action. While its main purpose is to lead directly to reactive management, good visibility also supports proactive management by making sure controls are in place and are effective. Visibility objectives are to:

Project Visibility is *how* you and your team know what's going on.

- Determine activity:
  —Planned tasks.
  —Unplanned tasks.

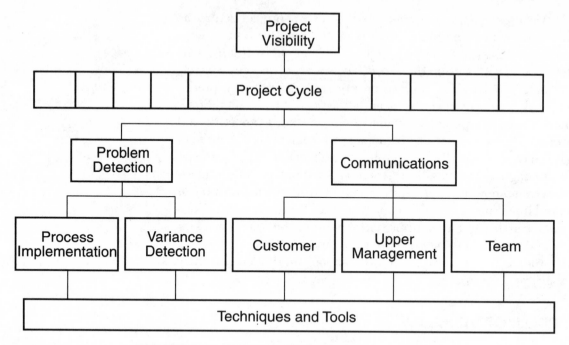

FIGURE 7.58   Project visibility decomposition.

—Work habits.

—Control process.

- Communicate—up, down, and laterally.
- Verify status—Is it as reported?
- Determine and influence morale and team spirit.

Project visibility is the implementation of information gathering techniques such as:

Meetings	Glance Management
Reports	Project Information Center
Tiger Teams	Top-Ten Problem List

These techniques are driven by the timing, need, and geographic location of the required data. They change as the project progresses through the project cycle.

GLANCE MANAGEMENT

Glance Management encompasses Management-By-Walking-Around (MBWA) and other informal techniques used for follow-up and daily awareness by an appropriate project member, particularly the project manager, chief system engineer, or experts. We chose the name to reflect a major visibility lesson learned. Far too many project failures caused by fatal problems or omissions could have been detected by a follow-up "glance" by the cognizant supervisor or expert. Experts can instantly identify small, yet critical details, not carried out correctly, that are rarely subjected to formal review—except as a part of a larger unit—which may obscure subtle deficiencies and delay their visibility to a much later event.

Glance management involves periodic sampling of work in progress by:

- Casual questions about a project detail . . . perhaps in a chance hallway meeting or in the parking lot.
- Engaging in conversations before or after meetings, or at group functions.
- Skip-level meetings—sitting in on a lower level meeting.
- Quick scans of FYI (for your information) copies of routine correspondence for key phrases.
- Maintaining a reputation for an open door and an open mind.
- MBWA—walking through the project area and actively observing.

Prior to the Challenger failure, an O-ring tiger team glanced at the booster joint design and proclaimed "wrong application of an O-ring." The O-ring was observed to be not under compression and the design allowed the O-ring groove to move and change dimension relieving the required compression of the O-ring. Although a recognized concern for almost ten years, no corrective action was taken until after the Challenger accident. Had someone used "glance management" to *initiate action* perhaps things would have turned out differently.

Management-By-Walking-Around is a visibility technique with important leadership and team building benefits. Even though its primary purpose is to improve visibility, it is useful for assessing morale and for obtaining general information. The MBWA method consists of stopping to talk while taking different routes through the project area. To promote openness, it is important to give answers to questions that may be asked and to inform the appropriate managers and supervisors of what you conveyed. But be sure to diffuse political situations and avoid immediate problem solving. Be careful not to usurp the authority you have delegated to those supporting you. Here are some MBWA guidelines and protocol:

- Make plant tours—your own facility and contractor/subcontractor facilities.
- Go where the action is.
- See and be seen.
- Observe, but do not direct.
- Talk to personnel working on your project.
- Verify status—spot check details and look for evidence of work in progress (drawings completed, software in test, parts machined).
- Use this opportunity for team building:
  —Show interest and ask people to tell you what they are doing.
  —Confirm that team members understand their part in the process.
- Carefully and decisively use the information gathered.
  —It may be used to assist the existing management in their management process or it may be used to change the existing management if they are found to be ineffective with no hope of improving.

MBWA can be especially effective when two or three work shifts are operating. The second and third shifts often feel left out of the mainstream: "Hardly anybody from day shift ever comes in." On one such project, the project manager and marketing manager, separately, made periodic visits to the work areas during second and third shifts. They were surprised by the number of valuable inputs they received. Even more surprising was the general morale improvement which even carried over to the day shift.

All glance management techniques share a common risk—giving the impression of invasive scrutiny. Everyone dislikes being interrogated or watched too closely. This is where leadership techniques come in to play. Glance management, especially MBWA, works best when visibility is both ways—when it includes recognition, praise, and casual advice—as well as questions.

THE PROJECT INFORMATION CENTER

A visibility system should include a project information center—a dedicated area or web page that displays the current status of all project activities against the plan. The use of a name like Short Cycle Room conveys an important message and is a constant reminder to project personnel of the importance of schedule (Figure 7.59).

FIGURE 7.59   A dedicated project information center.

Beware of stale data! The information center must be kept current, otherwise it is of little or even negative value.

The main benefactors of the information center are project personnel with schedule and budget responsibility and/or interest. All users benefit from this total visibility at a glance. It also provides a means for making the project more visible to stakeholders and others who may miss, or not be included in, meetings. By posting notices and selected correspondence, the observer can quickly scan for pertinent new information. The project information center is an ideal location for all-hands and project manager's reviews. On small projects, it can be the project manager's office or a conference room.

An alternative implementation method is to use a web-based information dissemination site with e-mail, baseline document libraries, and search capability. However, this approach lacks the opportunity for motivation, interaction, and cheerleading provided by a dedicated physical area.

TIGER TEAMS PROVIDE FOCUSED VISIBILITY ON CONCERNS

To maximize chances for success, the project team must be educated as to the purpose, methods, and expected positive use of Tiger Teams.

Tiger teams provide focused visibility on identified areas of concern. Usually composed of experts and/or experienced troubleshooters, their purpose is to objectively identify the problem sources and to recommend solutions. Solution implementation is the responsibility of the project team. While anybody can suggest the need for a tiger team, they are usually initiated by the project manager, upper management, the customer, or functional managers.

Typical Areas of Concern:
Design approach.
Interface compatibility.
Software approach.
Schedule approach.
Failures.
Management approach.
Quality.
Cost.
Personnel turnover.

Participants

Project personnel and invited experts with a demonstrated ability to accumulate the facts rapidly, objectively evaluate the status and impartially report their findings. Participants may include:

> Seller and/or buyer personnel.
>
> Outside consultants.
>
> Customer experts.

Tiger team members should be experts and "quick studies."

Benefits

Objective visibility on an area of concern.

Focused approach to improve performance.

Third-party assistance in securing increased resources.

Tiger team follow-up on success of recommendations.

Precautions

- Expected use of tiger teams should be publicized by project management at the outset and during the course of the project.
- Tiger teams must operate in a team (not adversarial) relationship with the project team.
- Tiger teams must have "free rein."
- Project manager must stay aware and support both project and tiger team personnel.

Tiger teams are for fixing problems, NOT for fixing blame.

MEETINGS—THE PROJECT MANAGER'S DILEMMA

Whether one-on-one or involving the entire project, meetings are a significant technique for gathering, and disseminating information. As such they can easily consume 40 percent to 60 percent of a project manager's time. Meetings are the major vehicle for performing many management roles:

Some informational objectives are better handled by other visibility techniques such as informal discussions, a telephone call, or a memo.

Informational	Interpersonal	Decisional
Gathering	Motivating	Investigating
Disseminating	Inspiring	Consensus making
Clarifying	Praising	Evaluating
Training	Committing	Decision making

High value meetings are critical to project success. However, expensive meetings that just waste the team's time can result in decreased morale. For meetings to be effective, they must serve a specific, well-defined purpose.[34] Too many meetings and poorly conceived and poorly executed ones, can be a major demotivator. When considering whether or not to hold a meeting, ask:

- What is the objective of the meeting?
- Is there a better way to achieve the objective?
- Is this meeting really necessary?
- What would be the consequences of not holding it?
- How to mitigate the consequences?

We will return to the interpersonal and decisional meeting aspects in the section on Leadership, along with the "how" to ensure meeting productivity. In the meantime, here's a summary of recommended conduct:

- Distribute an agenda well before the meeting.
- Invite only those required.
- State the purpose of the meeting and stick to it:
  —Exchange information.
  —Determine status.
  —Solve a problem.
  —Make a decision.
- Start on time—don't wait for late people.
- Keep the meeting on track and control the progress.
- Summarize the results and assign action items.
- Follow-up on action items.
- Ensure that all meetings are summarized including those you are not responsible for.

Informational Meetings   An informational meeting is the opportunity to update the team's collective knowledge and to inform other stakeholders. This knowledge includes perceptions and experiences as well as facts. As with traditional staff meetings, a series of smaller, nested meetings can be effective in matching the information range and depth of detail to the particular group. Examples of informational meetings are:

Type	Frequency	Typical Duration
News Flash	daily	10 to 15 minutes
All-hands	as required	several minutes to 20 minutes
One-on-one	weekly	one hour
Plan Violators	weekly	less than 30 minutes
Project Manager's Review	weekly	two hours
Executive Review	monthly or quarterly	one to two hours
Customer Review	monthly	varies widely

News Flash Meetings   News flash meetings are used to maintain a high profile for fast-moving developments and critical issues. Problems requiring immediate action are continued following adjournment. News flash meetings work best with a small group—usually the direct reports to the project manager. Some managers prefer that all participants remain standing throughout to instill urgency and discourage long-winded discussions. Others prefer to assign seats, making it easier to know who, or what organizations, are unrepresented and also to locate adversaries adjacent to one another.

> News flash meetings are most effective when conducted daily at the start of each shift or a few minutes before the lunch break.

The typical agenda is:

- What did not happen as planned?
- What action is required?
- What is not going to happen as planned?
- What action is required?
- What help is required of management?

All-Hands Meetings   All-hands meetings involve a larger group—usually the entire project team. Attendance by key personnel is mandatory. These meetings are typically convened to announce a major development such as a new contract, a technical breakthrough, or the need for extra effort. They offer a good opportunity for team building.

One-on-One Meetings   One-on-one meetings should be held weekly by every supervisor with each direct report to exchange information and deal with personal and performance issues. They are most effective when time limited. Therefore, the employee needs to prepare a priority list to ensure that the high priority items get addressed before the time limit is exceeded.

Headcount variance is often the earliest indicator of more serious problems.

Plan Violator Meetings   Plan violator meetings are held by the project manager to gain visibility and determine corrective action for areas not on plan. The manager that, for the prior week, is off schedule, headcount, or budget plan attends them. The violation, the cause, and proposed recovery are reviewed. Subsequent meetings update the recovery process. The business manager sets the variance threshold that triggers this meeting. The major benefits are:

- Causes task managers to pay attention to the plan.
- Provides review of previous week's headcount and schedule performance immediately following completion of the work week.
- Provides for prompt response to new problems.
- Keeps budget and schedule plans current.
- Keeps management knowledgeable.
- Lets the team know that you are watching and that you really care.

Project Manager's Weekly Review   The Project Manager's Weekly Review meeting extends beyond visibility to active statusing and corrective action. It involves all key project and functional support personnel. This meeting should be open to executive management as well as customer personnel. The agenda includes a thorough review of the status of the total project to surface conflict, areas of inaction, items awaiting disposition, and areas requiring special attention. The results include decisive actions by project management. The benefits include:

- Overall view of the project.
- Forum for organizational interaction to resolve project issues.
- Insight for support managers into project needs.

- Visibility into top project issues, concerns, and problems for all key participants.

Executive Management Review   The Executive Management Review is to provide upper management visibility into the status of the project. It usually consists of a presentation by the project's management on the overall health of the project. The format emphasizes accomplishments, particularly regarding contract requirements, and the efficient use of resources. This review is the opportunity for the project manager to alert executive management to bad news, potential risks, contingency plans or corrective action, and any additional resources required.

Customer Review   The purpose of the Customer Review is to provide the customer an opportunity for constructive challenge of the progress against plan. This applies equally well to contract customers and to internal customers—namely, marketing. This review can be avoided altogether, or reduced in content, by including the customer in the weekly Project Manager's Review. As with the Executive Review, key project team members present status against plan, problems analysis and recovery actions for problems, and seek concurrence from the customer as to the approach. Well-run projects routinely generate the type of data needed for this meeting, therefore, little new material needs to be prepared.

TECHNIQUES FOR ENHANCING VISIBILITY

Top-Ten Problem List   A Top-Ten Problem List heightens the visibility of the most important concerns of the customer, the project manager, functional managers, and task managers. These problems should to be coded by each identifier as:

> Publicize names of owners of the Top-Ten problems. It will help them get the priority they need.

- Minor—I'm in control.
- Major—I need help.
- Showstopper—emergency action required.

All problems on the Top-Ten List need to be statused daily by the responsible individual. The list is initiated by the task managers and propagates upward. The project manager's list should include majors and showstoppers that reach that level as well as pertinent items from the customer's list.

Use the Walls   Walls are an excellent display board for documentation review (RFP, proposals, user manuals, etc.) or design drawings. Use colored paper to indicate maturity (white for first draft, yellow for second, blue for the third). This technique has several benefits:

- Entire team has visibility.
- Helps identify inconsistencies, overlap, and so on.
- Highlights missing sections.
- Vividly illustrates document maturity and status.

Project Coordinators   Project Coordinators augment the project manager's visibility for larger projects. A coordinator is chartered as a representative of the project manager and proactively ensures future events will occur as planned. They signal problem areas and recommend solutions. Project Coordinators:

- Know how the organization "works."
- Provide expediting help to project and support organizations.
- Provide independent assessment of project information and status to the project manager.
- Ensure planning and milestones are satisfied.
- Ensure control procedures are being adhered to.

Customer Inplant Representatives   Customer inplant representatives reside with the supplier project team and provide two-way visibility because they:

- Understand customer expectations, needs, and capabilities.
- Provide continuous visibility into supplier and subcontractor activity and status.

The latter is accomplished by attending all inplant visibility meetings and by other techniques such as MBWA. The techniques of glance management are particularly pertinent to customer visibility. A customer inplant representative can address items that require guidance from the customer by immediately consulting with customer personnel. A secondary benefit is the escorting and briefing of customer visitors and their contacts.

TWENTY-FIRST CENTURY VISIBILITY TOOLS

Visibility tools include traditional devices and services such as:

—Telephone	—Cellular phone
—Teleconferencing	—Video conferencing
—E-mail	—Fax
—Courier services	—Mail
—Internet	

The last item in the first column, the Internet, will become perhaps the most important of all. Gates thinks so.[35] So do some project managers keeping abreast of a variety of projects overseas from their U.S.-based office. Photographs, taken twice a day with a digital camera, and sent daily via the internet, keep the team informed of progress, and provide focused visibility on trouble spots. The personal computers, together with local, wide-area networks, and the Internet have grown into powerful visibility tools.

WHEN DESIGNING YOUR VISIBILITY SYSTEM . . .

Keep an open door and an open mind. The concept of visibility cannot coexist with significant secrecy, avoidance, or exclusion. Yet these can take root and grow—particularly in the absence of strong leadership. The project manager needs to set an example by being open and willing to seek and accept expert advice, as well as bad news.

Avoid information overload. While it is better to be over-informed rather than under-informed, carried to the extreme, extraneous information causes overload and missed details.

Be selective. A visibility system can incorporate many techniques and tools. You need to determine the timing, critical need, and geographic location of the required information

> Visibility is only the beginning. The visibility system must lead to statusing and timely corrective action.

before designing and implementing the system you will use. These factors, and therefore the techniques, will generally change as the project progresses through its phases. It is important to carefully select the most cost-effective techniques and tools that get the job done.

PROJECT VISIBILITY EXERCISE

The real message of managing project information is not that "Information is power" but that "Shared information is empowerment." That is, the purpose for which project information is collected and disseminated is to enable those who can help the project manager successfully manage the project. The real issue with Project Visibility management from the perspective of a project manager is deciding what information is needed, when, in what format, and by whom in order to efficiently manage the project.

The purpose of this exercise is to design a project information system for a project that answers the following key questions:

- What information is needed?
- When is it needed?
- In what format is it needed?
- Who needs it?

Answer the questions for the following situation:

You've just been asked to plan this year's annual family reunion and picnic for all 95 of you. You've got to find the location, pick the time, notify everyone, feed that group, make sure the games and entertainment come off as planned, and especially make sure that Uncle Louie and Aunt Susan don't get stranded at the airport without a ride like they did last year. You know that Grandma will want to offer advice on the food even though she won't be doing any cooking and Uncle Fred always has ideas for games, some of which need to be tempered a bit. The football game last year was fun but did end in two sprained ankles and some hard feelings over the "enthusiasm" showed by Fred and Jan when they tackled people. Your two siblings have offered to help, Jack with the cooking and beverages, and Claire with the games. Claire's son, Ed, is old enough to drive and is a responsible young man.

As a way of starting this exercise, consider first what you want to control on the project. Project information should tell you if your control mechanisms are working or not. Information that doesn't help you or someone else control the project or parts of the project, is often either not useful or points to some aspect of the project about which you're concerned and for which you should have put a control mechanism in place. After considering areas to be controlled, consider the stakeholders and identify their roles and responsibilities. Use the items to be controlled and the list of stakeholders with their roles and responsibilities to begin to create the project information management plan. Note that in the case of the picnic the tools may be limited to e-mails, phone calls, a note to grandma, and a kitchen bulletin board but the principles apply to projects of all sizes and complexity.

8. PROJECT STATUS

Nothing is good or bad but by comparison.

Thomas Fuller,
Gnomologia

STATUS IS MEASUREMENT AGAINST THE PLAN

Project Statusing is the timely and comprehensive measurement of project progress against the plan to determine the potential seriousness of any variances left uncorrected. The main objective is to identify variances that require corrective action in order to recover to plan. To initiate corrective action quickly when deviations occur, the measurements must be:

- Relevant,
- Timely,
- Accurate,
- Comprehensive, and
- Compared to the plan.

> Statusing must accurately reflect reality against the plan—not how busy the project is.

In practice, many "status" reports merely recount activity, in which the intensity of the work reported is confused with progress.

Project activity without comparison to the plan may well be irrelevant, or even diversionary, to determining the need for corrective action. For example, the project manager may proclaim the team's long work hours and describe their dedicated efforts—even detailed work activities. Such reporting is often confused with statusing and contributes to information overload.

An effective statusing process:

- Collects performance of critical metrics—matched to project complexity and risk,
- Compares actual to plan,
- Tailors information to the needs of the team members interpreting it.

Status should be continuously known by task managers and their management—by all levels of project management. Others who can affect project success, such as customers, subcontractors, and vendors, should be statused as to their critical obligations. Brief monthly status reports for distribution to executive management and functional support managers are a powerful communication device for the project manager and the project team. Like many major corporations, Microsoft uses e-mail to distribute and comment on the monthly project status reports, and Gates and other top executives review them in appropriate detail. Gates reviews a hundred or so projects each month, and he "especially looks for schedule slips, cutting too many product features, or the need to change a specification."[36] The project manager creates the monthly status reports for management based on detailed knowledge of the project status. This section discusses the techniques and tools the project manager must have to maintain the daily awareness needed to effectively lead the project to a successful conclusion.

STATUS MEANS SCHEDULE, TECHNICAL, COST, AND BUSINESS—COMBINED

Conducting independent cost reviews is meaningless and can even be counterproductive.

Schedule, Technical, Cost, and Business factors should be evaluated together. The following lists are representative of the key metrics to be considered in each of the four factors. Not all are recommended or required since many are redundant.

Schedule

Progress summary
Master Schedule
Milestone accomplishments
Earned value
Assemblies and modules
Tasls
Subcontractors
Parts and material

Technical

Development results
Design release
Technical review (closure on action items)
Technical Performance Measurements
Interface control
 Quality
Design change rate

Cost

Actuals versus budget
Headcount
Earned value vs. expenditures
Burn rate and overtime ratio
Estimate to completion
Estimate at completion
Profit
Dispersion ratio°

Business

Contract change process
Actions to/from customers
Actions to/from management
Actions to/from contractors
Funding
Top-ten problems
Security clearances
Project manager's assessment

CONDUCTING THE MAJOR REVIEWS

This section addresses the details of format and agenda for the three reviews that facilitate the bulk of reactive management decisions. Detailed statusing does occur in smaller meetings—even one-on-ones—where corrective actions are sometimes decided. However, the Project Manager's Review is the best opportunity for all relevant stones to be overturned and assumptions to be challenged. The Executive and Customer Reviews have two purposes: to aid visibility and provide a forum for corrective actions that need higher level management or customer concurrence and support. Figure 7.60 provides a checklist for conducting these meetings.

These three important reviews can represent a significant expenditure of team time and effort. They should be working meetings to avoid wasting time, particularly the replaying of carefully rehearsed scenarios.

° Dispersion ratio refers to the equivalent full-time headcount divided by the number of different individuals charging to the project.

	Project Manager	Customer	Executive
General announcements	✓	✓	✓
Awards	✓		✓
Past and future meetings	✓	✓	✓
Organization (optional)		✓	✓
System concept overview (optional)		✓	✓
Action items from the customer	✓	✓	✓
Action items from upper management	✓		✓
Internal project action items	✓		
Master schedule with dateline and status	✓	✓	✓
Project milestone status	✓	✓	✓
Major accomplishments since last review	✓	✓	✓
Major customer-directed change status	✓	✓	✓
Engineering change request status	✓	✓	✓
Items awaiting customer disposition	✓	✓	✓
Top ten problem review	✓	✓	✓
Interface control action item status	✓	✓	✓
System engineering detailed status	✓	✓	
Technical Performance Measurement status	✓	✓	✓
Engineering release status	✓	✓	✓
Subsystem detailed status	✓	✓	
—component by component status			
—milestones accomplished vs. plan			
—funds expended versus plan			
Contractor/Subcontractor technical status	✓	✓	✓
Contractor/Subcontractor key milestones	✓	✓	✓
Contractor/Subcontractor detailed status by item	✓		
—Budget, EAC, Variance			
Top level cost performance vs. budget	✓	✓	✓
Financial status—top level	✓	✓	✓
—Budget, EAC, Variance			
Plan for handling the reported variances		✓	✓
Manpower status vs. plan—top level	✓	✓	✓
Funding status		✓	✓
Management reserve			✓
Profit analysis		if internal	✓
Summary of new action items	✓	✓	✓
Key milestones for next 6 months	✓	✓	✓
Calendar of planned meetings	✓	✓	✓
Future business opportunities	✓	if internal	✓
Project manager's assessment		✓	✓
Customer's closing comments		✓	

FIGURE 7.60   Typical status agenda checklist.

The typical symbols used for displaying schedule status are shown in Figure 7.61. To avoid wasted motion, however, learn to use the graphics format built into your scheduling software. This will reduce or eliminate the need to recreate data for management reporting.

STATUSING IS IDENTIFYING VARIANCES

The quantity of milestones can be used as a schedule performance metric (Figure 7.62a). The Milestone Deficiency Report (Figure 7.62b) should include an Estimated Completion Date (ECD) and a recommended corrective action for each milestone that is past due. This way of highlighting exceptions, problems,

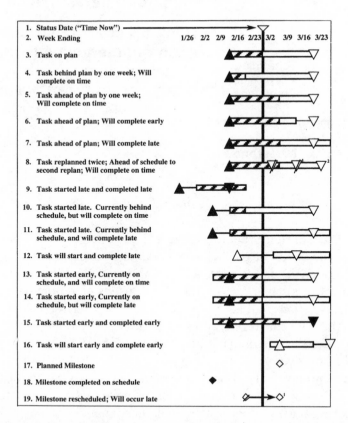

FIGURE 7.61 Typical symbols for reporting schedule status.

Milestone Status

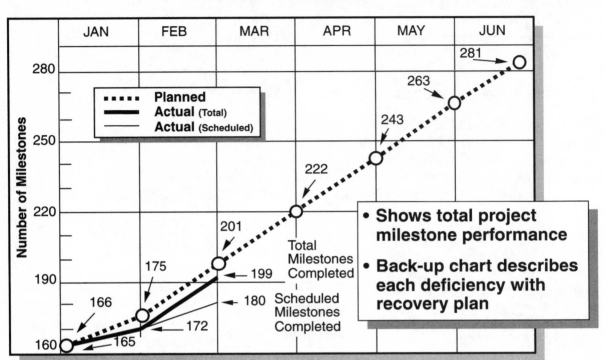

FIGURE 7.62a Milestone status report.

and actions is very effective for most status measurements and reporting.

The Configuration Item Status Report (Figure 7.63) demonstrates the utility of pulling together and focusing on the tasks related to each deliverable and combined schedule, cost, and technical reporting. Again, statusing consists of reporting exceptions and actions, not activities.

Material shortages represent another critical item to status shown here as a summary only (Figure 7.64). A separate sheet should be devoted to detailing each problem. Detail should include a summary of actions completed and remaining actions.

Before we cover several comprehensive metrics for statusing project cost, we will look at a simple headcount cost indicator for payroll-intensive projects (Figure 7.65). As with other areas, there

Milestone Deficiencies

Date Due	Project	M.S. No.	M.S. Title	Responsible	ECD	Plan
26 June	AJAX	SE-011	Release of Sys/Segment Design Document	R. Smith	3 Aug	Revisit trade studies per action item 1072
27 June	AJAX	SE-012	Interface Spec.	H. James	10 Jul	Close TBDs from Associate

FIGURE 7.62b Milestone Deficiency Report.

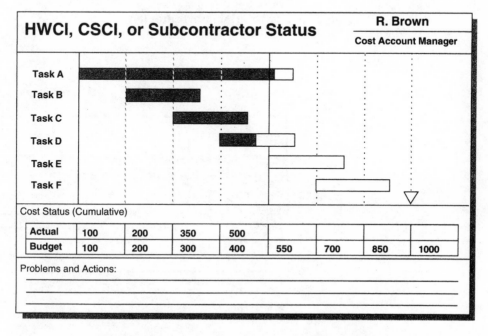

FIGURE 7.63 Configuration Item Status Report.

Part Number	Part Type	Quantity	Vendor	Next Assembly	Need Date	Prom Date	Resp. Individ.	Action
103-231	Elect.	42	Viking	1040	26 Sep	10 Oct	Fred H.	Visit vendor factory to pick up parts in person; daily phone calls to verify progress of tab and test of parts
621-040	Firm-ware	1	S/W Creations	7131	26 Sep	15 Oct	Jenny C.	Firmware coding requirements clarification to be delivered to vendor by 10 Sept. Check out tests to be witnessed by our QA and engineering at vendor facility.

The last part in paces the project.

FIGURE 7.64 Material shortgage list.

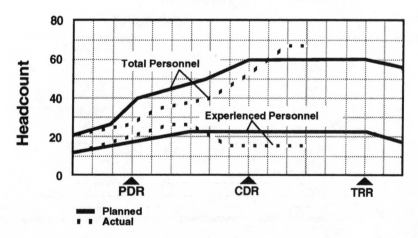

FIGURE 7.65 Headcount variance report.

are several formats and metrics for statusing headcount. Typical parameters include part-time headcount ratios, on-loan, and specific skill levels.

In this example, the project manager can use Total and Experienced headcount metrics to anticipate efficiency, cost, and schedule problems, because:

- Total personnel are exceeding plan.
- Experienced personnel are under plan.

With these expectations, the project manager needs to rebalance personnel through the functional managers and/or experienced contract resources.

The Top Ten Problem Summary (Figure 7.66) offers a means to highlight major problems which may result from a combination of factors. The summary should include the estimated completion date (ECD), the number of weeks on the list, and identify who is

Top Ten Problem Summary

No.	Problem Identification	Description	ECD	No. Weeks on list	Action/ Responsibility
71.	Update Project Products List (PPL)	Incorporate the changes from Rev A drawing release into the PPL	~~6/17,~~ ~~6/29,~~ ~~7/3,~~ 8/4	4	Frank A.
84.	Compatibility of SW with Rev A mechanical design	Ensure that software control system functions properly with Rev A mechanical modifications	8/1	1	Rich B.

◤——— **Detail Chart for each problem**

FIGURE 7.66   Top ten problem summary.

responsible for each action. A detailed chart should cover actions competed to date and actions planned with dates.

USING TPMS AND MARGIN MANAGEMENT TO OBTAIN TECHNICAL STATUS

Figures 7.62 through 7.65 display schedule performance against the plan, but they presume that the technical objective of the project will be achieved if the milestones are reached. For many projects where the technical issues are routine, such as in building a conventional house or revising a store layout, timely and successful accomplishment of technical objectives may be the only technical indicator needed.

In many new developments, however, more detailed technical statusing is needed to give early warning of design problems. For instance, if the integrated product team (IPT) responsible for performance of a new laptop computer decides to use a high-speed computer chip to meet their objectives, the higher heat load could force the IPT responsible for thermal control to use a larger cooling fan, which impacts system weight, physical volume, and power requirements, and so on. Cascading impacts such as this occur in almost every new design, and the risk of final system non-performance is managed by establishing reasonable subsystem or component margins early in the design process. The project team needs to identify the driving technical parameters of their system (weight, average power, peak power, thermal control, memory capacity, processing speed, system size, etc.). These key parameters are the technical performance measurement (TPM) set used to status and manage the technical development.

The microrover flight experiment on the Mars Pathfinder Project made very effective use of the TPM concept.[37] In their report the authors note that "by tracking the microrover's TPMs, the task manager gained insight into whether the delivered product will meet its performance requirements. There are several methods by which to track TPMs (i.e., system technical resources) and the task manager chose the time-phased margin management method. . . . The margin requirement is . . . expressed as a percentage of the TPM's allocation that declines toward zero over the design and development cycle. One of the advantages of margin management is that it allows management-by-exception—that is, so long as a TPM like mass has an actual margin that exceeds the requirement, specific risk management action is usually not needed."

Figure 7.67 illustrates one of the TPMs (mass) used on the microrover project (the team ultimately kept track of nine TPMs). The design margin requirement (established using the good judgment and experience of the team) started at 15 percent when the design was immature. It then dropped stepwise from 10 percent to 5 and finally to 1 percent, as the design details matured. As shown, at CDR (critical design review) in February 1994 the system design was in a risk zone because the 11 percent actual margin was below the 15 percent margin requirement. Six months later the best estimate indicated that the mass margin had fallen below the desired 10 percent limit, and weight reduction actions initiated at CDR were intensified. By February 1995

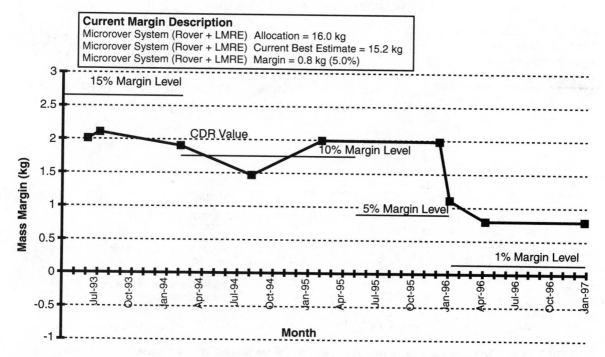

FIGURE 7.67 Example of a technical performance measurement (TPM) status chart (microrover mass).

the design modifications succeeded in recovering to the desired margin. When the now mature system was evaluated in April 1996 the margin was 4 percent, well above the minimum margin target of 1 percent. Early action 20 months before (in August 1994) prevented a crisis late in the system development.

The microrover team highlighted several lessons learned. "First, it was very useful to begin tracking TPMs *early* even though there were changes in the TPMs included and their allocations. . . . Second, TPM/margin management was one of the most cost-effective risk management methods for the microrover flight experiment. A collection of simple graphical displays made it extremely easy to see whether technical problems were looming. . . . Third, . . . the right number of TPMs to track in low-cost, high-risk . . . projects is small, but . . . should include key parameters used in any operations . . . ."

PERFORMANCE MEASUREMENT SYSTEMS QUANTIFY THE SERIOUSNESS OF THE VARIANCES

> Meaningful statusing depends on accurate and complete information.

Unless you are an accountant it is very hard to see trends in tabular data. With graphical displays significant items become vivid, and trivial data are appropriately obscured. Tufte, in his excellent work on the visual display of data,[38] has two figures that emphasize the value of graphics in detecting trends (Figure 7.68a and

I		II		III		IV	
X	Y	X	Y	X	Y	X	Y
10.0	8.04	10.0	9.14	10.0	7.46	8.0	6.58
8.0	6.95	8.0	8.14	8.0	6.77	8.0	5.76
13.0	7.58	13.0	8.74	13.0	12.74	8.0	7.71
9.0	8.81	9.0	8.77	9.0	7.11	8.0	8.84
11.0	8.33	11.0	9.26	11.0	7.81	8.0	8.47
14.0	9.96	14.0	8.10	14.0	8.84	8.0	7.04
6.0	7.24	6.0	6.13	6.0	6.08	8.0	5.25
4.0	4.26	4.0	3.10	4.0	5.39	19.0	12.50
12.0	10.84	12.0	9.13	12.0	8.15	8.0	5.56
7.0	4.82	7.0	7.26	7.0	6.42	8.0	7.91
5.0	5.68	5.0	4.74	5.0	5.73	8.0	6.89

N = 11
mean of X's = 9.0
mean of Y's = 7.5
equation of regression line: Y = 3+0.5X
standard error of estimate of slope = 0.118
t = 4.24
sum of squares X − $\overline{X}$ = 110.0
regression sum of squares = 27.50
residual sum of squares of Y = 13.75
correlation coefficient = .82
r^2 = .67

FIGURE 7.68a   Anscombe's quartet: All four of these data sets are described by exactly the same linear model. (Used by permission. © Edward Tufte, *The Visual Display of Quantitative Data*, Graphics Press, 1983.)

7.68b). He also warns against plotting data if it has no significance, as shown in Figure 7.68c.

In his 1997 book, *Visual Explanations,* Tufte revisits the information presented to the Launch Review Board on the night before the fatal 1986 space shuttle Challenger launch.[39] He makes a strong case that the way the data were displayed obscured significant facts. In fairness to the engineers involved, o-ring temperature had not been a focus in the prior studies, and the presentation was assembled in a short time. Still it is worth reviewing Tufte's displays; think about how better display of information could help you on your projects.

Formal Performance Measurement Systems like Earned Value quantify the seriousness of the problems you should have known about and acted on much earlier. Performance measurement

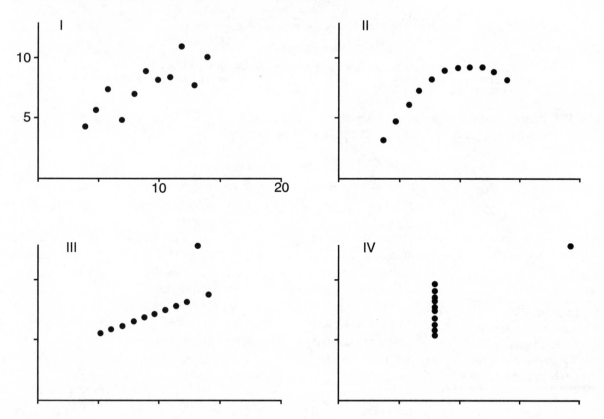

FIGURE 7.68b   Graphical display. (Used by permission. © Edward Tufte, *The Visual Display of Quantitative Data,* Graphics Press, 1983.)

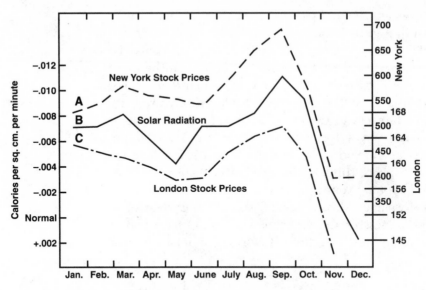

Solar Radiation and Stock Prices

A. New York stock prices (Barron's average), B. Solar Radiation, inverted,
and C. London stock prices, all by month, 1929 (after Garcia-Mara and
Shaffner)

FIGURE 7.68c   Solar radiation and stock prices. (Used by permission. © Edward Tufte, *The Visual Display of Quantitative Data,* Graphics Press, 1983.)

Garbage in—Garbage out.
Meaningful statusing
depends on good planning.
Poorly planned projects
simply cannot be statused.

systems vary widely, depending on the organization's management information system and the techniques and tools available to the project. In rapid growth years, many companies—especially technology startups where cost to capture a market is of little concern—use crude, informal systems. Figure 7.69 illustrates a cost status chart which fails to provide sufficient detail to decide on corrective action because schedule performance and technical milestone achievements are not included.

As competition increases and profit margins shrink, most organizations recognize the need to refine their performance measurements. Some commercial companies and many government agencies and their contractors use a system similar in framework to the one we describe here. This type of system requires detailed planning to predict cost and schedule expectations for each task. The insight provided is worth the effort, if the data are constructively used. In our experience, they've proved their value on projects with a budget as small as $500K.

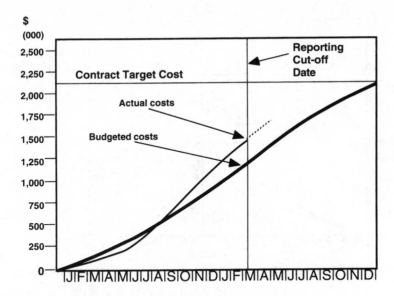

FIGURE 7.69   Superficial cost status.

The performance measurement system elements shown in Figure 7.70 are defined below.

BCWS	Budgeted Cost of Work Scheduled	The planned budget for the scheduled work.
BCWP	Budgeted Cost of Work Performed	The planned budget for the completed work.
		This is also referred to as the Earned Value.
ACWP	Actual Cost of Work Performed	Actual costs of performing the completed work.
BAC	Budget at Completion	The planned budget for all the work (a management reserve is often subtracted from the contracted or committed funding to arrive at a project budget).
EAC	Estimate At Completion.	Estimated total cost upon work completion
ETC	Estimate To Complete.	Estimated remaining costs to complete the work.

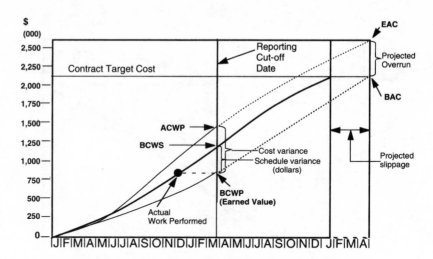

FIGURE 7.70   Performance measurement system elements.

Cost and Schedule variances can both be expressed as dollars or percentage. Using the definitions below, negative indicates an overrun.

	In Dollars	*In Percent*
Cost variance	BCWP − ACWP	(BCWP − ACWP)/BCWP × 100
Schedule variance	BCWP − BCWS	(BCWP − BCWS)/BCWS × 100

    The alternative methods for ETC (Estimate To Complete) and EAC (Estimate At Completion) are:

> Performance projections
> Managerial judgment
> Bottom up (grass roots)
> Statistical projections

Performance projections assume that performance will continue at the same rate:

$$ETC = (BAC − BCWP) \times (ACWP/BCWP)$$

$$EAC = ACWP + ETC$$

Managerial projections for ETC are a matter of judgment. Typical methods are:

- Original budget plan to go (if original plan is valid).
- Current burn rate multiplied by the estimated time to complete (if these factors are reliable).
- Burn rate multiplied by schedule slip plus the original plan including normal personnel roll-off for project shut down.
- Performance factor multiplied by the original budget plan to go (if efficiency rate is expected to continue).
- New bottom-up quote (scrubbed) (if time permits since personnel will stop work to produce it).
- The EAC (Estimate At Completion) is determined by adding the ETC to ACWP (Actual Cost of Work Performed).

There are several negotiable options for measuring work progress, expressed as the Earned Value (BCWP) by task. Four common definitions are listed below:

Option	Amount of Task BCWP (earned value)
0–100	Zero until task completion (For this method, work packages should be small, probably less than 100 hours). Distortion occurs since earned value is zero up until the task is complete.
50–50	One-half of Task BAC at start; final one-half is earned at completion. Distortion occurs since earned value is 50 percent at start with no work actually accomplished.
Percentage	Percentage of Task BAC based on interim milestones or task leader's estimate. (BCWP at completion = Task BAC) (for this method work packages can be 2 to 3 times larger than those for the 0–100 option) Lowest level of distortion.
Level-of-Effort	BWCP is earned as effort is expended (BCWP = BCWS at any time). Used for level of effort tasks (should not exceed 10 to 15 percent of the total contract value).

The 0–100 method is effective for small work packages. On large projects there is a significant administrative effort required to manage the individual task cost accounts.

These examples of using the 0–100 and Percentage Earned Value (Figure 7.71) are shown here for the same three tasks. The

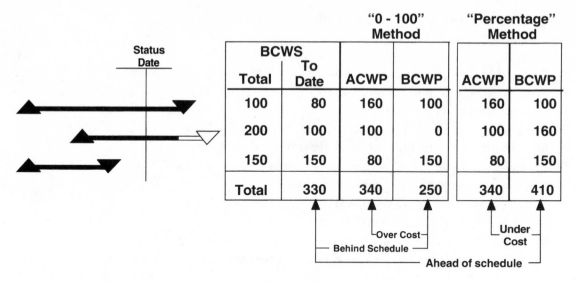

FIGURE 7.71   The 0–100 and percentage methods compared.

The percentage method based on milestone accomplishment is as accurate as 0–100 and it requires fewer charge numbers.

Interim milestones increase measurement accuracy.

Earned Value of the 0–100 option is distorted, since the second task is incomplete at the status date. The task Earned Value being zero makes the total look like bad news. In reality, the news is good. For the 0–100 method to be effective, the tasks should start and end within the reporting period so unfinished tasks will not distort the status.

The percentage example shows a more accurate status. With this method, the data reliability depends on the task leader's ability to accurately assess status of work progress. The preferred approach is to set milestones with accomplishment values and earned value is accrued when milestones are satisfied eliminating the need to estimate percent complete.

INTERPRETING THE TRENDS

In the previous sections, we selected charts that exemplify the key factors to status. These illustrations also provide a template which is adaptable to most projects. The performance of individual work packages is summed up to measure the aggregate performance of major WBS elements and the overall project. But status shouldn't be static. You need to pay careful attention to the trends, such as those in Figure 7.72, which can be leading indicators of trouble.

Two helpful indicators for trend analysis are CPI and SPI:

- CPI (Cost Performance Index) = BCWP/ACWP
- SPI (Schedule Performance Index) = BCWP/BCWS

These are interpreted in eight separate performance trend examples (Figure 7.73).

Timely, comprehensive project status information is important because it enables you to identify variances and quantify their seriousness. Differences between planned and actual results need to be reviewed on at least a monthly basis. Variances that exceed predetermined thresholds should be analyzed further to determine the reasons and the actions required to improve performance and recover to plan. The thresholds depend on the specific metrics. Example thresholds are:

$$\pm20\% \text{ and } \pm\$20K \text{ for the current period}$$

$$\pm10\% \text{ and } \pm\$40K \text{ for cumulative amounts}$$

Variance analysis reports need to be specific as to variance cause. The excerpt in Figure 7.74 illustrates the status for an example

> If you can't measure it, you can't manage it!

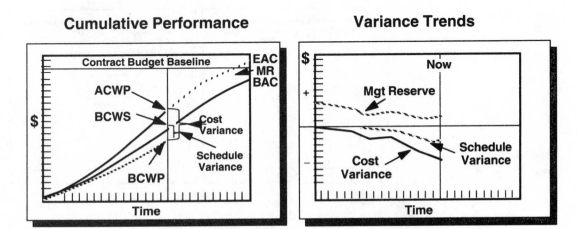

FIGURE 7.72 Trends provide leading indicators.

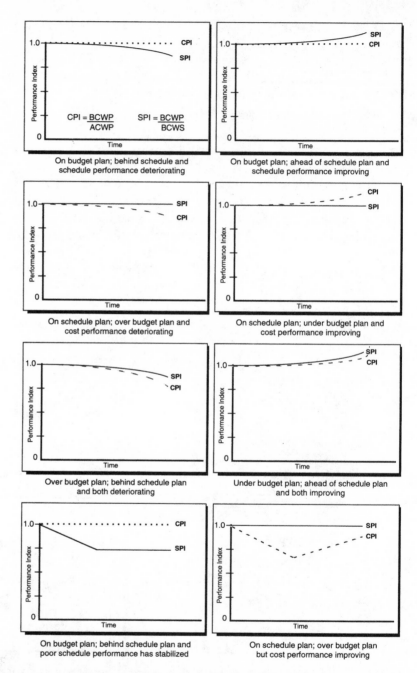

FIGURE 7.73   CPI and SPI trend analyses.

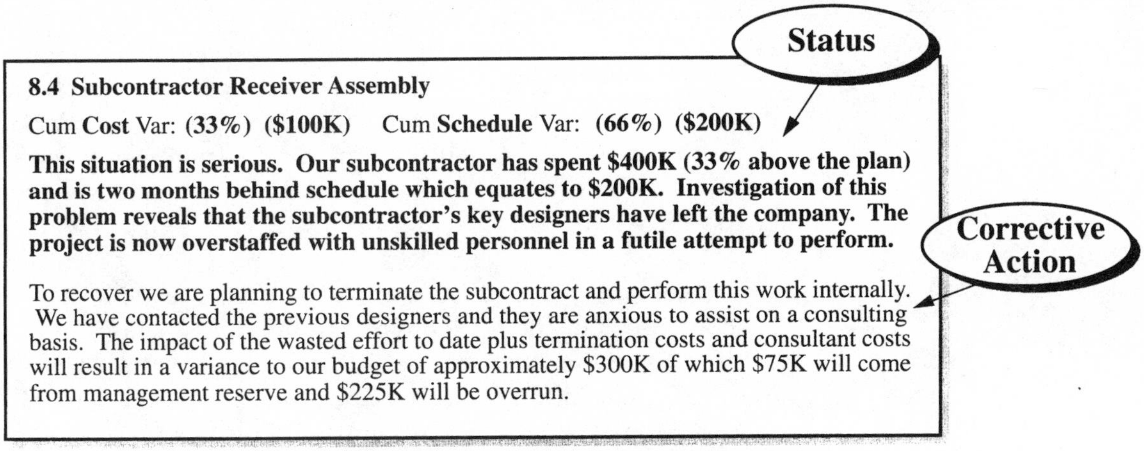

Status

8.4 Subcontractor Receiver Assembly

Cum **Cost** Var: **(33%)** **($100K)**   Cum **Schedule** Var: **(66%)** **($200K)**

This situation is serious. Our subcontractor has spent $400K (33% above the plan) and is two months behind schedule which equates to $200K. Investigation of this problem reveals that the subcontractor's key designers have left the company. The project is now overstaffed with unskilled personnel in a futile attempt to perform.

Corrective Action

To recover we are planning to terminate the subcontract and perform this work internally. We have contacted the previous designers and they are anxious to assist on a consulting basis. The impact of the wasted effort to date plus termination costs and consultant costs will result in a variance to our budget of approximately $300K of which $75K will come from management reserve and $225K will be overrun.

FIGURE 7.74   Status report example.

task, together with the corrective actions, the subject of the next section.

9. CORRECTIVE ACTION

A thought which does not result in an action is nothing much, and an action which does not proceed from a thought is nothing at all.

Georges Bernanos,
France Before the World of Tomorrow

CORRECTIVE ACTIONS ARE TAKEN TO FIX VARIANCES

Corrective Actions are the good and necessary reactive management steps to correct unacceptable variances detected (usually through statusing techniques) (Figure 7.74). Status without following through with corrective action is meaningless. Therefore, the process described in this section—corrective actions—usually takes place as a result of statusing.

There are many pressures to keep a project on schedule, and corrective actions are sometimes not applied because to implement appropriate action could cause unacceptable delay. Engineers were not allowed to pursue efforts to understand why some

Statusing is comparing current performance to the plan—corrective action is doing something about the difference.

test data on the Hubble telescope in 1981 showed the mirror met requirements, and other tests (on older test equipment) showed it did not. The already overrun program could "not afford the delay." Everything was assumed to be fine until eight years later when the telescope was put into orbit. The first use of the telescope revealed the defect, and we learned once again that repair of a system in operation is far more costly than a fix made during development.

Data have finally come to light that might explain the mysterious sinking of the USS Scorpion submarine 30 years ago. The evidence is strong, but the proof is not positive, that a battery in a Mark 37 torpedo burst into flames when a tiny foil diaphragm, costing pennies, unexpectedly ruptured in the battery. The crew of 99 died when the sub sank in May 1968. Earlier in 1968, a diaphragm failure occurred in the Mark 37-torpedo battery in a test lab, and six people were sent to the hospital. Tracing back to 1966, the Naval Ordinance laboratory had bypassed its own safety and acceptance procedures in order to meet the demand for deliveries of the Mark 37 torpedoes (with their batteries installed) to the fleet. The diaphragm in the battery even then was known to be a poor design, and difficult to make. The yield from one supplier was so low that 250 batteries had to be accepted without passing the required verification tests. One of these 250 batteries is the one that exploded in the laboratory. The on-going "corrective action" was to deny that a problem existed, to continue with deliveries to the fleet, and to discipline anyone who tried to link any operational problems to the procuring command.[40] A new safe design for the diaphragm was introduced into production in 1969.

Commercial products also find their way to the marketplace with design defects. Children's toys are often subject to recall for choking hazards, cars are recalled for mechanical or safety defects, software products are released for sale—followed shortly by bug fixes. Many of these defects are discovered in the development or verification process, but timely corrective action is often not taken. The pressure to be first to market is a driving force. However, producers of consumer products are increasingly being held accountable for consequential damage caused by defects, such as poorly designed car seats for children. Future investors will not be silent about an on-line trading company's liability, when Internet trading is shut down for four days due to the on-line company's software problems, as happened in 1999. Incomplete testing of software changes caused the stoppage. Associated Press reported in July 1999 that "sports equipment maker Shimano American Corporation agreed to pay a $150,000 civil penalty to settle allegations that it failed to report in a timely manner bicycle crank defects that caused 22 injuries." The cranks were put on more than 200 models of mountain bikes in 1994 and 1995.

Corrective actions may indeed have impact on project cost or schedule, especially if design flaws are not found until the product (hardware or software) is in final system verification or in operational use. The objective is to find problems early and fix them promptly. Schedule pressures, optimism, and the pressures by customers or management for the project manager to "be one of the team" are real issues that make effective corrective action easy to talk about but sometimes hard to do.

In theory, if there is sound visibility and a solid plan, the only time a project status meeting would be required is when corrective action is necessary, as determined by a continuously available status system. Generally, those team members who are on plan would not need to attend such meetings. In practice, however, periodic status meetings with key team members are essential, even if visibility and status systems appear to be sound and the project is right on plan. Status meetings allow the team to see the project as a whole, and omissions—in project integration, for instance—can be identified and corrected early.

The effective use of positive reactive management must consider many of the same attributes as does an automatic control system or servomechanism (depicted in Figure 7.75):

- Fidelity   —detection and accuracy
- Disturbances   —irrelevant data
- Noise level   —false input
- Time lag   —timeliness and validity
- Lead time   —early detection
- Gain vs. stability —too much gain can produce overreaction

Corrective Action begins with periodic variance analysis, to identify significant differences from the plan. The period and threshold

> The goal is to find problems early and fix them completely and correctly—the first time.

> Budget under-runs may be more critical than overruns.

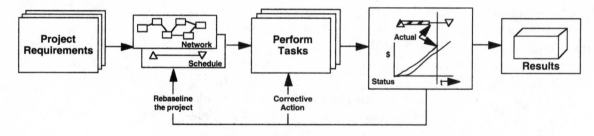

FIGURE 7.75   Corrective action closes the control loop.

for action is proportional to the criticality to the project. Near term critical issues may need to be statused daily with tight thresholds while non-critical issues are relegated to monthly statusing with broader thresholds. The business manager should determine the periods and thresholds. Cost thresholds should be expressed in both percentage and absolute terms—say, for example, 20 percent or \$20,000 for current periods and 10 percent or \$40,000 for cumulative measurements.

Schedule thresholds could vary widely, depending on the time remaining to task completion and whether the task is on the critical path, a low-slack path, or a high-slack path. One week slip is a reasonable threshold for a critical milestone with one year to completion.

> Repeated schedule slips require special attention, lest they become the critical path.

DETERMINING THE CORRECTIVE ACTION

Approach:

1. Analyze the problem:
   —The current impact.
   —The impact growth if no action is taken.
2. Prioritize all project problems from the most serious to the least serious.
3. Determine the best approach for each using analytical decision analysis.

> Problems may have several underlying causes.

In determining corrective action classical problem cause analysis is applicable. It consists of:

- What has changed from before the problem to after the problem?
- Were expectations unreasonable?
- Was the plan wrong?
- Were requirements ill-defined?
- Were resources insufficient?
- Was there a lack of interest?
- Was there conflicting direction?
- Were communications faulty?

Corrective action candidates include:

Cost overrun corrective actions (Figure 7.76) seek to *reduce:*

- Requirements.
- Labor rates and/or hours.
- Overtime.
- Project length.

> Corrective actions should decisively solve the problem. It may require out-of-box creativity.

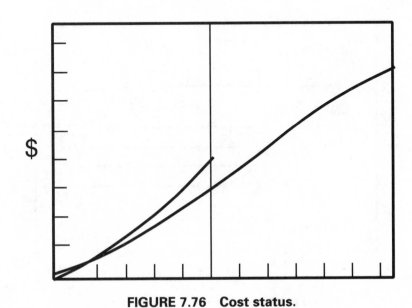

FIGURE 7.76   Cost status.

More imaginative cost options are to:

- Develop a more producible design.
- Install more efficient processes.
- Eliminate waste or superfluous tasks.
- Assign work to lower labor rate areas.

Schedule overrun corrective actions (Figure 7.77) *add:*

- Work shifts and/or overtime.
- Personnel.

and *improve:*

- Tools.
- Processes.
- Network (shorten critical path).

More imaginative schedule options are to:

- Overlap tasks.
- Use higher skilled personnel.
- Send work to high-efficiency specialty shops.

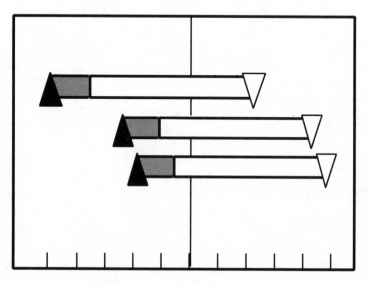

FIGURE 7.77   Schedule status.

Technical corrective actions seek to resolve shortcomings:

- Use tiger team of experts.
- Challenge requirements.
- Reduce quantities.
- Add skilled talent.
- Add more capable tools.
- Improve supplier(s).
- Add training.

Business corrective actions seek to improve the business process and eliminate bureaucracy. They involve:

- Experts.
- Consultants.
- Executive management.
- Customer involvement.

Selecting among alternatives, like any difficult decision process, may require an objective selection system. First, establish evaluation criteria (musts and wants). Then assign relative weighting factors and score the alternatives against the criteria. Figure 7.78 illustrates an approach for selecting schedule recovery action.

> Select the highest value solution.

The tentative choice is usually the highest scoring alternative. However, the evaluation criteria and weighting factors, being somewhat subjective, may lead to a close biased decision. A technique to evaluate the tentative decision is to assess the adverse consequences of implementing the tentative choice and to compare it with the closest alternative(s). The process should also consider the consequences of doing nothing different—always an alternative worth evaluating. It is important to document the decision analysis for later justification.

> In some cases, taking no corrective action may be the best of the alternatives.

Once the decision is made:

1. Develop an implementation plan.
2. Get the appropriate commitments.

The project manager approves the decision and is responsible for the timely implementation of the corrective action.

Evaluation Criteria		Alternative 1 One 12 hr shift			Alternative 2 Two 8 hr shifts			Alternative 3 Three 8 hr shifts			Alternative 4 Two 12 hr shifts		
Musts (Go-No Go): • Certified Software Testers • Available within 3 weeks								X X					
Wants	Weight (W)	Comments	Raw	Score R x W	Comments	Raw	Score R x W	Comments	Raw	Score R x W	Comments	Raw	Score R x W
Factors													
Maximizes productivity	10		5	50		7	70					10	100
Highly experienced in our software	8		10	80		8	64					8	64
Low average labor rate	8		7	56		10	80					5	40
Max Score (10xW)	260												
Total Score				186			214						204

FIGURE 7.78   **Evaluating alternatives by weighted scoring.**

SUCCESSFULLY IMPLEMENTING CORRECTIVE ACTION

Some problems require major actions.

The most prevalent error in reacting to variances is that corrective action is usually applied with too little, too late and with insufficient vigor. Problems must be dealt with promptly, decisively, and completely.

- Problems prevented are least expensive.
- Problems solved quickly are cheaper than delayed solutions!

Other common errors are:

Expensive expert consultants may be a real bargain . . . if they eliminate schedule slips during high "burn-rate" periods.

- Corrective action is usually insufficiently imaginative to consider all viable options.
- The effect of labor burn rate and schedule slippage is usually ignored.

Problems that occur during high burn rate periods are expensive (Figure 7.79). Extraordinary action may be justified to eliminate

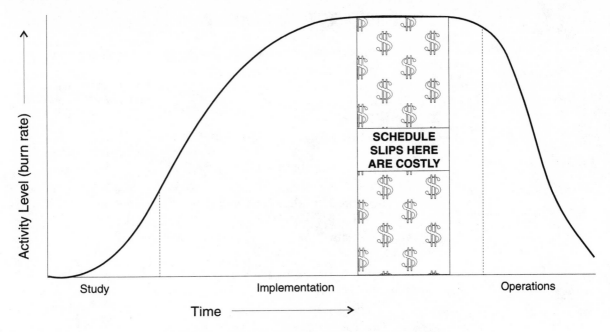

FIGURE 7.79   The high costs of schedule slips.

high burn rate slippages. If too many critical path activities are in variance, or if the burn rate renders the variances non-recoverable, it may be necessary to redefine the baseline plan since the current plan may be unachievable.

To ensure that all viable corrective actions are considered:

- Identify the total problem and impact.
- Develop alternative courses of action as strawman solutions.
- Select the highest value alternative.

Finally, to ensure that the plan is successfully implemented:

- Seek team consensus for the solution.
- Develop the implementation plan.
- Announce the plan.
- Status and control the corrective action plan along with the baseline plan.

> Re-baselining the project is often the first task of the "new" project manager.

10. PROJECT LEADERSHIP

The only way in which any one can lead us is to restore to us the belief in our own guidance.

Henry Miller,
The Wisdom of the Heart

THE ESSENCE OF LEADERSHIP

Distinct among the ten management elements, the proper application of leadership must ensure that the other nine elements are accepted, enthusiastically supported, and faithfully implemented. In this section, we address three primary aspects of project leadership:

- Situational leadership—the relationship of leadership to management.
- Techniques for inspiring and motivating individual and team performance.
- Style—determining and communicating your leadership style.

In the context of project management, leadership represents the ability to inspire—to ensure that project members are motivated—on both the individual and the team level. Several leadership professionals, quoted below, have captured the essence of inspiration and self-motivation. Regarding self-motivation, Peter De Vries wryly commented, "I write when I'm inspired, and I see to it that I'm inspired at nine o'clock every morning."

As Peter Drucker defines it, "Leadership is not a magnetic personality—that can just as well be a glib tongue. It is not 'making friends and influencing people'—that is flattery. Leadership is lifting a person's vision to higher sights, raising a person's performance to a higher standard, building a personality beyond its normal limitations." He contrasts leadership, "doing the right things," with management, "doing things right."

Efficiency is associated with management, even in climbing the ladder of success. But as Warren Bennis observes, "leadership determines whether the ladder is leaning against the right wall."

Stephen Covey reminds us that management is clearly different from leadership. "Leadership is primarily a high-powered,

"Leadership is primarily a high-powered, right brain activity."

"Leadership includes lifting a person's vision to higher sights."

Managing is doing things right. Leadership is doing the right things, like leaning the ladder against the right wall.

right brain activity. It's more of an art; it's based on philosophy. Management is the breaking down, the analysis, the sequencing, the specific application, the time-bound left-brain aspect of self-government." His own maxim of personal effectiveness: "Manage from the left; lead from the right."

Motivational experts seek to explain why some projects succeed while others do not. These studies result in leadership success models based on the project environment, the characteristics of the leaders being studied, and the leader's ability to influence others. Some have studied the basis for leadership power and influence, notably Hans Thamhain[41] and the Wilson Learning Corporation,[42] by having various influence factors ranked by managers, peers, and support personnel. To highlight the consistencies among their findings, we've focused on four influence categories. They're listed below in the order of their effectiveness as rated by team members:

- *Organizational position or formal authority.*
- *The manager's personal factors*—Expertise, interpersonal skills, information, connections and alliances, trust and respect.
- *The project work itself*—Work interest and challenge; future assignments.
- *Rewards and penalties*—Salary and promotion; coercion and penalties.

While the order varies somewhat among surveys and industries, most personnel rank the project manager's authority and expertise at the top along with the work itself. Surprisingly, salary and promotions are perceived only a little more positively than coercion and penalties, the later being seen as the least influential.

When we discussed forming the project team, we emphasized that the project manager should be given as much formal authority as possible. But we need to add one important caveat. The *existence* of the authority is considered to be a positive influence; however, its *undue exercise* can be perceived as coercion—diminishing the net influence. Selective use of formal authority only when absolutely required will produce the best overall results.

> In the absence of adequate formal authority, strong personal skills and leadership techniques are indispensable.

THE SITUATIONAL LEADERSHIP MODEL

Leadership techniques are nearly all situation-driven—they vary according to the task to which they are applied. To portray the situational nature of leadership, we use the orthogonal model we introduced at the end of Chapter 3. The cylinder shows the typical sequence of actions that occur in any well-managed task. After task work is assigned, a work plan is prepared. The plan may vary in detail from back-of-the-envelope ideas for a simple task, to a logic network detailing a complex project's sequence of resource-loaded work elements. Ideally, the plan is created by the team intending to do the work. Someone on the team—the team leader, a project manager, or a team member—provides oversight during execution, and work actually done is compared against the plan to note status. When unacceptable deviations in cost, schedule, or technical compliance are detected, corrective actions are taken to return the project to the plan. This work sequence is repeated throughout the project cycle, as represented by the axle in Figure 7.80.

The wheel (Figure 7.81) shows groups of leadership techniques and tools that may be needed to help the task sequence. The techniques include training, creating the environment, supervision maturity, interpersonal traits, reinforcement, setting examples, and rewarding achievement—all bonded together by the organization's vision. How the techniques and tools are applied can vary widely as a function of the skills and style of the leader and according to the situation.

Our model (Figure 7.82) positions the situational techniques of leadership orthogonal to the sequential management/supervision cycle. Leadership techniques must be applied situationally

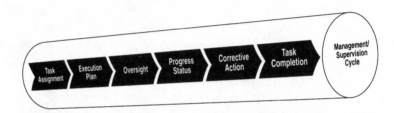

FIGURE 7.80   The sequential management/supervision cycle.

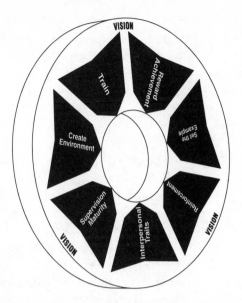

FIGURE 7.81   The situational leadership techniques.

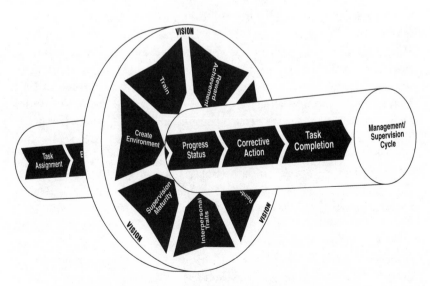

FIGURE 7.82   The orthogonal leadership model.

and responsively, relative to the active work phase and the specific team or individual circumstances at the time.

THE MOTIVATIONAL TECHNIQUES OF PROJECT LEADERSHIP

Nothing requires leadership skills more than the challenges of motivation. Yet the payoff is very high. According to the results of studies by The Public Agenda Foundation, a private research organization in New York, 88 percent of workers responded positively when asked if they considered it important to do their best job. However, 44 percent of those surveyed admitted that they "exert no effort over the minimum." And only 23 percent believe they work to their full capacity. The leader's motivation challenge is to tap that available discretionary effort.

The limitations of control and authority demand that project managers be able to differentiate motivational causes and effects, and be able to accurately relate them to the specific project team and member needs. Misplaced or ill-conceived motivation often turns into de-motivation—much worse than no motivation at all. The following groups of techniques, when properly applied, have proved effective in the project environment.

Vision portion in the margin:

> Vision pursuit is the glue that holds all the other leadership techniques together.

Vision   Above all else, we demand that our leaders have a vision and be able to articulate and structure its attainment. Whether it's successful task completion or a company reorganization, the ability to convey the vision and then affect its realization is the glue that holds all the other leadership techniques in tact. Leaders must accept the goals of the larger organization, of which their work is a part, and create the vision that supports the goals. They must understand the driving forces of the various stakeholders who will gain or lose by the vision's fulfillment. Finally, they must be able to communicate that vision to the team in relationship to their work. (Incidentally, visionaries who cannot lead to realization of their vision are called hallucinators.)

> The leader plans the work and works the plan.

Creating the Environment   How we manage vision attainment is the heart of the technique set. Attainment begins by creating the environment in which the work is to be accomplished.

Initially, this means defining management practices that will be used to manage the project and determining your style (discussed in detail at the end of the chapter).

In Chapter 5, we addressed to decision-making process as a major environmental and teamwork factor. The work of Douglas McGregor[43] is also useful in characterizing the leadership environment. He defined two types of environments illustrated in Figure 7.83, Theory X (authoritative) and Theory Y (challenge). Theory X is the militaristic environment based on the assumption that people really don't like to work and must be coerced into following orders, most of which originate with top management. But direct orders cannot always be depended upon, as the following story, originally appearing in the Naval Institute's *Proceedings,* illustrates.

Two battleships assigned to the training squadron had been at sea on maneuvers in heavy weather for several days. I was serving on the lead battleship and was on watch on the bridge as night fell. The visibility was poor with patchy fog, so the captain remained on the bridge keeping an eye on all activities.

Shortly after dark, the lookout on the wing of the bridge reported, "Light, bearing on the starboard bow."

"Is it steady or moving astern?" the captain called out.

This "beacon of information" provides several metaphors regarding position power, perceptions of authority, and the need to act on complete information.

FIGURE 7.83 Theory X (authoritative) and Y (challenge) environments.

Lookout replied, "Steady, captain," which meant we were on a dangerous collision course with that ship.

The captain then called to the signal man, "Signal that ship: We are on a collision course, advise you change course 20 degrees."

Back came a signal, "Advisable for you to change course 20 degrees."

The captain said, "Send, I'm a captain, change course 20 degrees."

"I'm a seaman second class," came the reply. "You had better change course 20 degrees."

By that time the captain was furious. He spat out, "Send, I'm a battleship. Change course 20 degrees."

Back came the flashing light, "I'm a lighthouse."

We changed course.

Theory X often results in an adversarial relationship between manager and subordinates—totally inappropriate for most project teams. Theory Y assumes that people want to work and can be highly self-directed with an appropriate work environment and reward system.

Subsequent to McGregor's original work, William Ouchi[44] introduced Theory Z to refer to the participative format that grew out of the Japanese "quality circles" movement and broadened with Total Quality Management. It is typified by closely knit teams that develop common goals to which they are committed through shared values (Figure 7.84).

For most projects each of these concepts has shortcomings. While Theory Z represents the project environment most closely—especially small, well-controlled projects—it has been found deficient in atmospheres of conflict. Larger projects involving multiple organizations, customers, subcontractors, and so on, work best when the environmental elements of both Theory Y (individual) and Theory Z (team) are combined. For your project, you need to determine the appropriate environment and decide how to set that environment in place.

Regardless of the specific style, a leader creates a problem-solving environment by:

- Building urgency and "admiring" the problem.
- Removing roadblocks so the team can do their things.

Variations in performance often stem from the leadership style used by the accountable person—the way the task work is assigned, planned, statused, etc.

Z - Management Environment

FIGURE 7.84   Theory Z (participative) environment.

- Eliminating window-dressing.
- Rising above bureaucracy and politics.

The same sequence of actions should be taken for a task managed by a self-directing team or by McGregor's worst nightmare X-style manager. After assessing the team and the stakeholder expectations, adopt or adapt a project cycle for the project and announce what tailoring the team is expected to do to that cycle. Identify the training needed, both on the team and individual levels, for the members to be able to work effectively together. You also need to define the balance of decision-making authority among the team, you as the project manager, and higher level management.

Due to the interdependent nature of project people and the teamwork culture, each team member wants to be involved and to feel responsible for proactive participation in management activities. These include planning, measuring, evaluating, anticipating, and alerting others to potential problems. To become committed to project goals, as Stephen Covey observes, ". . . they want involvement, significant involvement. And if they don't have involvement, they don't buy it. Then you have a significant

> The leader knows the people on the team and recognizes their needs.

motivational problem which cannot be solved at the same level of thinking that created it."

Project failures can frequently be traced to unrealistic technical, cost or schedule targets. Such targets may be entirely arbitrary or based on bad assumptions—setting team members up for failure. Furthermore, the goals that motivate one team member may not motivate another member. All tasks don't have to be inherently motivating—that's not sensible. But there have to be motivating factors, if by nothing more than participating in goal determination. This also helps ensure adequate risk analysis and acceptable risks.

We've found that it is better to aim high and to occasionally miss than to aim low. For example, one high-tech leader encourages employees to include goals in their MBOs for which there is at least a 50 percent chance of accomplishing. An overall MBO score of 75 percent is considered good—encouraging a stretch. Even overly aggressive goals, if set by the team member rather than the leader, can stimulate the extra effort needed to meet them. And they pay an extra dividend—On-the-Job-Training.

Meetings—lots of them—are an inherent part of the project management process. Nearly everyone complains about the time they waste in meetings. But meetings are the major vehicle for exercising leadership. In the section on Project Visibility, we provided conduct guidelines for the various types, from one-on-ones to formal reviews, but well conducted meetings can inspire and motivate the team. Too many meetings, or poorly conceived or poorly executed ones, can be a major demotivator.

Effective meetings are no accident. They demand management skills for preparation and leadership skills for conduct. For example, people who are needed for decisions, but who arrive late or not at all, waste everyone's time. Attendees who are not needed at all, also feel that their time is wasted. On the other hand, one of the most needless and damaging demotivators is exclusion. Occasionally, a team member will be "spared" from an important meeting or a difficult task with no explanation. With proper explanation, that person might have been relieved not to be involved, but may feel left out—perhaps even penalized.

A problem-solving meeting is a contest. The leader's challenge is to convince others to: change their positions or realign priorities, overcome prejudices and accept another point of view,

Involving team members in the goal-setting process has important benefits.

Goal-setting by team members ultimately leads to greater self-confidence and more aggressive goals.

Meeting format and conduct is a significant aspect of creating the environment.

A pattern of ineffective meetings is a sign of weak leadership.

extend commitments and increase vulnerability. But the leader needs to recognize and control counterproductive power struggles.

The leader should be an orchestrator, keeping the meeting balanced and on track (Figure 7.85). This often requires drawing out needed participation by others and preventing domination by overly vocal members, the leader included.

Studies by industrial psychologist Frederick Herzberg[45] examine specific factors that motivate people in their work environment—and those that don't. Herzberg and his co-authors identify several maintenance or "hygiene" factors that are not motivational. Pay and working conditions (safety, security, and comfort) reduce motivation when absent. But maintenance factors were found to lead to discontent only when they are missing or perceived as deficient, otherwise they have very little attitudinal affect. They are never motivators.

The presence of motivational factors, such as the work itself and recognition, can significantly improve job satisfaction, goal-orientation, and productivity. But they must not be manipulative. Alfie Kohn, in *Punished by Rewards*,[46] observed "Do this and you'll get that is not much different from do this or else."

> Major meeting demotivators include: lack of an agenda, indefinite start/stop times, and failure to stay on schedule.

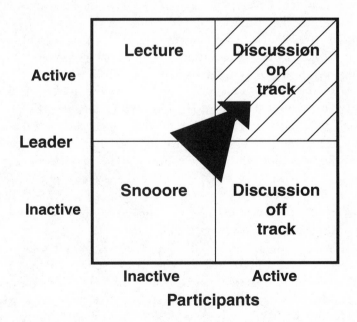

FIGURE 7.85   Keeping the discussion on track.

The maintenance and motivation factors are listed below in order of their relative importance revealed by Herzberg's research.

Motivational (Positive)	Maintenance (Negative)
Achievement	Policy and procedure
Recognition	Supervision
Work itself	Salary
Responsibility	Interpersonal relations
Advancement	Working conditions

Companywide employee relations campaigns involve maintenance factors, whereas motivational factors are generally in the domain of the project manager and others in a direct leadership role.

> A leader's effectiveness depends on the ability to assess maturity levels and to adopt the appropriate delegation style.

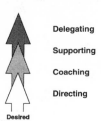

Delegating

Supporting

Coaching

Directing

Desired
Progression

Supervision Maturity A good leader evaluates each team member's ability to accept delegation and supervise others. Every opportunity should be taken to match the job assignments with interest and skills, keeping in mind that a perfect match is impractical. This means assessing every member's individual job knowledge and maturity, then planning desired growth so that *detailed direction* can progress to *coaching* on important points; where *coaching* can transition to *supporting* as needed; and where *supporting* can mature to full *delegation.*

As the maturity level moves from low to high, leaders need to vary their style from Directing to Delegating. Hersey and Blanchard[47] have developed a comprehensive situational leadership theory and process that helps in assessing maturity and determining the appropriate delegation style by considering the interaction between two major determinants (see Figure 7.86):

Task Behavior—the degree to which a leader *tells* people what, why, and how. Generally, task-oriented leaders set the goals and define the detailed steps to reach them.

Relationship Behavior—the degree of *support* provided by the leader and the extent of feedback sought. Relationship-oriented behavior is characterized by good bilateral communications and active listening.

Follower Readiness—the degree to which the followers need direction from the leader—individually and as a team. In

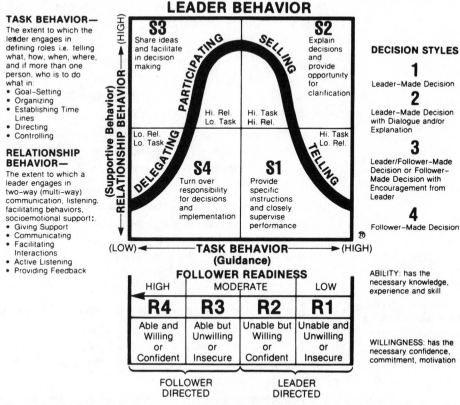

TASK BEHAVIOR—
The extent to which the leader engages in defining roles i.e. telling what, how, when, where, and if more than one person, who is to do what in:
- Goal-Setting
- Organizing
- Establishing Time Lines
- Directing
- Controlling

RELATIONSHIP BEHAVIOR—
The extent to which a leader engages in two-way (multi-way) communication, listening, facilitating behaviors, socioemotional support:
- Giving Support
- Communicating
- Facilitating Interactions
- Active Listening
- Providing Feedback

LEADER BEHAVIOR

(Supportive Behavior)
RELATIONSHIP BEHAVIOR — (HIGH)

S3
Share ideas and facilitate in decision making

PARTICIPATING

S2
Explain decisions and provide opportunity for clarification

SELLING

Hi. Rel.
Lo. Task

Hi. Task
Hi. Rel.

Lo. Rel.
Lo. Task

Hi. Task
Lo. Rel.

DELEGATING

S4
Turn over responsibility for decisions and implementation

S1
Provide specific instructions and closely supervise performance

TELLING

(LOW) ◄——— **TASK BEHAVIOR** ———► (HIGH)
(Guidance)

DECISION STYLES

1
Leader-Made Decision

2
Leader-Made Decision with Dialogue and/or Explanation

3
Leader/Follower-Made Decision or Follower-Made Decision with Encouragement from Leader

4
Follower-Made Decision

FOLLOWER READINESS

HIGH	MODERATE		LOW
R4	**R3**	**R2**	**R1**
Able and Willing or Confident	Able but Unwilling or Insecure	Unable but Willing or Confident	Unable and Unwilling or Insecure

FOLLOWER
DIRECTED

LEADER
DIRECTED

ABILITY: has the necessary knowledge, experience and skill

WILLINGNESS: has the necessary confidence, commitment, motivation

When a Leader Behavior is used appropriately with its corresponding level of readiness, it is termed a High Probability Match. The following are descriptors that can be useful when using Situational Leadership for specific applications:

S1	S2	S3	S4
Telling	Selling	Participating	Delegating
Guiding	Explaining	Encouraging	Observing
Directing	Clarifying	Collaborating	Monitoring
Establishing	Persuading	Committing	Fulfilling

FIGURE 7.86   The Hersey situational leadership model. Reprinted from Paul Hersey and Key Blanchard, *Management of Organizational Behavior: Utilizing Human Resources,* Englewood Cliffs, NJ: Prentice Hall, 1993, Sixth Edition, All rights reserved.

the project environment, readiness depends on the level of experience and knowledge available for the specific project and the interpersonal growth from working together as a team, all of which can be expected to grow as the project moves through its phases. The four basic situational leadership styles are summarized in Figure 7.86, followed by their appropriate application.

- Telling (S1): This style is most appropriate for followers who are unable or unwilling to take responsibility because they lack knowledge or experience.
- Selling (S2): This style can be practiced when selling concepts to top management and customers. It can be effective in obtaining team buy-in through selling the benefits of decisions. It is the natural training style.
- Participating (S3): This style is appropriate for a moderately mature team. The leader and followers share in the problem-solving, decision-making process, with the main role of the leader being facilitator.
- Delegating (S4): This style matches the needs of a team or individual which has reached a high maturity level. They have acquired both the motivation and ability to allocate project tasks and then to accomplish them with a minimum of supervision. The leader delegates and follows up.

Appropriate delegation is an effective technique for avoiding over-management while, at the same time, improving job satisfaction. As a project or task manager, a particularly strong motivator is the confidence demonstrated by turning over one of your own plums to another team member.

If they're not ready now, then consciously grow personnel to the point where they can accept delegation. Mismanaging this growth process can mean either delegating too early and experiencing performance problems or giving overly detailed directions and being branded a micro-manager. Whether a project manager or a junior team member, a sign of management maturity is knowing when to apply the following three approaches with one's boss:

- "It's my responsibility, and I am taking care of it."
- "It's my responsibility, and I am taking care of it. But you need to know what I am doing."
- "It's my responsibility, but the best solution is beyond my authority and I need your assistance."

Interpersonal Traits Leading people is, in part, the skill of knowing how to draw on the team's strengths and minimize the weaknesses. It takes time to understand others—to understand

---

| Delegate whole tasks—as large a piece as possible—not bits and pieces. |
| People that can handle delegation usually don't complain. |

why a single act of ours can have a positive effect on some and the exact opposite effect on others. It's not merely a one-time event of being type-cast by Wilson Learning[48] or Myers Briggs[49] or other good assessment tool, and then wearing a label. It requires conscious attention to the needs of each team member and hard work to understand their complexities of the team members so as to work with them and benefit from that complexity.

Much of traditional motivation theory is based on Abraham Maslow's five hierarchical levels (physical, security, social, status, psychic), each level becoming an intrinsic motivator after the lower-level need has been met. It has been our observation that any one of the levels may be dominant in a particular person. For example, some people are more responsive to psychic than to social incentives, regardless of how well their social needs have been met.

Needs can regress as the environment changes. Stephen Covey[50] dramatizes the point:

> If all the air were suddenly sucked out of the room you're in right now, what would happen to your interest in this book? You wouldn't care about the book; you wouldn't care about anything except getting air. Survival would be your only motivation.
>
> But now that you have air, it doesn't motivate you. This is one of the greatest insights in the field of motivation: Satisfied needs do not motivate. It's only the unsatisfied need that motivates.

Interpersonal clashes are inevitable, even in the most compatible teams. The techniques suggested here seek to channel the conflict in constructive ways so as to prevent a significant demotivator: prolonged or unresolved conflict.

The traditional conflict resolution methods are:

- Confrontation/Collaboration (Integration)
- Compromise (Negotiation)
- Smoothing (Suppression)
- Forcing (Power or Dominance)
- Withdrawal (Denial/Retreating)

Fact and issue based confrontation is the most favored mode for resolving conflicts, especially in dealing with superiors.

> The process of constructive confrontation can be honed into a significant asset.

Constructive confrontation has grown from a technique to a methodology complete with its own textbooks. But it is not a panacea.

Compromise is usually the best mode for dealing with functional support departments. At the other extreme, withdrawal is usually seen as capitulation, at best a temporary resolution. A skilled leader employs the full range of conflict resolution modes.

Brainstorming techniques are often used to attack the most difficult problems while enhancing interpersonal skills. The leader needs to ensure an open and non-critical atmosphere. For example, unusual or impractical ideas should be encouraged—they often lead to new combinations and improvements. Remember—the more ideas, the better.

The one-on-one meeting is one of the best techniques for exercising leadership on an interpersonal level. It provides the opportunity to demonstrate four important leadership qualities:

- Sensitivity to personnel issues
- Accessibility and friendliness
- Trust—respect for confidentiality
- Training and coaching.

> Group brainstorming can be very beneficial, but also very time consuming, so make sure it is time well spent.

Reinforcement   Reinforcement refers to techniques used to remind team members of the vision and the continuing requirements of working as a team. Because the project process includes difficult aspects which may not yet be intuitive, team members may resist or circumvent them. At every opportunity, the leader should emphasize the benefits of the project management essentials. Posters and slogans around a team room reminding people of important things are good if there is follow through to make them credible. The project leader's spoken words and body language, and especially job performance, can reinforce those points.

> A leader's spoken and body language, and job performance can provide reinforcement.

Setting the Example   "Walk the walk, don't just talk the talk," if you expect others to follow. It is less what you say that counts and more what you do that influences behavior. Your attitude and body language set the tone for the entire team. You need

> Every action you take sends a powerful leadership style message to team members.

to establish an atmosphere of openness by your willingness to seek advice, as well as bad news.

It's damaging to continually demand on schedule performance, and yet begin every meeting late. Act as you want your team to act:

upbeat, punctual, decisive, untiring, enthusiastic, fair, dependable

Group activities such as planning and problem solving offer ample opportunity for setting examples. Make sure that you begin meetings on time and operate by the same standards that the team has committed to.

Rewarding Achievement It may be time to put away the carrot and stick for good. Recent studies are calling into question the maxim of "You get what you reward." These studies show that, while some rewards can bring about short-term compliance, others often backfire in the longer term. Rather than getting sidetracked trying to resolve reward controversies, managers can benefit most by simply being aware of the issues. Much of the conflict confirms that different people respond to widely varying rewards. Some do not respond to external motivations at all. In the next chapter, we discuss the long-term implications of rewards such as salary increases and promotions. Our purpose is to characterize these forces so that they can be made part of everyone's awareness—managers and team members alike.

Some rewards can be perceived as denials of self-control and freedom of choice, especially if they don't address a need. Even though there are many techniques for finding out what people want, managers hesitate to pursue them. You may not be prepared to deal with the answer. But you'll discover that asking about motivations, whether by a formal survey or a simple one-on-one question, is motivating in itself. You need to follow-up to prevent being judged a hypocrit.

A Hilton Hotels Time Values survey revealed that 70 percent of people earning over $30,000 would trade a day's pay each week for an extra day of free time. This phenomenon exists even in the lower-pay brackets. Almost half of those surveyed earning less than $20,000 would also make the trade.

Never ask your team to do what you would be unwilling to do yourself.

Interesting assignments are often their own reward. People willingly work harder, as well as smarter, at interesting tasks.

Most people simply want to have interesting work and to be recognized for their accomplishments.

Most time-off incentives tied to productivity or schedule improvements get results.

It's important to recognize significant accomplishments frequently—but not routinely.

You should take advantage of every opportunity to recognize good performance, but it's most effective when done in a group environment such as at meetings or reviews—even off-site pizza breaks. Be sure you're aware of the supporting details and that you don't leave somebody out. A further note of caution: intrinsic motivation, so fragile in the team environment, can be destroyed by anything that is perceived as being manipulative or controlling—even praise. Those who receive excessive praise can become so self-conscious that they have trouble concentrating. They may even duck challenges to avoid potential failure.

Rewarding team performance can work as it does in sports—motivating stronger players to help weaker ones improve.

Rewarding individual performance doesn't necessarily result in a lack of teamwork. But cooperation does need to be one of the major performance rating factors. Accomplished leaders recognize and reward cooperation with teammates as an essential element of individual merit. One motivator for team performance is to do away with individual reviews. Some managers consider an entire task group's effort as one performance.

Regardless of your reward philosophy or the details of your rewards, they need to be systematically aligned with the goals and values of your project, environment, and company.

Training   Trying to do a job you haven't been trained for is no fun. This applies double to the project manager who needs to be trained to select appropriate project personnel, depending on the project type and size, and then to contribute to their career development.

Training does not work as a one-shot seminar, regardless of how long or how intensive it may be.

We are frequently retained by clients to train both their project teams and their executive management. We use techniques that bring groups together and encourages them to practice common goal-setting, problem solving, and acknowledge their interdependencies. We've used managed delegation exercises, joint buyer-seller project planning, project simulations, and a host of other techniques. We often train in-house trainers—a group responsible to train others. But this doesn't work unless the trainers have extensive—and successful—project management experience and can credibly address detailed issues from that perspective. As one of our clients asserted: "Someone with that kind of capability is usually very busy managing a hot project."

Not all people are emotionally or technically equipped to take on the teaching role. A teaching attempt at the wrong time, or by the wrong person, can be seen as a form of judgment or rejection. On the other hand, being taught by one's own management, if done well, can be extremely motivating. The higher the management doing the training, the more stimulating and effective it is in establishing a consistent culture (assuming that manager has progressed through the project trenches).

DETERMINING AND DECLARING YOUR LEADERSHIP STYLE

The practice of project management is increasingly influenced by human relations. Developing human relations skills, in turn, depends on awareness of one's own operating style and behavior patterns as well as a willingness to adapt those qualities to the specific project environment.

Firefighting provides a good metaphor for looking at how extreme a rigid personal style could be:

- Reactive—run for water
- Inactive—watch the blaze
- Counteractive—apply gasoline
- Distractive—send the fire trucks to the parade
- Retroactive—"I could have told you to install sprinklers if you'd asked."

The proactive manager would have already installed a sprinkler system.

The project manager's ability to get the job done usually depends more on operating style than on any other factor—even more than power or authority. A true leader knows what is going on at all times and anticipates situations, consciously operating in the appropriate style. While most leadership *techniques* are directed toward motivation, leadership *styles* characterize the methods for applying the techniques.

There are numerous texts and self-study guides for analyzing one's own style tendencies and preferences. We introduce two models below that have proved to be particularly effective. However, the details of any specific self-typing or group analysis scheme are less important than the process itself—exploring your

> As the leader, you need to be motivated to adapt your own behavior rather than to "shape up" someone else.

own preferences and stretching your range of styles. To benefit from that process you first have to be self-aware.

Before analyzing further, you may find it useful to jot down your own behavior patterns, both formal and informal. As Frankl says, we "detect" rather than "invent" our missions in life. Think about the way in which you respond to different situations. Think about the situations in which you're comfortable—and others where you're uncomfortable. In which kind of relationship problems do you invest time and energy on a regular basis—which ones need more of your time? Identify your motivation source (personal need served) in each.

Wilson Learning Corporation's Interpersonal Relations Model[51] has been widely used in the business environment for characterizing one's style. It is usually associated with a formal training seminar that includes a preliminary survey competed by selected peers. This is done through formal questionnaires similar in format to psychology and aptitude profiles. Your interpersonal style is determined by an evaluation of your peers' perceptions. The results are displayed relative to a four-quadrant model (Figure 7.87).

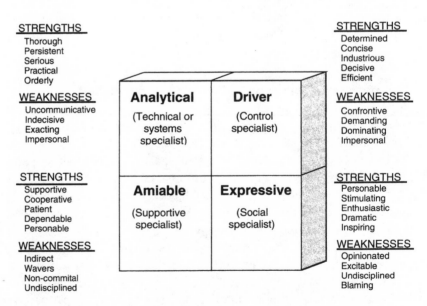

FIGURE 7.87   The basic Wilson Learning model.

Combining your primary style—Analytical, Driver, Amiable, or Expressive—with your secondary or backup style (one of the same four quadrants in the basic model), places you in one of the sixteen style categories, for example, an Expressive/Driver (Figure 7.88).

The utility of the Wilson model becomes clear when you consider the interactions among the various categories. The result is a much-improved insight and awareness, not only of your own styles, but of others' patterns as well. Perhaps most important is this newly acquired means to recognize behavior patterns and then anticipate interactions so as to extend your own personal behavior boundaries.

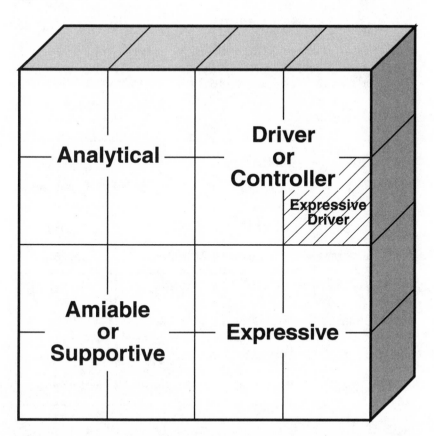

FIGURE 7.88   The sixteen Wilson Learning style combinations.

The Myers-Briggs model is broadly supported in psychology and self-help. It uses a questionnaire to help you determine your dominant trait in each of four pairs of traits:

E/I	Extrovert or Introvert
N/S	Intuitive or Sensing
T/F	Thinking or Feeling
J/P	Judging or Perceiving.

The model is based on the theory of psychological types described by C.G. Jung (1875–1961). Jung's model places you in one of sixteen categories based on combining that one dominant trait from each pair. The characterizations in Figure 7.89 are adopted from Keirsey and Bates,[52] one of several guides for interpreting the results.

Rather than consolidating peer- and self-review into one composite result, you are encouraged to characterize yourself and to independently have others respond to the same questions about you. Additional insight can thus be gained by comparing your

INFJ	INFP	ISTJ	ISFJ
Author	Questor	Trustee	Conservator
ENFJ	**ENFP**	**ESTJ**	**ESFJ**
Pedagogue	Journalist	Administrator	Seller
INTJ	**INTP**	**ISTP**	**ISFP**
Scientist	Architect	Artisan	Artist
ENTJ Field Marshall	**ENTP** Inventor	**ESTP** Promoter	**ESFP** Entertainer

FIGURE 7.89 Myers-Brigg's sixteen types, characterized by Keirsey and Bates.

results for each trait with the perception of others. As with the Wilson model, most authors provide detailed advice and insight regarding the dynamics of one style interacting with another (e.g., an ENTJ interacting with an ISFP), whether it be as team members, manager/subordinate, or spouses.

Regardless of your preferred style, your actual style at any time should be affected by such factors as the maturity level of team members and the gravity or priority of the situation. Variety and shifts in style are not only healthy—they're necessary. Leadership requires flexibility and adaptability in dealing with the task at hand, the personalities involved, events, and the situation.

This newspaper article in Figure 7.90 describes how Lt. General William G. Pagonis's leadership style literally moved

> You need to develop the ability to vary your style.

Gulf War Leader
Offers Lessons On Leadership

"In Moving Mountains: Lessons in Leadership and Logistics from the Gulf War" (Harvard Business School Press, $24.95), Lt. General Willian G. Pagonis tells how he served 122 million meals, moved 31,880 tons of mail, pumped 1.3 billion gallons of fuel, processed 730,000 personnel, set up 2,746 miles of main supply routes, and logistically supported an integrated military force equal to the population of Alaska.

The leadership style and techniques Pagonis used are equally fascinating. First he publicly gained the confidence of his boss.... (He) responded to the challenge... by signing his John Hancock on his logistical charts in front of Schwarzkopf and the rest of the command, as the latter stood by in disbelief and incredulity....

An expert on strategic mobility, it comes naturally to Pagonis to say, "if you have good people, and if you have the capability to expand and delegate, and you have a centralized plan, imagination and ingenuity will always win. I believe in centralized control and decentralized execution."

"Moving Mountains" explains... the outlines of Pagonis' demonstrated effective leadership style. **That style includes a constant, informational flow of communications on 3-by-5 cards, daily "stand-up" meetings and bulletins, and the necessary "articulation" of each leader's management style, so that subordinates need spend zero time and energy guessing how the manager manages.**

"If you can articulate your leadership style, you can cause a transition to go 20 times faster," he says. "Then everybody knows what you want. I am convinced too many chief executive officers want to keep their subordinates guessing, keep them at a distance and a little bit of an edge, and I think that's wrong."

—*San Jose Mercury News, 16 November 1992*

FIGURE 7.90 Leadership lessons in the Gulf War.

mountains in the Gulf War. Note the use of "daily 'stand-up' meetings and the 'articulation' of each leader's management style, so that subordinates need spend zero time and energy guessing how the manager manages." In his book Pagonis elaborates on his use of standup meetings (limited to 30 minutes and anyone interested, regardless of rank could attend) and 3×5 cards for communication with all levels of his organization.[53]

Anticipate necessary changes in your own style and declare what will trigger a change. A good time to announce these to the team is at the kick-off meeting. Here's an example: "I'll implement news flash meetings, plan violation meetings, daily stand-up meetings, and as needed, red teams and tiger teams. I'm an expressive/driver. I will operate in the Y-mode most of the time. I will be proactive and reactive—seldom inactive. I want to delegate as much as possible, but if I'm the one to recognize a slip in a delegated task, I'll switch to driver/directing mode."

LEADERSHIP ELEMENT EXERCISE

The objective of this exercise is to provide experience in describing your leadership style to others.

Based on the explanations of this chapter and your own leadership experiences develop a single bulleted chart that clearly describes to others your declared leadership style. If unfamiliar terms or jargon is used, explain for the uninitiated. Encourage feedback from peers, superiors, and subordinates as to its validity.

> Once you determine your preferred styles, declare yourself and lead consistent with your stated standard.

8

THE IMPLICATIONS FOR A SUCCESSFUL FUTURE

People ask for the secret to success. There is no secret, but there is a process.

Nido Quebin

That process, starting with our visual model, has been unfolding for several chapters. We've demonstrated the strong connection leading from a systematic process—our process—to successful projects, and by implication, to successful careers. The purposes of this chapter are to:

- Make evident the trends and forces that are shaping future management careers.
- Identify the barriers that need to be broken.
- Remove the need to take that leap of faith.

Project management is indeed the wave of the future. But that kind of broad claim has been made for other concepts that became popular, only to fade away. Why will the future of project management be different from, say, Total Quality Management?

THE FUTURE WAVES AND UNDERCURRENTS

In most industries, quality is still considered the top competitive success factor.

The bottom-line expectations for TQM have not been fulfilled—at least not in the short term. Japan's TQM culture shift took some 30 years.

In many ways, project management is evolving much like quality assurance did—from an obscure servant of line management; to broad consciousness; to formal disciplines, processes, and organizations with professional status; and finally, to the world's foremost competitive factor.

Total Quality Management and Continuous Quality Improvement developed great expectations on the part of project stakeholders, company shareholders, and all levels of users. But for many, the TQM bubble burst when The Wallace Company filed Chapter 11 bankruptcy shortly after receiving national acclaim for its TQM program (the Houston-based oil-supply company had just won the Malcolm Baldrige National Quality Award). Recent surveys on TQM results and attitudes have concluded that U.S. firms may not fully embrace TQM until it demonstrates more dramatic results at the bottom line. For example, the American Electronics Association found that 40 percent of the 455 companies it surveyed has realized less than a 10 percent defect reduction over 3 years (attributable to in-house TQM programs). That same survey found that Quality is by far the top competitive success factor, ranking far ahead of Service (#2) and Technology (#3).

The perceived value of high quality is increasing even while TQM programs are being abandoned! This apparent dichotomy can be explained by our cultural priorities which demand that bottom-line improvement initiatives bear significant fruit in the near term. The TQM concept will ultimately be successful, but only when embodied in disciplines such as system engineering, as part of an integrated project management process.

Project management is not a single idea or campaign. It's a confluence of several concepts (quality management being an important one) that offer both short-term and long-term bottom-line performance improvements. Waves (management du jour) which roll into project management include:

- Right-sizing the organization.
- Re-engineering the business process.
- Reducing middle line management.
- Shifting toward project teams and product teams.
- Using comprehensive, integrative processes.

Project management is moving from a specialty to the mainstream—from a management or organizational option, like a task force, to the way the enterprise is run. We're just beginning to feel the potential impact. The wave, building from many synergistic currents, is between the stages of broad consciousness and professional formalization.

Many associations and conferences are devoted to furthering project management development and recognition. The growth of project management's professional status and its reservoir of practitioners is reflected by international associations such as the Project Management Institute, the Performance Management Association, and the International Project Management Association. For example, the Project Management Institute membership is now growing at some 36 percent annually (Figure 8.1).

A solid career path depends on the ready availability of education and training. To that end, project management is being widely recognized as a fundamental management process with specific professional competency and knowledge criteria, including graduate programs at several universities. The Project Management Institute certifies those who have passed a rigorous eight-hour exam, as a Project Management Professional. Almost

Thousands of independently certified Project Management Professionals are now advancing the field.

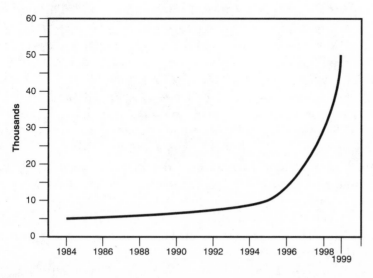

FIGURE 8.1 The accelerating Project Management Institute growth.

half of the members have applied, with just over half of those being certified. In addition, many corporations offer competency-based certification of project managers.

The U.S. government strongly supports project management training and education, usually at the agency level. As Undersecretary of Defense, David Packard, co-founder of Hewlett Packard, initiated the formation of the Defense System Management College at Fort Belvoir. While the 14-week curriculum emphasizes negotiation techniques and contract management for DoD and industry managers, the principles of project management are covered as well.

> It remains for system engineering to be recognized as a process integrator rather than as a technical specialty.

Another encouraging sign of professional growth, at the process and discipline level, is the formalization of system engineering practices through organizations such as INCOSE, the International Council on Systems Engineering. From a modest beginning in 1990 as NCOSE, a national organization with 30 members, INCOSE membership now exceeds 3,500 and is growing annually. Even though the American Management Association encouraged its formation, it is only loosely connected with the project management profession.

> When challenged to call on personal power to marshal the troops, some project leaders may feel like responding as did Shakespeare's Hotspur: "So can I, and so can any man; but will they come?"

Even though that beleaguered middle level of line management appears convinced that the future lies in project management, just what that implies is not clear to those more comfortable with conventional power structures. That problem is not new, as evidenced by this heated exchange related by David McCullough.[1] In 1904, after the Panama Canal project team had protested an international mandate for a sea-level canal, Lord Kirchener reacted to President Roosevelt's support for team authority by saying: "I never regard difficulties, or pay heed to protests like that; all I would do in such a case would be to say, 'I order that a sea-level canal be dug, and I wish to hear nothing more about it.'" Roosevelt's retort strikes a familiar chord for any present-day project manager: "If you say so, I have no doubt you would have given such an order; but I wonder if you remember the conversation between Glendower and Hotspur, when Glendower says, 'I can call spirits from the vasty deep,' and Hotspur answers, 'So can I, and so can any man; but will they come?'"

> With all this knowledge and intensity, why aren't major projects more consistently successful?

That anecdote sums up the major leadership challenge facing the new breed of project managers: obtaining a full and

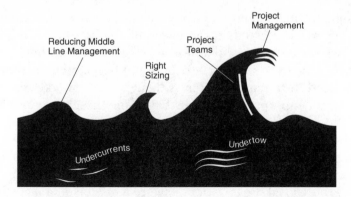

FIGURE 8.2   A treacherous undercurrent: The hidden enemy of project management.

continuing commitment by the team. An undercurrent of dissatisfaction, based largely on past exposure to flawed processes and inconsistent implementations, continues today. We call this undercurrent the hidden enemy of project management (Figure 8.2).

EXPOSING THE UNDERTOW—THE HIDDEN ENEMIES OF PROJECT MANAGEMENT

A negative attitude and lack of confidence in project management often turns out to be a self-fulfilling prophecy:

> At a software engineering course for aspiring managers, the participants were asked: "If your team of programmers developed airplane on-board flight control software, and one day when you were flying, you found out before take-off that this plane was one of those equipped with *your* software, how many of you would get out?"
>
> All except one person raised their hands. The course instructor asked the only one left whose hand was not raised, "What would you do?" She said, "Stay in my seat—if my team wrote the software for this plane, it wouldn't move, let alone take off."

While this story is told with tongue in cheek, it comes close to characterizing the attitudes of many frustrated team members in this era of "vaporware" and getting to market at any cost. In an

Project success depends on the team members' attitude as much as on the leader.

attempt to understand why some teams succeed and others do not, experts have studied the magic of the natural-born leaders who have been successful at leading project teams. These studies produced project manager attribute models similar to those we referenced in the last chapter. Although relevant and important, this leadership approach alone, based on the characteristics of the leaders in the studies, cannot yield teams that are consistently successful. This approach fails to consider the importance of the process and tools, and the team members' attitudes toward essential project management techniques.

Professional organizations have recently taken a more scientific approach to understanding project success and failure. They evaluate work practices, and then develop and apply maturity models. For example, the Carnegie Mellon Software Engineering Institute has developed the SEI Capability Maturity Model (CMM) to assess the work practice maturity of software development teams (Figure 8.3).

This model has been in use since 1987 and is becoming the de facto standard for software development maturity. Five levels of maturity are used to rate organizations as to their ability to reliably produce software based on four evaluation areas: Processes, People, Technology, and Measurement. The model is based on the theory that the more effective the people, processes, tools, and measurement, the higher the probability for project success.

The capability approach to success needs to account for the team's attitude.

We reported above on the expanding use of competency-based and knowledge-based certifications for project managers. Currently, the International Council on System Engineering (INCOSE) is crafting a maturity model for system engineering to be used to assess organizational capability in that domain and the Project Management Institute is working on a Project Management Capability Model. Unfortunately, while these capability models assess the presence of practices within an organization, they fail to examine the team's underlying support or resistance to these practices.

We support the leadership approach to success and the need for a comprehensive project management maturity model, but we caution against their use without assessing and accounting for the team's underlying resistance to the fundamental practices of project management and system engineering. Even though effective leadership can provide the direction and a capable team can

Implications of Advancing Through CMM Levels.					
	Level 1	Level 2	Level 3	Level 4	Level 5
Processes	Few stable processes exist or are used.	Documented and stable estimating, planning, and commitment processes are at the project level.	Integrated management and engineering processes are used across the organization.	Processes are quantitatively understood and stabilized.	Processes are continuously and systematically improved.
	"Just do it"	Problems are recognized and corrected as they occur.	Problems are anticipated and prevented, or their impacts are minimalized.	Sources of individual problems are understood and eliminated.	Common sources of problems are understood and eliminated.
People	Success depends on individual heroics.	Success depends on individuals; management system supports.	Project groups work together, perhaps as an integrated product team.	Strong sense of teamwork exists within each project.	Strong sense of teamwork exists across the organization
	"Firefighting" is a way of life.	Commitments are understood and managed.	Training is planned and provided according to roles.		Everyone is involved in process improvement.
	Relationships between disciplines are uncoordinated, perhaps even adversarial.	People are trained.			
Technology	Introduction of new technology is risky.	Technology supports established, stable activities.	New technologies are evaluated on a qualitative basis.	New technologies are evaluated on a quantitative basis.	New technologies are proactively pursued and deployed.
Measurement	Data collection and analysis is ad hoc.	Planning and management data used by individual projects.	Data are collected and used in all defined processes.	Data definition and collection are standardized across the organization.	Data are used to evaluate and select process improvements.
			Data are systematically shared across projects.	Data are used to understand the process quantitatively and stabilize it.	

FIGURE 8.3   The implications of advancing through the capability maturity model.

**Team empowerment
depends on winning over
the hidden enemies of
project management.**

provide the vehicle, these hidden enemies can still cause the trip
to be bumpy, if not downright hazardous.

In the early 1980s, we became aware that most project failures were not caused by the problems of advanced technology,
but rather by the failure to implement fundamental and basic
project management techniques. Teams within companies, known
for their expertise in project management, would violate basic
practices and as a result would experience failures of the worst
kind. For example:

Failure	*Poor Practice*
NASA Challenger disaster	Inadequate qualification
Hubble defect	Ignored conflicting test results
Intelsat VI failure to achieve orbit	Inadequate change controls
Denver International Airport debacle	Failure to rebaseline with added requirements
FAA air traffic control system failure	Inadequate risk management and ever-changing requirements
AT&T long-distance system shutdown	Failure to test after change

In each of these cases, a fundamental project management
practice was overlooked, ignored, or circumvented. In every case,
the properly applied project management technique would have
prevented the project failure.

We set out to discover what caused project teams to ignore
proven practices. Fortunately, our business causes us to routinely
interface with substantial numbers of skilled project personnel
from government agencies and contractors, commercial hardware
and software companies, and with graduate students, at several
universities, pursuing project management careers.

**No competent project
manager would think of
managing a project
without these important
techniques, effectively
practiced.**

We designed a survey to be administered to participants entering our training room. The survey collects the participant's
candid attitudes about "how they value" a selected group of important project management techniques prior to receiving training. The summary of responses (Figure 8.4) from some 20,000
participants represent the percentage of "Positive" responses for
some of the most important techniques. Our premise with this
questionnaire is that personnel who are negative, neutral, or have

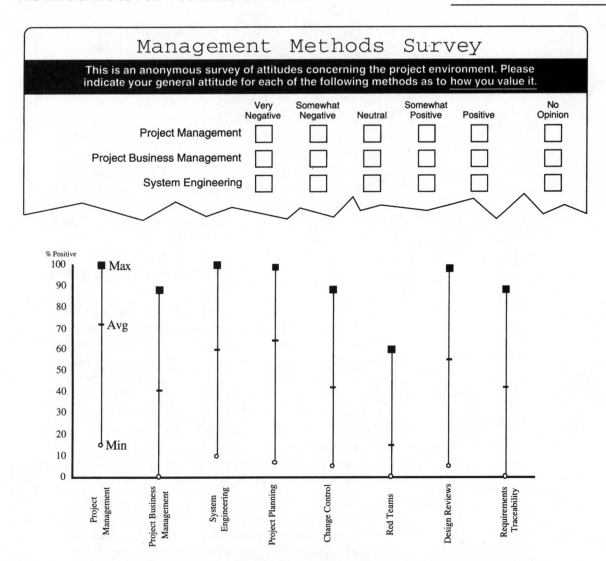

FIGURE 8.4 Management methods survey form and summary results.

no opinion toward a technique cannot be expected to pursue and support the technique in the project environment. The "Somewhat Positive" person may support the technique if implemented by others, but will usually not be the initiator. The only person who is a possible candidate for championing the technique and cultivating its effectiveness in the project environment is the person who checks "Positive." And even if positive, the person might not have the leadership skills to instill a technique in a resistant climate.

The survey results are sobering on two accounts, the wide range of group results and the low averages. The negative biases carried into the room when the survey was taken are a major cause for concern. The 45 percent averages for Project Business Management, Change Control, and Requirements Traceability means that less than half of the 20,000 participants felt solidly positive toward these techniques. Inadequate attention to one or more of these specific techniques caused the failure of the Intelsat commercial satellite, the Challenger disaster, and the Denver airport delay and cost overrun. Thus the results of this survey are particularly alarming when you consider that clients send only their best project personnel to a week or two of project management training.

Further analysis reveals that the main factors contributing to the nearly 85 percent dynamic range for most factors is the corresponding knowledge/experience with the technique and the management level of the respondent. The perceived value of project management techniques diminishes with descent into the organization hierarchy (Figure 8.5).

Fortunately, this trend can be reversed with proper training and positive experience with the techniques. In early applications of the survey, we administered it both before and after training without discussing the reasons for the survey. The results showed a positive attitude increase to 70 percent or higher for most techniques as a result of understanding the use, and the application of the technique. This attitude improvement demonstrates the power of training. It is important for project leaders to measure the attitudes of their team at project start-up by applying this survey. Then, armed with this knowledge apply selected training to improve the understanding of the techniques that received low scores.

SO MUCH TO LEARN—SO LITTLE TIME

Our surveys and personal experiences reveal a strong tendency for people to abandon discipline in favor of ad hoc practices if given

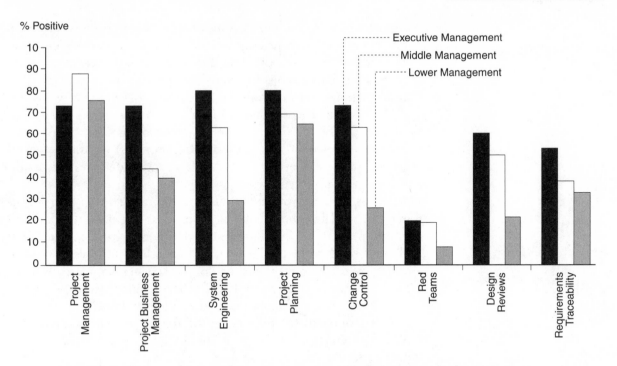

FIGURE 8.5   How three management levels value important techniques.

the opportunity. Thus, it is incumbent on all organizations to establish a culture based on fundamentals and to maintain it through training and consistent practice. While campaigns and promotions can help get everyone's attention, they are a reinforcement, not a substitute, for continuously reinforced fundamentals.

The broadest concepts may not work well without systemic changes from the top down. Effective and lasting process renovation requires a far greater commitment than banners, hype, and a 5-day seminar. A growing consensus believes the system changes have to begin at the public education level and include "remedial" training at all levels and by all levels of the organization.

The declassified Corona reconnaissance satellite program,[2] considered by many to have given birth to the integrated product team concept, illustrates the sweeping changes that may be required for successful project management. Since all subsequent U.S. space reconnaissance evolved from the CIA's Corona program (1960 to 1972), which spanned 13 years and 145 launches, its

> To some organizations, assimilating the new processes is like learning that the earth is round.

importance to U.S. security is inestimable. However, it very nearly didn't succeed, with 12 failures in a row, and only two successes in the first two years of operation. Eventual success is credited to the establishment of a project management process based on integrated project teams and many of the fundamental techniques we've included in our process. The failures were corrected with only two failures during the last 8 years of the program. In spite of the amazing success of the Corona program, most of the powerful project management concepts, such as integrated project teams, did not get widespread attention until the 1990s.

But very few organizations could survive a two-year hiatus in order to effect the acculturation process. We need to attain the intuition and level of commitment that comes from several years of successful projects, but without expending those years. As the saying goes, "We have the technology." We can systematically learn from the successes and failures of others. And we can develop our intuition through conditioning and mental gymnastics.

There needs to be a mechanism for the lessons learned to get into the hands (and minds) of those who would benefit most. If project teams are prematurely dispersed to other projects, just at the time they should be documenting those learning experiences, it goes undone.

Many government and industry standards and regulations have been inspired by lessons learned and are maintained and updated as a means of promulgating those experiences. Training and cross-project technical meetings are major techniques for communicating lessons learned.

Lessons learned developed by the project team after a project is complete can be invaluable to other project managers, present and future. Current U.S. Government request for proposals require bidders to explain how they will apply past lessons learned to the management of the proposed project. An example of an excellent lessons-learned document is the DoD's Best Practices Manual.[3] Any project's requirements should include the relevant lessons from prior projects and they should be managed as equally important to the customer's requirements. A database of lessons learned should be readily available to all team members (Figure 8.6). Lessons learned should be formally required to be prepared at project closeout, regardless of the size or complexity of the project.

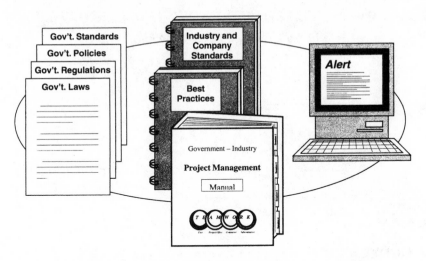

FIGURE 8.6   Lessons learned can take many forms.

Albert Einstein has been quoted as saying, "Everything should be as simple as possible—but no simpler." One corollary might be, at any level of complexity, make sure you have a management process up to the task, and that you follow it to the letter. Management formality increases with the project size, risk, or complexity as illustrated in Figure 8.7. In general, more complex or higher risk projects require tighter controls, such as requirements traceability and baseline management. Furthermore, as size and risk increase, so do the needs for planning and documentation (Figure 8.8).

Kinder's book, *Ship of Gold in the Deep Blue Sea,* provides an interesting example of a successful project that highlights the tailored application of the principles we have discussed.[4] The book is a thought-provoking study of the recovery of gold from a ship, the Central America, that sank in 1857 in water 8,000 feet (2,440 meters) deep. Treasure hunters usually work in an ad hoc fashion with no detailed project plan. In stark contrast, Tommy Thompson, the entrepreneur and project manager, ran the multi-year recovery project in the 1980s in a very business-like and structured way, as carefully described by Kinder. There were few guidelines from prior projects as to how to proceed, and there were many obstacles to success. First was the challenge of finding the ship, with no precise recorded location at the time it sank in

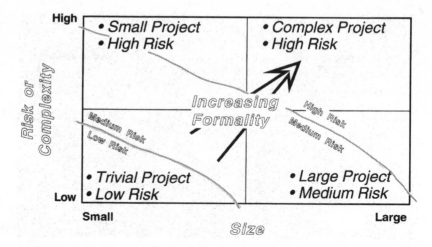

FIGURE 8.7   Management formality increases with size, risk, or complexity.

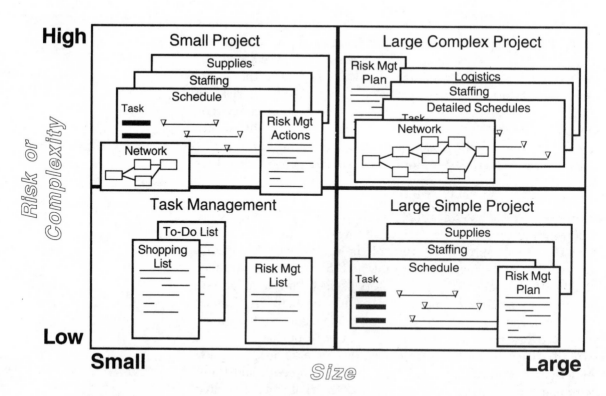

FIGURE 8.8   Planning increases with project size, risk, or complexity.

one of the nineteenth century's worst hurricanes. Second was the challenge of designing recovery equipment when intuition of deep-sea experts said, "it cannot be done." Third, the project had to be run in a business-like fashion because investors expected a clear accounting of the way their funds were expended, and they expected a positive return on their investment. Expert opinion in the mid-1980s was that deep-sea recovery would cost hundreds of millions with little chance of success. Thompson's project cost less than 15 million dollars for his highly successful effort. Fourth, the project required secrecy because other ventures were actively trying to beat Thompson to the gold. Although Thompson did not use our terminology, he intuitively recognized the need for an incremental development with periodic control gates. His intuitive tailoring of the process emphasizes the objective we have: to see the process applied appropriately without drowning in unnecessary detail.

"Overwhelming complexity" is often cited as the reason project management processes defy our intuition. But complexity alone does not preclude intuition. Intuition develops from observing and understanding key principles. For example, the behavior of a gyroscope is not intuitive to most of us. But to an inertial guidance specialist, gyroscopes are second nature.

> In project management, familiarity breeds intuition that dissolves contempt.

Intuition is developed by observing the environment, understanding the driving characteristics, and learning reasonable ranges for them. As an example, consider the plight of the main character in an old movie. As part of the plot he was to pretend that his sister had just given birth to a baby. A woman asked him how much the newborn weighed. Caught by surprise, he suggested the baby weighed 20 pounds. The woman reacted in horror, "Oh, no!" Our hero quickly corrected his mistake, "Oh, of course I meant 20 ounces." The woman reacted in horror, "Oh, no!" If you don't have sufficient intuition to get within an order of magnitude, you are in the wrong position. Take heart—intuition can be developed if you work at it and pay attention.

Managing a project without some intuition is like looking at a road map through a drinking straw. Generating that intuition is perhaps the most important contribution of our visual model. Effective empowerment is confirmed by the positive attitudes on the part of team members who embrace the model and the process. The obvious correctness of the model instills confidence in

> Being able to internalize the overall project management process removes the need to follow the individual steps on faith, or by edict.

the process. A team that understands the value of a credible process, and follows it because they believe in it, will be far less likely to omit an important step or to perform a practice incorrectly.

Project management is the best training ground for general management.

THE PAYOFF

- Successful projects
- Satisfied clients
- Improved bottom lines
- Successful careers
- A healthy stand of highly-qualified executive timber.

9

APPLYING
THE PROCESS

**We must push out beyond our comfort zone, and make
ourselves build . . . better, faster, cheaper.**

Daniel S. Goldin,
Administrator, NASA, 1992

The continued thrust to increase competitiveness and shorten
time-to-market in commercial industry, and the more recent
effort to reinvent the procurement process in government, has
created sustained pressure to adopt new paradigms for development projects. The banner of "better, faster, cheaper" places emphasis on the use of commercial off-the-shelf (COTS) systems
and components, nondevelopment items (NDI) (previously developed products that are not commercially available), and advanced, state-of-the-art components.

This chapter reviews two successful and two unsuccessful
projects, examining the processes they followed compared to the
traditional approach used during the 1960s through the 1990s.
The results illustrate that, without a valid and comprehensive
process, faster and cheaper does not automatically lead to better,

This chapter is based on a paper by Forsberg and Mooz, "System Engineering for
Faster, Cheaper, Better," presented at the ninth annual symposium of the International Council on System Engineering (INCOSE), Brighton, England, June 1999. The
paper was designated one of the five best papers at the symposium.

and, conversely, that an intelligently tailored process can greatly improve the success rate for projects.

It has been suggested that the sequence be revised to "faster, cheaper, better," because doing the first (faster) usually leads to the second (cheaper), but cannot guarantee the third (better). This is the reason that the administrator of NASA, Dan Goldin, has insisted that *better* comes first, because without focus on the technical quality, the project may fail. A low-cost, on-time failure satisfies no one.

"Better, faster, cheaper" has become the new buzz word for the new century. It follows in the proud footsteps of terms such as total quality management (TQM), concurrent engineering, and integrated project teams. All of these are excellent concepts and, if properly implemented within the context of an overall project management and system engineering philosophy and process, the improvements in project performance can be dramatic. Out of context, however, these terms become hollow slogans that do little to help the project, the product, the user, or the team. Worse, the slogans can become excuses for deviating from essential project management and system engineering disciplines needed to succeed.

A "better, faster, cheaper" process is essential to our continued competitiveness in an era of tight budgets and global markets. The objective of this chapter is to identify the essence of "better, faster, cheaper," to highlight the lessons learned, and to emphasize that success depends on a valid and properly tailored, comprehensive process.

Two well-publicized projects that exemplify the "better, faster, cheaper" approach are the Clementine project (1994)[1] and the Mars Pathfinder mission (1996).[2] Both projects are reviewed with conclusions validated through interviews with the Clementine project manager and with key team members on the Mars Pathfinder project. This chapter also contains a review of the Buyer Procurement System (BUYER) project that, after three different attempts in a span covering more than a decade, failed in its goal to implement a commercial off-the-shelf product as a key piece for a large software development upgrade. The conclusions for BUYER were obtained through interviews in 1996 and 1997 with two of the project managers involved, plus a review of the project documentation. Finally, the chapter draws on the accident investigation of the Therac-25 radiation machine.[3] The Therac-25 used previously developed products that are not commercially available (NDI). Since both of the failed projects reviewed here used COTS or NDI, the causes of their failures are relevant to this chapter, even though neither were initiated under the banner of "better, faster, cheaper."

"BETTER, FASTER, CHEAPER"

When the first satellites were designed and built in the late 1950s, there were no commercial products available for space use. Everything had to be created from scratch or commercial products had to be adapted for use in an environment for which they were never intended to be used. This led to both performance and reliability problems. The first 12 launches of the Corona satellite (the first U.S. reconnaissance satellite) were all failures.[4] Yet, the project survived (a total of 145 launches were made), and today the Corona project is considered very successful and a remarkable achievement. The key to ultimate success of aerospace projects in the early 1960s was the creation and implementation of project management and system engineering processes that were ultimately applied to all such development efforts. Procedures were developed that became the best practices of the 1960s, 1970s, 1980s, and 1990s. These defined the traditional approach used on most projects to the present time.

As technology matured, our expectations matured as well. Now, over 40 years later, any system failure is considered unacceptable. One of the consequences of the successes of the process models of the 1960s is that in the 1970s and 1980s they led to more process formalization and often to unnecessarily rigid adherence to a generic (untailored) process.

One view of the traditional approach can be represented as the Technical Aspect of the Project Cycle (or Vee), as depicted in Figure 9.1. This approach is requirements-driven, and starts with identification of user requirements. When these requirements are understood and agreed-to, they are then placed under project control and the system concepts and system specification are developed in response to them. The system decomposition and definition process is then applied and repeated over and over until,

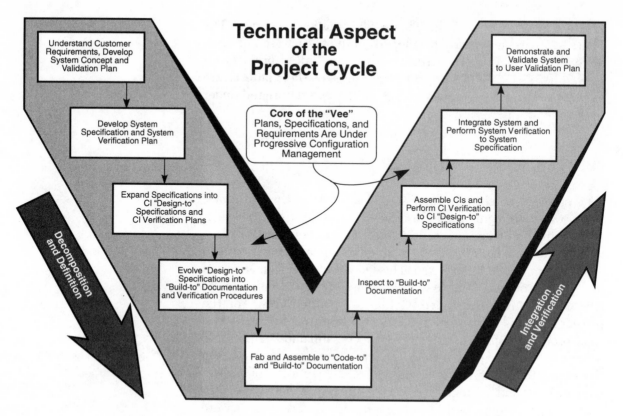

FIGURE 9.1   **The technical aspect of the project cycle (the Vee).**

ultimately, lines of code and piece parts are defined. Agreement is reached at each level, component interfaces are defined, and the decisions are placed under project configuration management before proceeding to the next level. When the lowest level is defined, we move upward through the integration and verification process on the right side of the Vee to ultimately arrive at the complete verified and validated system. At each level, there is a direct correlation between activities on the left and right sides of the Vee—the rationale for the shape. Everything on the left and, at the appropriate time, on the right side of the Vee are sequentially placed under configuration control, and hence this has been designated the core of the Vee. The generalization of the model to include incremental and evolutionary development is discussed in Chapter 6.

While the core of the Vee is sequential, concurrent development is an essential part of the process. The concurrent off-core analyses, investigations, and tests of critical issues are engineering studies necessary to manage opportunities and risks inherent in higher level on-core candidate concepts. These studies ensure that the higher level requirements can be met, and that the team is not committing to develop an antigravity device. Upward iteration with the user ensures that the solutions being considered will be acceptable in the completed system (in-process validation). Upon approval, the higher level on-core solutions become part of the baseline, but the supporting studies (that prove feasibility of the core decision) *do not;* they are documented, however, as a part of the decision-support process.

Today, the management processes that led to past successes are viewed with suspicion and are being targeted as the villains in the drive to produce the next generation of systems. Under management pressure, several projects have adopted the banner of "better, faster, cheaper," and have had significant success. To say that they were successful because they used previously developed products (COTS or NDI) misses the point; from the late 1960s to the present, there has always been pressure to use previously developed products. What is new today is the range of useful products available for incorporation into the next generation of aerospace systems. However, these recent projects did break the 1970 and 1980-era rigid interpretation of the traditional approach by creatively tailoring the project management process to their specific needs. Their legacy is important to us all. Their lessons apply to all projects, commercial as well as aerospace. We will examine how we can use their success to improve on the traditional project management and system engineering approach.

CLEMENTINE

According to the project manager, the Clementine spacecraft was smaller (508 pounds dry weight), built faster (22 months), and cheaper ($80 million) than any previous deep space mission.[5] The spacecraft, launched in 1994, had the mission objectives of photographing the earth, the moon, and an asteroid.[6] It met two of these three objectives, and the radar returns from the lunar South Pole strongly suggested the presence of ice in a large lunar crater. A fourth objective of this project was to prove that using a streamlined acquisition and management process, and maximizing the use of COTS, would substantially reduce the development cycle and development costs. These latter objectives were successfully demonstrated.

While the macro-objectives for the Clementine project were fixed, the detailed capabilities of the spacecraft were determined by what could be achieved with available equipment. So while "better, faster, cheaper" was the goal, the lower decomposition level requirements were not determined by the mission, but rather by available capability. The Clementine team used existing products for over half of their subsystems. Since the team did not need to develop the designs, the Vee for COTS used in their system would descend only to the component level (Figure 9.2). However, off-core critical issue studies below the component level were required to investigate capability, to ensure interface compatibility, and to determine required modifications to achieve desired performance.

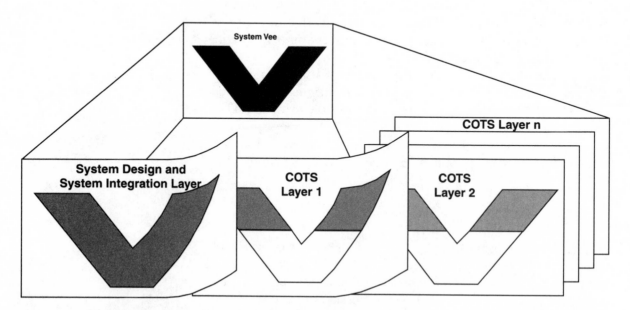

FIGURE 9.2   The Vee, in layers, for a COTS system. The full-depth Vee is required for component interfaces.

In one example, the project team relied on traditional high-reliability piece-part and component procurement to achieve the necessary reliability levels. According to the project manager,[7] "commercial diodes, transistors, and integrated circuits were pre-screened prior to selection (approximately 4% of all diodes, 3% of all transistors, and 1% of all integrated circuits failed the screening test). . . . Sensor reliability analysis was conducted using (traditional) reliability standards to identify potentially weak elements for replacement." These risk management activities are the off-core critical issue studies shown in Figure 9.3.

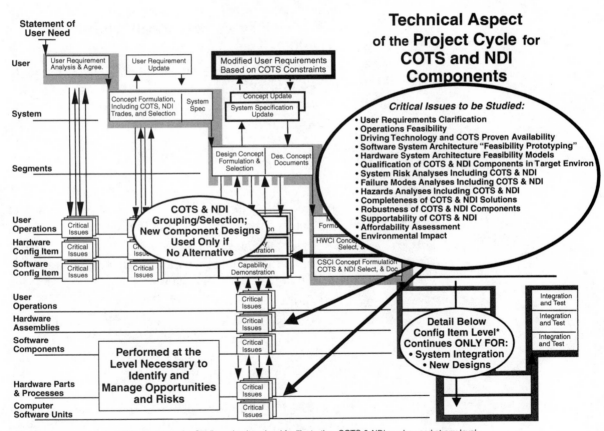

FIGURE 9.3 Critical issues to be studied for Commercial Off-The-Shelf (COTS) and Nondevelopment Items (NDI).

The pressure on the Clementine project to meet the January 1994 launch date, which had been set in January 1992, caused some software testing to be restricted in scope. Incomplete low-level testing failed to detect the software error that caused the spacecraft to miss its third objective of photographing the asteroid. The Clementine team allowed schedule pressure to cause them to circumvent proven software development discipline. In every project, technical risk must be balanced against project schedule.

When asked to describe the top five factors contributing to Clementine's success, the project manager, Pedro Rustan, replied:

1. Empowerment, where the project manager has full authority (executive management didn't meddle).
2. Leadership.
3. Availability of a significant amount of hardware from previous projects.
4. Managerial, technical, and financial skills and motivation.
5. Burning desire to succeed!

In an earlier article,[8] Rustan also identified several other factors necessary to the success of his project:

6. Collocate the team (including all the engineers and technicians) for all essential functions.
7. The project manager should control the procurement process; the government contracting officer should be responsible to the project manager.
8. Build and test an engineering model.
9. Reduce formal controls (on component traceability, quality, and documentation) to the minimum acceptable—based on risk.
10. Use a small team with clear responsibilities.

A comparison of Rustan's points with the operating procedures for the Skunk Works, a highly efficient aircraft development organization, shows a significant commonality.[9]

The operating rules for both Clementine and the Skunk Works are also consistent with the *essence* of good, traditional project management. The reason they succeeded is not that they abandoned obsolete processes, but rather that they intelligently tailored and streamlined the project management and system engineering processes to their needs.

MARS PATHFINDER

Like Clementine, the Mars Pathfinder project also introduced several new approaches to project implementation.[10] Key was the early and comprehensive use of computer modeling and simulations during the study period, which facilitated concurrent engineering.[11] The team also focused on the integration of previously developed products. Some items such as a heat shield for Mars atmospheric entry are not commercially available (as yet). To take advantage of prior experience developed 20 years earlier on the Viking missions, heat shield design and fabrication experts were recalled from retirement. The Mars Pathfinder team successfully reduced the development cost by about one-half, compared to similar projects, and shortened the development schedule from five years to three years.

The Mars Pathfinder mission is one of the first NASA projects to be developed under the "better, faster, cheaper" banner. Discussions with Dr. Robert Shisko at the Jet Propulsion Laboratories (JPL) confirmed that there was a well-developed project management process and risk mitigation activity for the entire project development span, even though it was a departure from the approach used on previous large JPL projects.[12] Dr. Shisko stated:

They implemented new things, combined in new ways, with the following highlights:

1. Flatter management structure, which shortened decision times.
2. Collocation of the entire team.
3. Greater authority given to subsystem managers.
4. Necessary documentation was created, but in a nontraditional, less formal way.
5. Preference for testing rather than analysis during development.

6. The focus on "cheaper" caused careful management of cost and schedule reserves.

In addition, the team had a well-defined quantitative risk analysis process. For instance, they modeled the entry, descent, and landing sequences, and used Monte Carlo analyses to provide data for risk management decisions. Although the team did not express it this way, the details of Figures 9.2 and 9.3 apply here.

The observations by Dr. Shisko match very closely the areas emphasized by Rustan in his articles on spacecraft project management.

THE BUYER PROJECT

Although not initiated under the banner of "better, faster, cheaper," the BUYER project focused on one of the key avenues of success for "better, faster, cheaper": the use of COTS products.

BUYER is a multimillion dollar software system designed to provide procurement support throughout a medium-sized commercial organization. After attempting unsuccessfully to build a home-grown system in the 1980s, a decision was made to purchase a COTS product and tailor it to the organization's needs. Three unsuccessful attempts over a decade led to project termination in 1997. Had the project team used the concepts in Figures 9.2 and 9.3, problems would have been revealed earlier and more systematically instead of being a continuous string of surprises. A list of lessons-learned was compiled, from which the following points have been extracted:

- Poor requirements lead to poor plans.
- For COTS software projects, use incremental, phased development.
- For COTS software, pick the product, *then* pick a contractor based on their experience with *that* COTS product.
- Use of COTS products may require performance compromise.
- A COTS product is not really COTS if the vendor is modifying it.

- COTS software is not really COTS if it doesn't run on your target hardware and system software.
- Involve the user in the development process.

In the first two attempts, the BUYER project failed because the selected COTS packages did not meet user requirements; in an environment of continuously changing user requirements, however, no development approach could succeed. In the third attempt to produce a system, the team finally got the necessary management support to baseline a stable set of solution-independent user requirements.

The last iteration of the BUYER project failed because, unknown to the team, key software that ran successfully in a commercial UNIX environment was only available in an alpha version for the new target environment (Windows NT). The problem was *not* the use of COTS, but rather the incomplete implementation of system engineering. The project team jumped on an attractive COTS solution, without performing off-core studies (Figure 9.3) to identify and mitigate the risks associated with the Windows NT opportunity.

Intelligent hard-working people devoted years to make the BUYER project a success to no avail. They certainly displayed a burning desire to succeed (Rustan's success factor number 5 above). In fact, the BUYER team did most things right. But, as the saying goes, "close only counts in hand grenades and horseshoes." This is *not* an example of problems caused by "better, faster, cheaper" concepts; rather, the BUYER team simply failed to implement proven system engineering and project management principles.

THE THERAC-25 PROJECT

Therac-25 is a computerized radiation therapy machine used to treat cancer patients. It was first used in commercial hospitals in 1982. The goal of the manufacturer was to replace two older models with a new design that was more useful to the hospital because it combined both low- and high-energy modes of operation into a single unit. It was also designed to be cheaper to produce and operate. The Therac-25 project used NDI software in its design. Although not developed under the banner of "better, faster, cheaper," this project is relevant because use of NDI is a primary means for achieving "better, faster, cheaper" results, but NDI risks are often overlooked.

An excellent study of the cause of the Therac-25 failures reported that "between June 1985 and January 1987, six known accidents involved massive overdoses by the Therac-25—with resultant deaths and serious injuries. They have been described as the worst series of radiation accidents in the 35-year history of medical accelerators."[13] This 24-page article should be mandatory reading for any system engineer involved in reuse of hardware or software for new applications.

The Therac machines provide two modes of operation: low-energy, long-time exposures and high-energy, short-time exposures. The energy settings were controlled by software on a PDP-11 computer. The software had software interlocks to prevent long exposure at high-energy levels. For the first three years of operation, the eleven machines then in use performed as expected. However in 1985, a patient in Georgia "received one or two doses of radiation in the 15,000- to 20,000-rad (radiation absorbed dose) range. . . . Typical single therapeutic doses are in the 200-rad range. Doses of 1,000 rads can be fatal. . . . " After two years of investigation (and 5 accidents later), it was found that a fast typist could enter data and move to a new screen faster than the computer cycle time for polling the screen entry data. Thus, input data were lost and so the software safety interlocks were bypassed. This allowed high-energy, long-exposure times to be accidentally activated.

The Therac-25 development used software from two earlier models (Therac-6 and Therac-20). Both earlier systems used the PDP-11 computers (as did the Therac-25), and both older systems had been in use for a decade without problems. Selected software was used without modification in the new machine. The developer did not recognize that this "previously developed product" was not being used in exactly the same way, however. Both of the Therac-6 and Therac-20 models had software and hardware safety interlocks. The new Therac-25 had only software safety interlocks to save cost. After the Therac-25 accident investigation was completed, a re-examination of the Therac-20 showed that the old software had exactly the same failure mode, but the hardware interlock intervened to prevent the hazard.

Leveson and her co-author highlighted important lessons about software reuse: "A naïve assumption is often made that reusing software (NDI) or using commercial off-the-shelf (COTS) software increases safety because the software has been exercised extensively. Reusing software modules does not guarantee safety in the new system . . . and sometimes leads to awkward and dangerous designs. . . . Rewriting the entire software to get a clean and simple design may be safer in many cases." In addition, they found that, along with other problems, good system engineering was lacking in the Therac-25 design and development, and proven software engineering practices and processes were not followed. *There was no effective peer review during the Therac-25 system development phase.*

The Therac development team used previously developed software to save development cost, to save development time, and to create a better product (the same goals sought by advocates of "better, faster, cheaper"). In this case, faster and cheaper did not lead to better.

GENERAL OBSERVATIONS

PRODUCT RELIABILITY

How good does the COTS product have to be? A score of 96 percent (success rate for diodes screened for use in the Clementine) is an excellent test score in school, but is it satisfactory for your project? Consider Mikel Harry's assessment of the consequences of an even tighter 99 percent successful performance requirement:

- 20,000 lost articles of mail per hour
- Unsafe drinking water almost 15 minutes each day
- 5,000 incorrect surgical operations per week
- Two short or long landings at most major airports each day
- 200,000 wrong drug prescriptions each year
- No electricity for almost 7 hours each month[14]

Most consumer COTS products fail to some degree, whether we talk about new cars or new Microsoft Office 2000 applications. The issue for system engineers to resolve is whether or not the failures are of importance to their project. Most people would refuse medical treatment from a device or medical system that had a reliability level equivalent to current commercial software products sold for use on desktop computers.

The COTS product being reviewed for a specific application may not be suitable for its new use as it comes off the shelf. System engineering has the obligation to evaluate the risks and to decide on the appropriate actions. As the Therac-25 accidents revealed, assessing the suitability of a COTS or NDI solution is nontrivial.

SHORTENED PROJECT DEVELOPMENT SCHEDULE AND REDUCED COST

Project teams for both Clementine and Mars Pathfinder tout their success in reducing project schedule from the traditional 5 or 6 years to an "amazing" 2 to 3 years. What is new? America's first operational fighter jet, the P-80, was developed from concept to first flight (in 1945) in 143 days.[15] The U-2 went from concept to first flight (in 1955) in just eight months. The SR-71, still one of the most advanced aircraft in the world in 2000, 38 years after its first flight, was developed from concept to its first flight (in 1962) in 32 months. The SR-71 also pushed the state of the art in many areas, including the structural use of titanium. The Corona project, America's first reconnaissance satellite, took 3 years and 11 months from project start to the first totally successful flight (in 1960); this span includes 13 launches before full success was achieved. The Corona program was started before any manmade objects had been put into orbit so everything from concept to reliability was first of a kind. These 4 projects share a common trait in that all had a national mandate and resources (which had to be continuously justified) to get the job done right.

The P-80, U-2, and SR-71 were all developed in the Lockheed Skunk Works.[16] The Corona was developed in a Skunk Works-like environment, with Kelly Johnson, founder of the Skunk Works, as an advisor.[17] While Lockheed seems to be the only organization to sustain a Skunk Works for an extended time (50 years), David Aronstein discusses three other independent aerospace Skunk Works operations (two American, one German) which embodied the same rules and outstanding successes.[18] The

Skunk Works concepts were also common and effective in the computer industry. IBM, Control Data, and Intel all maintained significant Skunk Works-like operations.

One of the characteristics of the Skunk Works is that it is a small part of a larger organization and they were able to "skim off the cream of the crop" for engineering and manufacturing talent. There is not enough "cream of the crop" for all projects to operate in this way, so there is a challenge in making the Skunk Works concepts a general approach. However, the principles of a thoughtfully tailored system engineering and project management process, a small, empowered, collocated team, and tailored documentation, to name a few areas, can apply to any project. The factors highlighted as elements in the success of Clementine and Mars Pathfinder are consistent with the Skunk Works guidelines, and Skunk Works operating principles are indeed a model paradigm for the "better, faster, cheaper" projects to follow.

One of the consequences of the successes of the process models of the 1960s is that they led in the 1970s and 1980s to more formalization of process and often to unnecessarily rigid adherence to a generic (untailored) process. As noted by Cialdini,[19] Ralph Waldo Emerson in his essay "Self-Reliance" said, "A *foolish* consistency is the hobgoblin of small minds" (italics added). There are many instances in the experience of the authors and our colleagues where unthinking adherence to process led to wasted time and money. In the 1970s and 1980s, projects typically stretched out many years and costs grew significantly. Average project spans are shown in Table 9.1.

Table 9.1 Average Project Span for Major Defense Acquisition Programs Based on Data from the Acquisition Reform Benchmarking Group[20]

Decade	Average Span from Project Start to Initial Operational Capability
1960s	74 months
1970s	104 months
1980s	107 months
1990s	97 months

Lest we think that these problems are unique to the military or space industry, there are many examples from commercial experience as well. In one instance, a project team in a major U.S. corporation, working in a dispersed environment (over 10 sites), shortened key internal processes from 30 days to 2 days; the overall project span decreased from a predicted 5 to 6 years to a completion in 18 months. The secret: improved communication and interaction through collocation of the key project team members. Breaking the mold of past practices is key. The advances in the Internet and the evolving use of distributed, collaborative engineering (DCE) concepts and tools will allow similar effective team interaction, even when they are not physically collocated. The ability to have informal, frequent, ad hoc technical dialogue is the essence of collocation, which is one of the powerful principles of a Skunk Works.

In another instance, a corporation desired to introduce a "hot new idea" for a food product. At the time the idea was proposed, they were well ahead of the competition and could have captured a majority of a very lucrative business. However, it took eight years for them to get this high-priority product to market, longer than it took to build the Golden Gate Bridge in San Francisco or to build the world's first satellite! The problem was that they had no process. The general attitude is that the military and NASA have cumbersome processes and the government could realize great savings if only they would adopt tailored commercial practices. Beware; you cannot tailor a process if it does not exist.

In the early 1990s, the Department of Defense (DoD) mandated that DoD standards and specifications be replaced by commercial ones—even though commercial counterparts do not always exist. The objective was to break down barriers between the DoD and the commercial market place. A side benefit is that it forces everyone to break the constraints of their old paradigms and rethink the processes from scratch. That is also one of the challenges the "better, faster, cheaper" advocates have given us. NASA has demonstrated that "better, faster, cheaper" can lead to dramatic success as demonstrated in the Mars Pathfinder mission.[21] The key is that any process must be tailored to the project at hand, and the system engineer must thoughtfully perform this tailoring.

The penalty for inappropriate deviation from the process can be severe, however. The GOES NEXT project, which started in 1985, was designed to provide the next generation of weather satellites with the first launch planned for 1989.[22] A five-year development should have been more than adequate. The first launch actually occurred in 1994, five years late and with a four-fold increase in costs (to $1.2 billion). The GOES NEXT management team decided early in the development that since satellite production was almost routine they could skip the study period. The consequence was that critical development issues, which should have been found in the off-core studies of the Study Period (Figure 9.3), were not discovered until the project was well into the implementation phase. Use of COTS or NDI would not have mitigated this failure to follow a proven process.

Another example of the consequences of inappropriate tailoring of the project cycle is found in the Lewis spacecraft launched by NASA in August 1997. This spacecraft was not simply the first of a new generation—it was to be a pathfinder in a new way of doing business. Two of the business objectives were to validate a new approach to acquisition and management of spacecraft systems, and to reduce cost and development time of space missions for science and commercial applications. Developed under the banner of "better, faster, cheaper," the Lewis spacecraft achieved the second two. Lewis was launched on 23 August 1997. The first problem was found 20 minutes after launch. All contact with the spacecraft was lost on 26 August 1997. There are specific engineering and operational causes of the failure.[23] However, from a process standpoint, one of the primary causes was *the abandonment of informal peer reviews* two years prior to flight. (Note that this was a root cause of the Therac failure cited earlier.) The contractor reduced the number and scope of internal reviews to save costs, and could do so because the customer did not require them. From the perspective of our model, they did inadequate off-core risk management. The lack of peer reviews allowed the risk areas to go unchecked to orbit.

Creeping elegance is another culprit in derailing a project. Reaching back 250 years, the history of the development of the maritime chronometer is an excellent object lesson for us in our modern era. This critical device could have saved literally thousands of sailors' lives in the 1700s, but John Harrison, the inventor, delayed release of his design for 40 years, because he had "not perfected the details."[24] In that 40-year span, Harrison created five working models that were field-tested and met all critical requirements, but each time he discovered a way to improve the product before its release.

Conversely, the Clementine project manager insisted that the team use the existing capability of the COTS products to drive the system capability. The desire to "improve" on the COTS products was prohibited. As noted in the BUYER lessons learned, use of COTS products will usually require performance compromise. The system engineer must control the requirements management process.

BACK TO BASICS

The success of the "better, faster, cheaper" approach confirms the original purpose of the process models as represented by Figures 9.1, 9.2, and 9.3. Nothing in the actual experience of the projects reviewed here contradicts the value and intent of the traditional view. In fact, they forcefully remind us that any process must be *understood, tailored appropriately,* and *aggressively managed.* The multisegment model (Figure 9.2) can be combined with an incremental or evolutionary approach to suit the needs of a project. However, inappropriate pro forma application of any process will be counterproductive. *Avoid foolish consistency.*

When we started the study of projects implementing the "better, faster, cheaper" paradigm, we expected to find a new way of doing business. We planned to map that new process against the traditional project management process to highlight and learn from the differences. What we found was that the project champions had thoughtfully tailored the old way of doing business to eliminate waste and overturn irrational or unnecessary barriers.

The real breakthrough by the project teams on Clementine and Mars Pathfinder was to apply appropriate tailoring of the project cycle and effective implementation of concurrent engineering on the off-core opportunity and risk identification and mitigation studies. In the failed projects, many smart people worked very hard to achieve success; however, to save time and cost, they omitted key steps which lead to their downfall. You have to understand the project management and system engineering process before you can successfully tailor it. To tailor without understanding is to invite disaster.

At the request of the NASA administrator, the Enterprise Safety and Mission Assurance Division studied 14 projects that used the "better, faster, cheaper" approach to product development in order to assess the lessons learned.[25] Some of the projects were within NASA, some were jointly managed by NASA and industry, and several were entirely contractor-managed ventures. The projects took place in the 1990s, and they were mostly successful, but the report included several significant failures as well. Some of the projects are still under way and will not be completed until the first decade of the new century. The author of the report, Charles Cockrell, summarized his findings in nine lessons:

1. Use cohesive technical teams with authority to do the job.
2. Maintain visibility through reviews.
3. Use a design-to-cost philosophy.
4. Apply risk management techniques.
5. Use experienced personnel.
6. Establish good communication.
7. Conduct better up-front planning.
8. Have clear requirement definition.
9. Use technology with appropriate readiness level.

None of these lessons are unique to the high-tech world of NASA. In fact, Cockrell's conclusions in his report also have universal application:

1. Foremost, the new way of doing business isn't really new.
2. Doing things under a better, faster, cheaper approach has not negatively impacted the quality of the (products).
3. There is a fine line between having too much organizational structure . . . (so) that processes become bureaucratic sponges . . . versus having too little structure that we repeat costly mistakes of the past.

4. Dynamic, interactive, multi-dimensional communication is essential . . .

5. Lessons learned apply equally to projects assigned to the aerospace industry, to (Principal Investigators), to government in-house projects, and to projects undertaken totally as a commercial venture with no government involvement.

6. Better, faster, cheaper approaches should be considered another tool in how we carry out our mission, not the only tool.

Properly applied, the experience of the past four decades is entirely relevant to today's drive for "better, faster, cheaper." The Skunk Works experience is also relevant to our goals here. Thoughtful application of the principles underlying the traditional project management cycle and system engineering management process will yield success if we are alert to the need for tailoring and implement an aggressive opportunity and risk management policy. The Clementine and Mars Pathfinder projects have proven it can be done. The other projects cited illustrate the risks if the process is not carefully tailored. System engineers and project managers now need to be proficient in the approach so the successes can be repeated and failures avoided.

NOTES

INTRODUCTION

1. Thomas A. Stewart, "The Corporate Jungle Spawns a New Species: The Project Manager," *Fortune,* (July 10, 1995), p. 17.

CHAPTER 2

1. Henri Fayol, *General and Industrial Management* (New York: IEEE Press, 1984). A translation of the original French version published in 1916.

2. Winston W. Royce, "Managing the Development of Large Software Systems," *Proceedings, IEEE WESCON,* (August 1970), pp. 1–9.

3. B.W. Boehm, "A Spiral Model of Software Development and Enhancement," *Tutorial: System and Software Requirements Engineering,* eds. R.H. Thayer and M. Dorfman (Washington, DC: IEEE Computer Society Press, 1990), pp. 513–527.

CHAPTER 3

1. Michele Jackman (with Susan Waggoner), *Star Teams, Key Players* (New York: The National Association for Female Executives Professional Library, Holt and Company, 1991).

2. Dennis Kinlaw, *Superior Teams* (Hampshire, England: Gower Publishing Ltd., 1998).

3. K. Forsberg and H. Mooz, "The Relationship of System Engineering to the Project Cycle," *Proceedings of the National Council for*

System Engineering Symposium, (Chattanooga, TN: October 1991), pp. 57–65.

4. Dennis M. Buede, *The Engineering Design of Systems—Models and Methods* (New York: John Wiley & Sons, 2000).

5. Ben R. Rich and Leo Janos, *Skunk Works* (Boston: Little, Brown & Company, 1994).

6. David C. Aronstein and Albert C. Piccirillo, *Have Blue and the F-117A* (Reston, VA: American Institute of Aeronautics and Astronautics, 1997), Appendix C, pp. 232–241.

CHAPTER 4

1. *Report of the Presidential Commission on the Space Shuttle Challenger Accident,* (1986), p. 95.

2. John L. Beckley, *The Power of Little Words* (Fairfield, NJ: The Economics Press, 1984).

3. Simon Winchester, *The Professor and the Madman* (New York: HarperCollins, 1998).

4. Sybil Parker, ed., *McGraw-Hill Dictionary of Mechanical and Design Engineering* (New York: McGraw-Hill, 1984).

5. R.H. Thayer and M. Dorfman, eds., *Tutorial: System and Software Requirements Engineering* (Washington, DC: IEEE Computer Society Press, 1990), pp. 606–676.

6. *A Guide to the Project Management Body of Knowledge* (Sylva, NC: Project Management Institute, 1996), pp. 159–171.

CHAPTER 5

1. Stephen R. Covey, *The Seven Habits of Highly Effective People* (New York: Simon & Schuster, 1989).

2. Michele Jackman (with Susan Waggoner), *Star Teams, Key Players* (New York: The National Association for Female Executives Professional Library, Holt and Company, 1991).

3. Peter F. Drucker, *People and Performance: The Best of Peter Drucker on Management* (New York: Harper & Row, 1977).

4. Deborah S. Kezsbom, Donald Schilling, and Katherine A. Edward, *Dynamic Project Management* (New York: Wiley, 1988).

5. Dennis Kinlaw, *Superior Teams* (Hampshire, England: Gower Publishing Ltd., 1998), pp. 201–233.

CHAPTER 6

1. Michael Cusumano and Richard Selby, *Microsoft Secrets* (New York: Simon & Schuster, 1995), pp. 192–207.

2. Frank Addeman, "Managing the Magic," *PM Network, The Professional Magazine of the PMI,* (July 1999), pp. 31–36.

3. Eberhardt Rechtin and Mark W. Maier, *The Art of Systems Architecting* (New York: CRC Press LLC, 1997).

4. R. Stevens, P. Brook, K. Jackson, and S. Arnold, *System Engineering—Coping with Complexity* (Hertfordshire, England: Prentice Hall Europe, 1998).

5. Jim Lovell and Jeffrey Kluger, *Apollo 13* (New York: Pocket Books, 1994), Epilogue, pp. 372–378.

6. Kevin Forsberg, "'If I Could Do That, Then I Could . . .'—System Engineering in a Research and Development Environment," *Proceedings of the National Council for System Engineering Symposium,* (St. Louis, MO: July 1995).

7. Kevin Forsberg and Hal Mooz, "Application of the 'Vee' to Incremental and Evolutionary Development," *Proceedings of the National Council for System Engineering Symposium* (St. Louis, MO: July 1995).

8. Ben R. Rich and Leo Janos, *Skunk Works* (Boston: Little, Brown & Company, 1994).

CHAPTER 7

1. Stephen R. Covey, *The Seven Habits of Highly Effective People* (New York: Simon & Schuster, 1989).

2. "Advertisement and Specification for a Heavier-Than-Air Flying Machine," U.S. Army Signal Corps Specification No. 486, (Washington, DC: Smithsonian Institution, December 1907).

3. Tom D. Crouch, *The Bishop's Boys—A Life of Wilbur and Orville Wright* (New York: Norton & Company, 1990), p. 347.

4. Cynthia Monaco, "The Difficult Birth of the Typewriter," *American Heritage of Invention & Technology,* (Forbes Inc., summer 1988), pp. 10–21.

5. John R. Hauser and Don Clausing, "The House of Quality," *Harvard Business Review,* (May/June 1988), pp. 63–73.

6. L. Guinta and N. Praizler, *The QFD Book: The Team Approach to Solving Problems and Satisfying Customers through Quality Function Deployment* (New York: AMACOM Books, 1993).

7. Bill Gates, *Business,* (Warner Books, 1999).

8. Michael Cusumano and Richard Selby, *Microsoft Secrets* (New York: Simon & Schuster, 1995), pp. 192–207.

9. Richard E. Fairley and Richard H. Thayer, "The Concept of Operations: The Bridge from Operational Requirements to Technical Specifications," *Tutorial: Software Requirements*

Engineering (2nd ed.), eds. R.H. Thayer and M. Dorfman (Los Alamitos, CA: IEEE Computer Society Press, 1997), pp. 73–83.

10. Thomas L. Saaty, "Priority Setting in Complex Problems," *IEEE Transactions on Engineering Management,* vol. EM-30, (August 1983).

11. Charles H. Kepner and Benjamin B. Tregoe, *The New Rational Manager* (Princeton, NJ: Princeton Research Press, 1981).

12. Suzanne K. Bishop, "Cross-Functional Project Teams in Functionally Aligned Organizations," *Project Management Journal,* (Sylva, NC: Project Management Institute, September 1999), pp. 6–12.

13. Bishop, "Cross-Function. . . ."

14. Peter F. Drucker, *People and Performance: The Best of Peter Drucker on Management* (New York: Harper & Row, 1977).

15. Deborah S. Kezsbom, Donald Schilling, and Katherine A. Edward, *Dynamic Project Management* (New York: Wiley, 1988).

16. James P. Lewis, *Team-Based Project Management* (New York: American Management Association, 1998), p. 71.

17. Lewis, pp. 22–28.

18. Tom I. Peters and R.H. Waterman, Jr., *In Search of Excellence* (New York: Harper & Row, 1974).

19. Harold Kerzner, *Project Management* (New York: Von Nostrand Reinhold, 1984).

20. Kerzner, *Project. . . .*

21. Kerzner, *Project. . . .*

22. Stephen R. Covey, *The Seven Habits of Highly Effective People* (New York: Simon & Schuster, 1989).

23. Kezsbom, *Dynamic. . . .*

24. Robert Shisko, *NASA Systems Engineering Handbook, SP-6105* (Washington, DC: NASA Headquarters, 1995).

25. Sunny Baker and Kim Baker, *The Complete Idiot's Guide to Project Management* (New York: Alpha Books, 1998), pp. 97–100.

26. J. March and Z. Shapira, "Managerial Perspectives on Risk and Risk Taking," *Management Science,* vol. 33, no. 11 (November 1987).

27. Robert T. Clemen, *Making Hard Decisions* (Boston: PWS-Kent Publishing Co., 1991).

28. Jon Krakauer, *Into Thin Air* (New York: Doubleday Dell, 1997).

29. K. Forsberg and H. Mooz, "Risk and Opportunity Management and the Project Cycle," *Proceedings of the National Council for System Engineering Symposium,* (July 1995).

30. B.W. Boehm, "A Spiral Model of Software Development and Enhancement," *Tutorial: System and Software Requirements Engineering,* ed. R.H. Thayer and M. Dorfman (Washington, DC: IEEE Computer Society Press, 1990), pp. 513–527.

31. Cusumano, *Microsoft. . . ,* p. 192.

32. Leonard J. Kazmier, *Principles of Management* (New York: McGraw-Hill, 1969), p. 309.

33. Drucker, *People . . . ,* p. 498.

34. Michael Doyle and David Straus, *How to Make Meetings Work* (New York: Berkley Publishing, 1984).

35. Gates, *Business. . . .*

36. Cusumano, *Microsoft. . . ,* pp. 28–29.

37. Ed Jorgensen, Jake Matijevic, and Robert Shisko, "Mars Pathfinder Project Microrover Flight Experiment: Risk Management End-of-Mission Report," Jet Propulsion Lab report JPL D-11181-EOM, (September 23, 1998).

38. Edward R. Tufte, *The Visual Display of Quantitative Information* (Cheshire, CT: Graphics Press, 1983).

39. Edward R. Tufte, *Visual Explanations* (Cheshire, CT: Graphics Press, 1997), pp. 38–53.

40. Sherry Sontag and Chistopher Drew, *Blind Man's Bluff—An Untold Story of American Submarine Espionage* (New York: Public Affairs, Perseus Books Group, 1998), pp. 88–120.

41. G. Gemmill, H. Thamhaim, and D.L. Wileman, "The Power Spectrum in Project Management," *Sloan Management Review,* vol. 12 (fall 1970), pp. 15–25.

42. The Wilson Learning Corporation, Eden Prairie, MN.

43. Douglas McGregor, *The Human Side of Enterprise* (New York: McGraw-Hill, 1960).

44. William G. Ouchi, *Theory Z: How American Business Can Meet the Japanese Challenge* (Reading, MA: Addison-Wesley, 1981).

45. Frederick Herzberg, Bernard Mausner, and Barbara Snyderman, *The Motivation to Work* (New York: Wiley, 1959).

46. Alfie Kohn, *Punished by Rewards* (Boston: Houghton Mifflin, 1993).

47. P. Hersey and K.H. Blanchard, *Management of Organizational Behavior: Utilizing Group Resources* (Englewood Cliffs, NJ: Prentice Hall, 1993).

48. The Wilson Learning Corporation, Eden Prairie, MN.

49. Consulting Psychologists Press, Inc., Palo Alto, CA.

50. Covey, *The Seven. . . .*

51. The Wilson Learning Corporation, Eden Prairie, MN.

52. David Keirsey and Marilyn Bates, *Please Understand Me, Character & Temperament Types* (Del Mar, CA: Prometheus Nemesis Book Company, 1984).

53. William G. Pagonis (with Jeffery L. Cruikshank), *Moving Mountains* (Boston: Harvard Business School Press, 1992), pp. 185–191.

CHAPTER 8

1. David McCullough, *The Path Between the Seas, The Creation of the Panama Canal 1870-1914* (New York: Simon & Schuster, 1977), p. 488.

2. Kevin C. Ruffner, ed., *Corona: America's First Satellite Program* (Washington, DC: CIA History Staff, Center for the Study of Intelligence, 1995).

3. W.J. Willoughby, Jr., ed., *Best Practices—How to Avoid Surprises in the World's Most Complicated Technical Process* NAVSO P-6071 (Washington, DC: U.S. Government Printing Office, 1986).

4. Gary Kinder, *Ship of Gold in the Deep Blue Sea* (New York: Vantage Books, 1999).

CHAPTER 9

1. Pedro L. Rustan, "Clementine: Measuring the Results," *Aerospace America,* (February 1995), pp. 33–38.

2. Craig Sholes and Natalie Chalfin, "Mars Pathfinder Mission," *PM Network,* (January 1999).

3. Nancy G. Leveson and Clark S. Turner, "An Investigation of the Therac-25 Accidents," *IEEE Computer* (July 1993), pp. 18–41.

4. Kevin C. Ruffner, ed., *Corona: America's First Satellite Program* (Washington, DC: CIA History Staff, Center for the Study of Intelligence, 1995).

5. Rustan, "Clementine. . . . "

6. Jeffrey Lenorovitz, "Clementine to Mark U.S. Return to Moon," *Aviation Week and Space Technology* (January 17, 1994), pp. 66–67.

7. Rustan, "Clementine. . . . "

8. Pedro L. Rustan, "Spacecraft Project Management," *Technology Management,* vol. 1 (1994), pp. 17–23.

9. Ben R. Rich and Leo Janos, *Skunk Works* (Boston: Little, Brown and Co. 1994).

10. Sholes, "Mars. . . . "

11. David B. Smith and Mike Vertal, "Flight Project Reengineering: A Modeling Approach," *International Council for System Engineering (INCOSE) Symposium* (August 1997).

12. Ed Jorgensen, Jake Matijevic, and Robert Shisko, "Mars Pathfinder Project Microrover Flight Experiment: Risk Management End-of-Mission Report," Jet Propulsion Lab report JPL D-11181-EOM (September 23, 1998).

13. Leveson, "An Investigation. . . . "

14. Mikel J. Harry, "The Nature of Six Sigma Quality," (Motorola Inc., Government Electronics Group, 1987).

15. Rich, *Skunk.* . . .

16. Rich, *Skunk.* . . .

17. David C. Aronstein and Albert C. Piccirillo, *Have Blue and the 117A* (Reston, VA: American Institute of Aeronautics and Astronautics, 1997).

18. Aronstein, Appendix C.

19. Robert B. Cialdini, *Influence, The Psychology of Persuasion* (New York: William Morrow, 1993).

20. Acquisition Reform Benchmarking Group, "1997 Final Report, Part 2—Measuring Cycle Time Improvements," Prepared for the Under Secretary of Defense, Acquisition and Technology (June 30, 1997). Available: www.acq.osd.mil/ar

21. Sholes, "Mars. . . ."

22. Frank Kuznik, "Blundersat," *Air & Space Magazine* (Washington, DC: Smithsonian Institution, December 1993/January 1994).

23. Lewis Spacecraft Mission Failure Investigation Board Final Report (Washington, DC: NASA Headquarters, February 1998).

24. Dava Sobel, *Longitude* (New York: Penguin Books, 1996).

25. Charles Cockrell, "Lessons Learned from Better, Faster, Cheaper Concepts As Applied to Selected NASA Programs" (Internal Document), (Washington, DC: Office of Safety and Mission Assurance, NASA Headquarters, May 1998).

ACRONYMS

The acronyms that are included are those that are undefined in the text, or that appear more than once, with or without a definition. (We have not duplicated those that appear with their definition in one section only.)

Acronym	Name and Definition
AR	**Acceptance Review.** A control gate to ascertain verification and acceptance.
COW	**Cards on the Wall Planning.** A planning technique in which team members interact to create a project strategy, tactical approach, and resulting network by locating and interconnecting task cards using walls as the work space. The wall data are transferred into a computer for scheduling, critical path analysis, and iteration.
CCB	**Change Control Board.** A board established to approve all proposed changes to an approved baseline.
CEO	**Chief Executive Officer.** A company's most senior manager, responsible and accountable for a company's performance.
CSC	**Computer Software Component.** An element of a Computer Software Configuration Item (CSCI). CSCs may be further decomposed into Computer Software Units (CSUs).
CSCI	**Computer Software Configuration Item.** A software component of a system that is designated for configuration management to ensure configuration integrity. It may exist at any level in the hierarchy, where interchangeability is required.
CI	**Configuration Item.** A hardware, software, or composite item at any level in the system hierarchy designated for configuration management.CIs have four common characteristics:

1. Defined functionality,
2. Replaceable as an entity,
3. Unique specification,
4. Formal control of form, fit and functionality.

Each CI should have an identified manager and may have CI-unique design reviews, qualification certification, acceptance reviews, and operator and maintenance manuals.

CDR	**Critical Design Review.** A series of control gates to approve the build-to and code-to documentation, associated draft verification procedures, and readiness and capability of fabricators and coders to carry out the implementation. All hardware,

software, support equipment, and tooling should be reviewed in ascending order of unit to system. More appropriately called Production Guarantee Review.

CPM   **Critical Path Method.** A project network and schedule development approach that analyzes the network and determines the project's critical path. A single estimate is made for the duration of each task in the network. This distinguishes CPM from PERT, which uses three estimates for the duration of each task: earliest, nominal, and latest finish.

DoD   **Department of Defense.** A department of the executive branch of the U.S. Federal Government. DoD is responsible for the armed forces and provides for the common defense.

ECR   **Engineering Change Request.** A request to the Change Control Board to consider a change to the technical baseline.

EAC   **Estimate At Completion.** Actual cost and schedule of work completed to date plus the predicted costs and schedule for finishing the remaining work.

ECD   **Estimated Completion Date.** The predicted date for task completion.

FAA   **Federal Aviation Authority.** The agency of the executive branch of the U.S. Federal Government that manages the national airways.

FQR   **Formal Qualification Review.** A control gate, to review test and analysis data to prove the design will survive the expected handling and operational environment with margin. The FQR includes approval of the qualification certificate. Also called Qualification Acceptance Review.

FCA   **Functional Configuration Audit.** An engineering audit of a Configuration Item (CI) to verify that the test results of the "As- built" item satisfy the item's specification. The FCA, with the results of the Physical Configuration Audit (PCA), is the decision point to confirm that the design is ready for either integration or replication.

HWCI **Hardware Configuration Item.** A hardware component of a system, designated for Configuration Management to ensure integrity. It may exist at any level in the system hierarchy where interchangeability is required. Each HWCI is to have (as appropriate) design reviews, qualification certification, acceptance reviews, and operator and maintenance manuals.

HMO   **Health Maintenance Organization.** A commercial business that combines a health insurance program with health care delivery.

IEEE **Institute of Electrical and Electronic Engineers.** A professional organization dedicated to the disciplines of electrical and electronic engineering. Members exchange technical information, promote standards, and otherwise advance the knowledge base of their disciplines.

MBO   **Management By Objectives.** A management technique used to manage people based on documented work statements mutually agreed to by manager and worker. Progress is periodically reviewed, and in a proper implementation, the worker's remuneration is tied to performance.

MBWA **Management By Walking Around.** Part of the Hewlett-Packard legacy and popularized by management theorist Tom Peters, MBWA works on the assumption that a manager must circulate to fully understand the teams' performance and problems. The best managers, according to Peters, spend 10 percent of their time in their offices, and 150 percent of their time talking and working with their people, their customers, and their suppliers.

NASA   **National Aeronautics and Space Administration.** The agency of the U.S. Federal Government responsible for air and space exploration.

PCA   **Physical Configuration Audit.** An engineering audit of a Configuration Item (CI) conducted to verify that the item "As-built" conforms to the "Build-to" documentation. Results of the PCA are part of the Acceptance Review.

PDR   **Preliminary Design Review.** A series of control gates to approve the design-to specifications, associated verification plans, and approaches to developing build-to and code-to documentation. All hardware, software, support equipment, facilities, personnel, and tooling should be reviewed in descending order of system to assembly. More appropriately called Performance Guarantee Review.

PERT   **Project Evaluation Review Technique.** A technique for scheduling and statusing a project by constructing a network diagram of tasks and events and periodically evaluating progress against the network. Estimates are given for the most optimistic, nominal, and most pessimistic duration of each task in the network. These data allow statistical evaluation of critical paths for the project and a statistical prediction of project completion dates. The three-point estimate on each task is the primary distinguishing feature between a PERT network and a Critical Path Method (CPM) network that uses a single estimate for the duration of each task.

PIR   **Project Initiation Review.** A control gate at which the provider's executive management reviews, approves, and commits the company to the provider's project plan and approves the project start.

PPL   **Project Products List.** A summary of all deliverable and development versions and quantities of all hardware, software, support equipment, tooling, support services, and documentation. The PPL is the baseline for Work Breakdown Structure (WBS) development and for planning, budgeting, and scheduling.

PWAA   **Project Work Authorizing Agreement.** Documents that define and authorize work tasks to be performed within a company for a project. The PWAAs and subcontracts are the end product of implementation planning.

The PWAA must contain the following five elements:

1. Task description (input required, task to be performed, and output resulting from successful completion).
2. Time-phased budget.
3. Schedule, with appropriate intermediate milestones, and if appropriate, detailed work packages to enable earned value reporting.
4. Signature of the task leader indicating commitment to do the task within the time and budget constraints.
5. Signature of the Project manager indicating that the task is authorized.

QA   **Quality Assurance.** The design and implementation of design features and procedures to ensure that specifications can be verified. This includes specification analysis, quality engineering for inspectability and testability, manufacturing process control, and the use of techniques and training to implement the measurement and testing process.

RFP   **Request For Proposal.** A buyer document used to solicit proposals from potential bidders. The Request For Proposal consists of a Solicitation Letter, Instruction to Bidders, Evaluation Criteria, Statement of Work, and a System Specification.

SWCI   **Software Configuration Item.** See Computer Software Configuration Item.

SQA   **Software Quality Assurance.** The control of the development environment to produce quality code.

SSR   **Software Specification Review.** A control gate to approve the specifications for the software and firmware. Software Development Specifications for the Computer Software Configuration Item(s) are released after approval at the Preliminary Design Review (PDR). See also Configuration Item Specification Review (CISR).

SOW   **Statement Of Work.** The part of the Request For Proposal and resulting contract that describes the work required by the contract. Includes a description of the tasks that must be performed and the identification, quantity, and schedule of the deliverable contract end items.

SCR   **System Concept Review.** A control gate to approve the recommended system concept and validation plan conceived to satisfy the requirements of the System Requirements Document.

SDR   **System Design Review.** A control gate to review and approve the top-level design solution and expected decomposition into hardware and software configuration items. See also Design Concept Review (DCR).

SRR   **System Requirements Review.** A control gate to review and approve the System Requirements Document that identifies which needs of the total User Requirements Document will be satisfied by the proposed project. The SRR is the decision point to allow the project to proceed with the in-depth analyses and tradeoffs necessary to select a preferred system concept with associated "Should Cost" (budget) and "Should Take" (schedule) estimates.

TRR   **Test Readiness Review.** A series of control gates to demonstrate readiness to conduct acceptance or qualification tests during which official verification data will be produced. Since TRRs are conducted to approve the conduct of official data gathering tests, they will occur at whatever integration level the last opportunity for verification is experienced.

TBD   **To Be Determined.** Contract content such as dates, specifications, or criteria that have yet to be defined. Contractors cannot be expected to accurately propose to TBDs. When defined, they become the basis for an Engineering Change Proposal (ECP).

TBR   **To Be Resolved.** Contractual content, such as dates, specifications, or criteria that are not final, and are to be resolved by the contractor or by the buyer as part of the development effort. When resolved, they may be a basis for an Engineering Change Proposal (ECP).

TQM   **Total Quality Management.** An approach to quality predicated on viewing all coworkers as customers who must be satisfied and all work processes as needing continued improvement.

WBS   **Work Breakdown Structure.** The hierarchical division of the system into elements of the system and the associated work tasks.

INDEX

CUSTOMER NOTE: IF THIS BOOK IS ACCOMPANIED BY SOFTWARE,
PLEASE READ THE FOLLOWING BEFORE OPENING THE PACKAGE.

The enclosed disk contains files to help you utilize the models described in the
accompanying book. By opening the seal, you are agreeing to be bound by the
following agreement:

This software product is copyrighted, and all rights are reserved by Kevin
Forsberg, Hal Mooz, and Howard Cotterman. You are licensed to use this disk on
a single computer. If the software is to be used on more than one computer in a
company or educational institution, additional copies of the diskette(s) may be
made for each person in the company or educational institution. However, this license does not extend to the material in the accompanying book which may not
be copied except with the written permission of John Wiley & Sons, Inc.

This software product is sold without warranty of any kind, either expressed or
implied, including but not limited to the implied warranty of merchantability
and fitness for a particular purpose. In developing this software, neither the authors nor the publisher are engaged in rendering legal, accounting, or other professional services. If legal advice or other expert assistance is required, the
services of a competent professional should be sought. Neither the publisher nor
the authors or owner of the copyright assume any responsibility for errors, omissions, or damages, including, without limitation, incidental, special, or consequential damages (including lost profits) which may result from use of the
information in the book or on the diskettes. (Some states do not allow the exclusion of implied warranties, so the exclusion may not apply to you.)